Alison Johnson grew up in Aberdeen and gained her first degree, an MA in Medieval and Renaissance English, at Aberdeen University. After picking up a second degree at Oxford, she married Andrew Johnson and moved with him back to Scotland, where they both found jobs as teachers on the Isle of Harris. On the west coast of the island they found Scarista House, a decaying manse which they converted into one of the most highly acclaimed hotels in Scotland, receiving accolades from all the major hotel guides.

They sold the hotel in 1989 and now run The White Horse Press, publishing books and journals on environmental and social subjects.

ALISON JOHNSON

A House By The Shore

Scarista Style

A free-range and humane approach to cooking and eating

WARNER BOOKS

A *Warner* Book

A House By The Shore first published in Great Britain in 1986
by Victor Gollancz Ltd
Published in 1987 by Futura
Reprinted 1988, 1990, 1991
Published in 1994 by Warner Books
Reprinted 1995
Copyright © Alison Johnson 1986
Illustrations © Christine Dodd 1986

Scarista Style first published in Great Britain in 1987
by Victor Gollancz Ltd
Published in 1988 by Futura
Reprinted 1991
Published in 1995 by Warner Books
Copyright © Alison Johnson 1987

This edition published by Warner Books in 1998

The moral right of the author has been asserted.

A CIP catalogue record for this book
is available from the British Library

ISBN 0 7515 2336 4

Printed and bound in Great Britain by
Clays Ltd, St Ives plc

Warner Books
A Division of
Little, Brown and Company (UK)
Brettenham House
Lancaster Place
London WC2E 7EN

A House By The Shore

In memory of my father,
James Inglis Rice

Thanks are due to many people in Harris
and elsewhere for their help and advice while
I was writing this book: but especially to
Finlay J. Macdonald, without whose
encouragement I should never even
have started.

Contents

Foreword

One stormy December evening when we were discussing alternative careers, Andrew decided it was time I wrote a book.

"But how would I start?"

"I'll give you the chapter headings," he volunteered, hopefully. "One: How I Married Andrew and Had to Keep Him for the Rest of His Life. Two: Why We Came to Harris—why did we come to Harris?"

"Not for the weather," I said, glumly, as a cloud of smoke gushed into the room, rammed down the chimney by the usual Force 9.

"Get away from it all? Disillusioned with urban society, perhaps."

"We couldn't get a job anywhere else," I pointed out, but Andrew said he didn't think that sort of thing would sell.

"Anyway," he continued, "it shouldn't be difficult to scrape up enough of the sort of rot books are full of. How we found the house—did it up—the first hotel guests—guests and pests—Problem will be keeping it short enough. Now how long is a book?" he went on, selecting one at random from the shelves. "About twenty chapters—you wouldn't want *that* many: ten is plenty. Two hundred pages—about 500 words a page. Good Grief! That's about 100,000 words!"

He looked horrified. I think he had an awful vision of me running to 150,000 or 200,000, unstoppable as the sorcerer's broom, once chopped into chapters. There was a short silence.

"How could you finish it off?"

*

He was quite right: it was difficult to get started, having written nothing for many years but letters of complaint to dilatory suppliers of plasterboard and groceries, but it was much more difficult to keep it short enough, and very hard indeed to finish it off. This was supposed to be a book about the evolution of Scarista House from ill-thought-out daydream to hotel of good repute, but many other things happened on the way, which would not be left out. I hope those who read it will see why we came to Harris, and why we are still here twelve years later, in spite of the weather.

Part One

THE WEST LOCH

1

Dropping Out

Andrew and I met at Oxford, where we were both taking further degrees. Collecting degrees, however, did not really seem to be an end in itself, and it soon became obvious that neither was it a means to an end. What employer would willingly hire overgrown children of 23, who were totally ignorant of the use of the 8-hour day? Our friends gritted their teeth and became tax inspectors, or research assistants in dismal universities from Abu Dhabi to Ohio. Some got married and bred immediately in urban semis. Their lives filled us with dismay. Could one survive an office desk? Could one really change nappies and push a pram? One plainly could not. Like the rest, however, we applied to enter the civil service, to take worthy teacher training courses, to be second under-tea-boy to assistant lecturers at nameless seats of learning. To our relief, no-one wanted us. We would have to gather our talents together and make what we could of ourselves. What would it be?

Andrew was a good handyman. I was greatly impressed by the alacrity with which he painted the bathroom of my Oxford flat. He did the bath a tasteful shade of yellow, giving it several coats, and was incensed by my flat mate's choice of mauve toilet paper. In fact, he has hardly held a paintbrush since: but even painting was preferable to writing up his thesis. As for me, my chief hobby was cooking. I liked to entertain friends lavishly, and in between such spending bouts, I positively enjoyed using the cheapest food-stuffs as a basis for interesting meals. "Have you any brains?" I would ask the jolly butcher in Oxford market, causing him to bellow with laughter. He always had, or if not, he would produce tripe or hearts or some other cheap leavings. Andrew ate his way stoically through whatever I put in front of him, even dandelion

15

leaves from the garden in Park Town where we lived. They were very bitter, but we were usually very hungry.

It was worth eating dandelions in order to be able to pay for lodgings in Park Town, rather than in the cheaper parts round the canal and up the Cowley Road. Park Town is a graceful Georgian double terrace containing an oval garden, the houses joined by a roof balustrade the entire length of each side, hiding the attic windows of the former servants' quarters. Friendly cats prowled along here, and would jump onto my bed through the open window. We could picnic in the gardens, and walk away from the traffic down through the University parks and Mesopotamia, enjoying an illusion of rural peace. There were ducks to feed and cows on the far bank of the river. Mooning around here between abortive interviews we tried to combine our interests into a workable future. The list ran something like this: living in the country, opera, sailing, architecture, religion, joinery, cooking. It did not at first seem like a hopeful combination. Gradually a plan emerged. We could buy a large and derelict old house (architecture) near the sea (sailing) and in the country (rural living), restore it (joinery) and run it as a hotel (cooking). Opera and religion would have to struggle for survival.

On the whole this seemed satisfactory. With typical academic arrogance, we assumed that what we had thought, would be. The fact that we had no money and no relevant experience did not disconcert us. We would earn some money and look for houses suitably beautiful and derelict. The teaching profession suddenly appealed: teachers can live in the country, where large ruinous houses abound, and they have plenty of free time in which to sail around contemplating religion and opera. We decided to head for Scotland, which has a lot of coastline.

In Aberdeen, where my mother lives, we got fixed up with a teacher training course which mercifully lasted only three months: it was intended for big-headed postgraduates with at least two degrees, whom the staff and other students would be heartily glad to get rid of after one term. With this to look forward to, we got married and spent our honeymoon touring the West of Scotland in my mother's borrowed car, looking for suitable ruined houses. Andrew seemed to have a liking for McCaig's Folly in Oban: it is an unfinished replica of the Colosseum. I discounted it on the grounds that its surroundings are insufficiently rural. We camped in incessant West Highland rain and midges. Andrew had not known about either, and I felt secretly guilty. Fortunately, my mother had paid for us to spend a couple of nights at Ardfenaig House in the Isle of Mull. This was breathtaking. The proprietors were running just the sort of hotel we imagined: secluded, welcoming, full of lovely furniture and objets d'art. The meals were delicious and the views superb. All around was the worn pink granite, the green machair and the white beaches of the Ross of Mull. The experience was irresistible: our plan was vindicated.

Back in Aberdeen, the midges lessened and the rain turned to snow, and we began to look for the jobs that would take us to the West again. Oban High School needed teachers of English and Science, and so did Sir E. Scott school in Tarbert, Isle of Harris. No other applicants seemed to want such posts at that time: it would be different now, I suspect.

We visited Oban. It seemed ideal for our purposes. It is situated on the West Highland tourist route, with access to interesting sailing including the Corryvreckan whirlpool for the adventurous. Rambling Edwardian houses and small estates abound in the area. It is not an impossible journey either to Andrew's relatives in Cornwall or mine in Aberdeen. Furthermore, there was local authority housing available for teachers, which would enable us to save towards our derelict mansion, and the High School was large and important enough to allow for promotion and rapid salary increase. We decided Oban was the place, but curiosity sent us to have a look at remote, unsuitable Harris, with its 100-pupil school and no teachers' houses.

In Inverness, we broke our train journey to see the deputy director of education. Yes, the Tarbert jobs were ours if we wanted them: no-one else had, in the six months they had been advertised. The train to Kyle of Lochalsh was nearly empty: no-one wanted to go West in November. In desolate Strath Bran a sleety mist pulsed across the wintry russet slopes. One felt it was always like that. At Strathcarron the pub was shuttered and dilapidated; at Strome the ferry no longer ran, according to an already faded notice. But the Western sea began to reveal itself around Drumbuie, brilliant in the low winter light, with a scatter of black tidal rocks and green-capped islets. The world became wider, lower and brighter, the colours translucent as a rainbow. And what colours! The deer-grass on the hills at this season is burnt orange with a tinge of scarlet where the sun hits, fading to cream on the summits. The flashing white of many waterfalls intersects bottle green conifer belts, always shimmering with recent rain. If there is sun at all, rainbows and hints of rainbows brighten and fade, and the sea is intensely blue. The very seaweeds that fringe it are as varied as a garden of flowers—brown, orange, ochre and emerald green. From this weed-fringed shore come the most exciting sounds and smells: the yelling of gulls, the puttering of little boats heading for the horizon, the shouting of men at the ropes of ferries and fishing craft, and everywhere the pungent, salty, oily seaweed tang. To anyone who loves the West, that smell is like a stiff dram.

On the train drawing near Kyle, I stood at the open windows whiffling like a dog. The western rain began, relentless, soft and dark. The rattling bus taking us to Portree was nearly empty, too. Not so the bus from Portree to Uig: it was almost full of blue-eyed old men in tweed jackets and caps, all of whom knew each other and spoke softly and courteously together. There was not a word of English: the conversation was all in Gaelic. I felt we were in a foreign country. Andrew, on the other hand, brightened up visibly as the rain and darkness thickened outside.

"These people look just like the Cornish!" he said, and seemed quite satisfied thereafter. To him, the non-Celtic, fast-spoken, quick-moving Aberdonians we had been living amongst were the foreigners.

At Uig pier, we clambered up the gangway of the *Hebrides*, just us and twenty Harrismen, who for the most part retired to the bar, where we could not afford to go. It was twilight at 4.00 p.m., wet, and very mild on deck. The bow-wave surged past us with a lovely even hiss and a gleam of white to each swell. The ferry rounded out of Uig bay quickly, and was immediately out of sight of habitation. Nearly two hours later came the little winking light of Eilean Glas lighthouse, and soon after in the far distance the tight cluster of Tarbert's street and pier lights.

Everyone disembarking greeted everyone on the pier, softly and in Gaelic, and dispersed into the rainy night. I felt too noisy, too jerky and too brightly coloured.

Andrew Beattie, the English headmaster, met us and entertained us hospitably that night. Next day, in the rainy morning light, the little school, with its litter of non-matching buildings, looked dreary and enclosed. A few hardy sheep stalked across the playground; I could see them from the windows of the classroom that would be mine if we came to Harris. Of course we wouldn't: it was unsuitable in every respect.

The Beatties kindly took us by car all over the island. On the single-track road round the east side we stopped in a passing place to picnic. The landscape was incredible: distant hills, long promontories and near hummocks were all bare pale grey rounded rock. Narrow ribbons of red deer grass or black peat-squelch ran between them, and some of the rocks gradually resolved into small hairy sheep, busily grazing on nothing at all. On terrace after terrace of rock sweeping down to the shore, many small pools and lochans reflected the pallor of the misty sky. Beyond was the Minch, calm and silver, with the distant escarpments of Skye hiding their crests in the mist. How on a wet winter's day, could this barren land be so full of light? There was a strange iridescence, as if the sun were just about to shine through; but looking up at the low clouds, there was no sign of it. Rocks and water seemed brighter than the sky.

Mr Beattie returned us to the ferry. We felt guilty about not telling him we would not be coming back. Consequently the ferry trip was not as enjoyable as it should have been. We told each other of the impossibility of Harris and praised Oban.

"Harris is really too remote. The houses are all tiny. There would never be anything worth buying."

"And you'd never see a tourist. Do you think anyone goes there?"

"Not many. Anyway, we'd miss the trees. There doesn't seem to be a single tree on the island."

"Yes there are! There are some in the Beatties' garden."
Silence.

"It's funny. The sea makes up for the lack of trees."

"That incredible light."

Silence again.

"It's much more exciting than Oban, isn't it?"

"But not really practical."

"No."

Twenty-four hours later impractical Harris had won the toss.

In the New Year, we stuffed as many of our belongings as would go into our ancient Land-Rover and set off from Aberdeen. We had on so many clothes as to make movement difficult; I remember I had a poncho on top of my duffel coat and three pairs of socks. Even so our feet soon lost all feeling against the aluminium floor of our unheated vehicle. One could see the slushy road through the holes in the floor. We rattled slowly across the snowy north of Scotland. Nothing moves in the Highlands in the week after Hogmanay; it was difficult to get petrol, of which our Land-Rover drank a great deal, and impossible to buy a cup of hot coffee. The only other travellers were respectable family groups driving between villages to visit relations. The less respectable had succumbed to the festivities days before: abandoned cars in the ditches bore witness to their fate. By now we are well used to the singularities of the Highland festive season, but on this first visit we were somewhat dismayed by the cold and solitude, as by the exhaust-fume sickness and aching bones produced by our shaky old vehicle. I am sure both of us had second thoughts, and wondered about Oban.

Our ferry sailed at 9 the next morning. We had a puncture in the dim morning light. As Andrew flung himself in the mud to deal with it wearing his one respectable outfit (a white pullover and trousers) I began to despair, and possibly even to wail. But we made it to the ferry, and the sun not only rose, it actually appeared, warm and golden. It shone all the way across the Minch, and on all the little green islands, each with its half dozen sheep, in East Loch Tarbert. The pale grey hills of East Harris looked friendly and familiar, and the little croft houses dotted along the shore sent up straight sweet-smelling plumes of peat smoke. Already we felt as if we were coming home.

Through Mr Beattie, we had rented a furnished house at Leachkin, just out of Tarbert on the West Loch. It was very large by

Harris standards, and looked south west across the water. To the south east was Tarbert, at the isthmus between east and west lochs; to the north west, the loch broadened out to the open horizon, with the enticing little island of Isay lying in the way. It looked like good boating. There was some ground we could cultivate for vegetables. The sun was still shining. Everything was delightful.

2

Tarbert

Everything continued delightful. As town dwellers, we were in a state of constant wonder at how romantically far north we were. At about 10 o'clock after a long morning twilight, we would see the sun top the rocky edge of Ben Luskentyre to the south. It trundled uncertainly along it for perhaps four hours, casting fantastic shadows on the pale wind-wearied tussocks of grass. By two o'clock it had rolled out of sight, and the west loch was plunged into shadow. As the steep shores darkened, the water paled and gleamed, holding the last reflections of a pearly sky.

The earliest part of the Hebridean year is often our most beautiful time. The weather can be more still and clear than at any other season. By night, the sky is full of stars, stars where one never knew there were any, extra stars in Orion, the Pleiades hopping and jumping to crowd themselves all in. When the full moon shines, she is so bright that the stars recede as if by day. The sea reflects a silver swathe of light. You can distinguish colours clearly, and if you preferred reading by moonlight to looking at the moon, I dare say you could. The Aurora Borealis is visible most nights, once the eye is attuned. Usually it is only a wavering pallor in the Northern sky, but sometimes strong pulses of pink and green shoot rhythmically to the zenith over an arc of 180°. By day, sea and sky are cloudless blue, and every bone and wrinkle of the grey and tawny land is highlighted by the low sun. There is not a scrap of green. Nothing grows yet, in spite of the low incidence of frost: there is not enough sunshine at this latitude. But the days lengthen faster and faster after mid-January, and there is a sense of happy expectancy, like waiting for Christmas. Everyone's small talk is full of it: "The nights are getting shorter." "Aye, we'll know the difference in a week or so." "It's lighter in the mornings, too." Small talk, but no small matter: islanders long for the light nights of summer and dread the onset of winter darkness. At first we thought this quaint, but now in our eleventh winter we are as much in awe of solstice and equinox as everyone else.

For winter in Harris is not all starry nights and clear days. Indeed, I think we have the most vicious winter weather in Europe. Well-informed visitors often tell us how mild our winters are: we have the Gulf stream; we have little frost and snow; how much warmer we are than Kent or Norfolk or Cumbria! But they have forgotten the wind. Winter gales, which usually means the first Force 8 or upwards since perhaps April, can start at the beginning of September and rage for 7 months, in a bad year. The winter incidence of gales in exposed parts of the island is one day in three on average. The violence of these gales is astonishing. The huge seas and white water are no surprise—they happen on any coast in lesser storms. The effects on land are more extraordinary. Motor vehicles are regularly pushed off the roads or flipped over by the wind. Debris flies through the air as if in some hurricane-hit shanty town: slates, sheets of corrugated iron, bits of caravans and hen-houses. Roofs are ripped off and windows smashed in. We used at first to be horribly fascinated by the behaviour of our kitchen window. The glass would bulge out and in, alternately sucked and blown by the gale, with a dull popping sound, but it never gave way. During one worse than average storm, when I was attempting to teach some rudiments of grammar to a class of unwilling boys, I was disturbed by shouts of "Miss, Miss! The roof's blown off!"

"Nonsense! Get on with your work!" I snapped.

"But Miss—"

As I turned to clip the ear of the disruptive element, I saw he was quite right: chunks of the gymnasium roof were sailing past the window.

Such gales blow from any quarter, except due east. Southwesterly is the commonest and fiercest, but land and buildings have evolved to accommodate it. Less of a wind from an unusual quarter may cause more damage, bouncing off high bluffs and catching the corners of buildings, to the detriment of rones and downpipes. It

SCARP

HUSHINISH

AMHUINNSUIDHE

ARDVOURLIE

CLISHAM

BUNAVONEADER

WEST LOCH
TARBERT
ISAY

ARDHASAIG
GILLAVAL
LEACHKIN

TARANSAY

BEN LUSKENTYRE STIOCLETT

TARBERT

LUSKENTYRE

EAST
LOCH
TARBERT

BORVE

TOE
HEAD
CHAIPAVAL

SCARISTA

NORTHTON

"THE BAYS"

LEVERBURGH

RONEVAL

SOUND
OF
HARRIS

RODEL

HARRIS

was the northerly wind we feared at Leachkin. The West Loch is a comparatively narrow inlet with high sides, pointing south east to north west. A north west to west wind was straightforward, screeching gleefully up the loch and over the isthmus to Tarbert, leaving the high wire fences of the school playing-field plastered with flotsam of polythene sacks and broken fish-boxes. A south-westerly reared up over the mass of Ben Luskentyre, hit the centre of the loch in a massive catspaw, or perhaps a smallish tornado, and had spent its rage before lashing our front windows. But the nearly-north wind clawed up the sheer crags on the far side of Gillaval, the mountain which loomed behind our house, often showing a wild spiral of cloud in a blue sky before we felt a breath of its descent. Then it was on us with a shriek and a bang. Its alternate lulling and moaning was restless and sinister. This was the wind that sucked at our kitchen window, flipped our boat over on her mooring, and hurled small birds against our back door. Andrew, in particular, hated it. I disliked it less, as it usually came with drier, brighter weather. During our first few years in Harris, it was the continual dampness I found a misery, as I was used to the hard frosts and dry snow of Aberdeen. The southerly wind was my enemy. It brought evil-smelling mist in summer and a fiendish cocktail of rain, hail and sleet in winter. Occasionally, which was better, it graced us with a snow blizzard. This always resulted in a power cut. The electricity cables run down the road from Stornoway, over a mountain pass, and the iced-up wires soon break in high winds. Indeed, they do not need to be iced up: long power cuts are common and frequent for much of the year.

During our first school term in Harris, we were busy with the new experience of being employed, and it was not until friends and relatives began to visit us in the spring that we explored the island to any extent. The fortunate visitors were treated, on these trips, to the front seats of our beloved Land-Rover, from one of which we had recently extricated a dead mouse and its nest. The cab still smelt rather of rancid mouse. The Land-Rover was our first ever vehicle and we were very proud of it. Usually it started, and even progressed, with a great deal of noise and smoke, but sometimes there was a difficulty about remaining stationary, as the hand brake was chronically inefficient. Once on, it required a hammer blow to knock it off again, so we tried to avoid applying it. Andrew is fond of driving backwards at top speed, rather than turning round; and as some previous owner had reversed the canvas to separate the cab from the back, thus reducing rear visibility, the procedure was hazardous. Soon we had very few rear lights, and as spares were locally unobtainable, we did without. In the damp climate of Harris, thick green moss grew up inside the base of the windows, which I thought pretty, but I doubt if our visitors liked it. Worst of all, sometimes strange explosions took place under the bonnet. I shall never forget my mother leaping out of the moving vehicle, clutching her handbag, as smoke belched from the dashboard.

On these safaris, I usually sat in the open back, and until overcome by exhaust fumes enjoyed the views immensely. Harris is small, only about 25 miles long, but the scenery is varied. To the north, above the waist of Tarbert (Tairbeart means a place where a boat can be hauled overland) lies a range of grim mountains, a sort of no-man's land between Harris and Lewis. The highest summit, Clisham, is only 2600 feet, but the whole range is spectacularly steep and craggy, conveying a powerful impression of malevolent and watchful old age. The rock is Lewisian gneiss, the oldest metamorphic rock in the world, worn by wind and water to gaunt ribs and ridges. Gillaval and Sgaoth Iosal with their long steep corries crouch like evil old giants over their sour peat bogs. They claim occasional victims, too: sheep, children, shepherds. Beyond them the road climbs over the shoulder of Clisham, whose pointed and tilted summit is always crowned with a streaming scarf of cloud, even on a clear day, for the mountains make their own weather in the moist Atlantic air. North of Clisham, the road zig-zags down to Ardvourlie on Loch Seaforth. On the landward side lies a great natural amphitheatre through which the Scaladale river winds, overhung by misty crags and corries, a fit subject for the most romantic Victorian landscapist. To seaward the prospect is less awesome: a mundane assortment of power-lines, fences, land-drains and "done up" croft houses, typical of island life.

South of the mountains Harris spreads out lower and rounder. A single track road switchbacks out to the western promontory of Hushinish. Here a sandy beach on the south side looks out over many small rocks and islands. The tiny village huddles on the machair above the bay, and beyond it is the high island of Scarp, quite recently depopulated. The shore to the North rises in steep cliffs towards the mountains. There are more inaccessible sandy beaches, more cliffs, more mountains, till habitation begins again 25 miles round a roadless coast in Lewis.

At Hushinish we would pile the Land-Rover with driftwood for our fires. The visitors turned blue and shivered: having learned from Andrew's optimistic reports that Harris has a mild climate thanks to the Gulf Stream, they never brought enough clothes. They didn't realise he only meant milder than Hudson Bay or Okhotsk which are comparable latitudes. How they must have dreaded the driftwood, too! It spat and cracked and gave no heat. We liked it: it produced lovely green and blue flames, and was free.

Back over the lurching road, past the Edwardian baronial pile of Amhuinnsuidhe, with its salmon falls and neglected gardens, past Bunavoneader with its solitary factory chimney, at the head of a deep bay. A whaling concern operated from here in the first half of this century. Many of the old people can remember it—stinking, bloody work but work nevertheless, in an area of chronic unemployment. In our more whale-sensitive age, the abandoned brick stack has an air of lonely reproach, a cenotaph to many dead. There is another memorial here, too: the Norwegian manager who earned his bread from the death of whales erected a fine tombstone to his beloved dog, Sam. I often think of that contrast; it has followed me through all our years on the island.

To go further south, one has to return to Tarbert, where the island is only about ¼-mile wide between the east and west lochs. Eastward the whole length of the island is the Bays, the fantastic rock wilderness which had so astonished us on our preliminary visit. The shoreline is very indented, and in every little cove and creek are houses, stuck precariously on the bare rock. At first we were puzzled as to why so many people lived in the Bays, where only a few narrow strips of hard-won soil are available for cultivation. The answer, as so often in the Highlands, is that the fertile land on the west of Harris was cleared for sheep farming in the mid-19th century, and any of the population who could not be encouraged to emigrate were forced back to the rocky east coast.

It is picturesque enough now, in an age of subsidies and unemployment benefit, but it is impossible to forget the abject misery of that overcrowded population, as refugees without homes, possessions or seaman's skills descended on the original fishermen who scratched a living here from the sea.

For the modern householder, though, there are certainly fine views. In clear weather, Skye looks within touching distance, and beyond it, fifty miles away, are the whole line of mountains from Applecross to Scourie. Often their tops are striped white with snow, and sometimes the whole range is entirely covered, floating like icebergs in a blue sea. When we first saw the Alps across the lagoon from Venice, we felt at home: they looked very much like Suilven and Canisp from Scadabay. That is the islander's dream, to find somewhere that looks just like his own island. Gaelic songs are full of nostaglia for home: "If I had given my heart to it altogether, what made me ever leave the place of my love?" Scalpay men who have sailed the world over will tell you proudly that the seas around Scalpay are the worst in the whole ocean. A class of bored children shown a picture of York Minster shrieked with delight: "it's just like Rodel Church, Miss!" How passionately people here love their native place! All the more misery for the evicted populations of Luskentyre, Seilebost, Horgabost, Scarista: forced into surroundings only a day's walk away, but as alien as Patagonia.

"The grass on the West side is most Clover and Dasy, which in the summer yields a most fragrant smell." So wrote Martin Martin in 1716. This is the distinctive Hebridean machair. In our first summer, we were astounded by the beauty of these coastal pastures. Where the sour peat is sweetened by shell sand blowing from the beaches, there is great fertility. At the end of April, primroses and daisies appear on the seaward slopes. In a week or so the tidal salt-flats at Luskentyre and Northton are entirely pink with thrift, and thereafter comes a succession of bloom—bird's foot trefoil, white and red clover, ladies' bedstraw, poppies, pansies, centaury, meadow rue, harebells, knapweed and many more. The sheep are taken up to the hills in late May, and immediately these meadows are sheets of pink and white and yellow, with scarcely a leaf of green showing. The air is laden with honey and lark-song. The flowery pelage extends into the marram of the dunes, and patches of fragrant mauve sea-rocket appear almost at the tide line, mingling with shells and black twirls of dry seaweed. The long clean beaches start white at Luskentyre, and gradually change through cream to pinky gold as one goes south. The colour change is attributable to the different proportions of various shells which compose the sand. At Luskentyre it is mainly cockles. By Scarista, there is a preponderance of bright pink thin tellins. In places delicate swirls of blue-grey resolve into crushed-up mussels. Whatever the colour of the sand, the sea, even on a dullish day, is clear turquoise inshore and deep blue towards the horizon.

No one can fail to be impressed by these beaches. Our visitors shot reels of film, to our gratification. Some even joked about going swimming, and one or two did remove their shoes and paddle.

During our first few months, if we had no friends staying with us we did not move around much. We told everyone that teaching at Tarbert was very easy, and so it was, for classes were small and the pupils docile. All the same, it was quite an adjustment. We had been well on the way to perpetual studenthood, and it was difficult to adjust to punctuality and toeing the line. It was difficult to do as we were told, and difficult to imagine our charges would, or should, do as we told them. Mine never did. I was not surprised. Andrew had slightly more success; as he taught General Science, he could always arrange an explosion if interest was flagging, or wire up the baddest boy for a few electric shocks, to the delight of the rest of the class. But the study of English and History does not lend itself to colourful disciplinary measures. I gave out thousands of lines and they wrote them in science lessons. They did their science homework in English. On the whole, though, they were good-humoured and tried not to spill the beans to the rest of the staff; indeed, they were embarrassingly conspiratorial, once they discovered that we did not have "the Belt" and anyway didn't know how to use it, which we were forced to confess after cross-examination.

"Miss! You'd better not get one. Mr M— belted Queerie and Queerie took his hand away and Mr M— got it on the thigh."

My sympathies were not with Queerie, a boy whom I would cheerfully have hanged, but I couldn't trust myself to aim straight, as I can't even hit a ping-pong ball, and so procured no Belt. I pulled out tufts of hair, which can be done from the back when the victim is unsuspecting, and confiscated mountains of sweets and comics. The latter punishment hurt me more than them: if left with sweets and comics, they would at least keep relatively quiet, so that other teachers passing by would think I had a grip on things. On demoralised Friday afternoons, confiscations dwindled. Andrew soon made an interesting and helpful discovery about the effects of fresh air, too. Our first action in the morning was always to turn off the heating and open the windows in our respective classrooms, causing vociferous complaints from our pupils.

"No one else does that! Only you and Mr J. It's freezing!" We assured them it was healthier that way. However, experiment and observation led Andrew to realise that a rise in temperature and lack of oxygen could be made to induce a condition of stupor, most heartily wished for as 4 o'clock drew near: so on went the heating and the windows were shut. I gratefully adopted this procedure, but Andrew was better placed, really, as the soporific fug was increased by leaks from calor gas cylinders and other scientific fumes. Also, he could always escape to his prep room for a few gulps of air. Sometimes, when he overdid things, the air became so noxious that he had to evacuate the whole class to the playground. As the lab was next to the infant classrooms, this caused great delight among the little children, who hung at the windows waving to their older brothers and sisters. Further alarms were caused by his explosions. On one occasion, after a particularly loud bang followed by screams, the primary school headmistress rushed in to the rescue, expecting wreckage and blood, but it was only some conjuring trick.

The other staff treated us with tact and kindness, which we did not really deserve, for we were undoubtedly both arrogant and ignorant. We started from the unfortunate position of feeling that much of the work we were asked to do was pointless. We knew that many of the children would never get jobs, and that even those who did would not obtain them by growing copper sulphate crystals or perusing *Julius Caesar*. The greatest embellishment of a good pupil would be a crown of "O" grade passes, perhaps three or four. After that, there was a chance of two years at the Nicolson

Institute in Stornoway, Higher grade passes, possibly a college course, possibly university: but very few would get that far, and for those that did, the future was far from assured. They might still be unemployed at the end of it, and at any point along the route, the attempt to cram in more than natural ability would really allow could lead to crestfallen failures. This is not, of course, particular to pupils in Harris. It pertains across the whole country. Being fresh from lengthy education, and sick of it, we were very conscious of this. As for children who were not set on examination courses, their case was even more discouraging. At 12 and 13 they were still childish, eager for anything new. After that a curtain came down. The girls were dreaming of boys and babies, and the boys of sheep and whisky. They were intensely bored. What could one do to raise a spark of interest? School could never be the adult world after which they hankered, so for them it was meaningless, try as one might. Their boredom cowed me, but I could see no alternative for them. Certainly one cannot encourage 14-year-old girls to breed, and even in Harris there are not enough sheep for all the boys to chase, though there is enough whisky to drown them.

I am sure our lack of conviction showed, and it must have made us a nuisance to everyone, to pupils as well as teachers. After all, there is no point in attacking, or even in not defending, established standards unless one has something more relevant to offer. Educationists are forever propounding some new and "more relevant" scheme, of course, but in fact each is as worthless as the last—or as worthy: the success or otherwise hangs entirely on the conviction and dedication of the individual teacher. What is taught hardly matters at all; it is the spectacle of an adult devoted wholeheartedly to an ideal that impresses young people.

Well, I was not wholehearted. When a certain youth fell asleep and slid off his seat in a history lesson, I was sorry for him, but not surprised. The pathos of this moustached young giant, trapped in his little school desk, haunted me (and my history lessons) all my teaching days. But really, I was probably wrong. I expect he had been dreaming happily enough of sheep, to which he soon afterwards escaped two months short of his official leaving date. The school attendance officer did not take ship for the offshore

31

island where he lived, so he was safe enough. Good luck to him. But no *real* teacher could have felt any good would come of his truancy, and no real teacher would have bored him into slumber, either.

On the whole, though, I think the children quite enjoyed us. We were an entertaining double act. Andrew is tall and thin and I am short and fat—a good start from a youthful point of view. Our appalling cut-price clothing was another source of glee. I made skirts from hideous-coloured remnants, and Andrew had a very long-legged pair of large-check trousers and a very short-sleeved small-check jacket (in non-matching colours) which he wore for most of his teaching career. I had to listen to so many remarks about these trousers that eventually I put them in the dustbin.

Our other attraction was that we put a lot of time and effort into the school Youth Club. There is very little entertainment for youngsters in Harris. The population is too small and scattered to make the usual clubs and societies possible, as school transport takes the children home at 4 o'clock. Consequently, Youth Club meetings were the longed-for goal of the whole week. We needed no fancy amusements. We encouraged them to sell refreshments, to raise money for equipment, and they were immensely pleased with the things they bought – a dartboard, a home-made snooker table, disco lights, and records. Our club members were very unsophisticated compared with city children. When we took them on a summer barbecue to Hushinish, boys and girls tore off their shoes and paddled rapturously, or chased a football on the sand. We had been expecting drinking in the bus and fornication in the sand dunes, but there was no trouble at all.

It was through the Youth Club that our previously much-ridiculed Land-Rover reached the summit of its fame. The children in outlying districts had never been able to attend meetings, but as we could pack a dozen into our bone-shaking vehicle, on different weeks they could be picked up from the Bays, the West Side, Kyles Scalpay or Hushinish. They came with a will, collected money spontaneously to pay for petrol, and were astonishingly grateful. Our battered old wreck now became an object of the greatest affection and esteem.

Unlike teaching, the Youth Club was immensely rewarding,

simply because they enjoyed it so much. Out of that enjoyment, we tried to encourage them to do something for other people. We held sponsored litter collections, with the redoubtable Land-Rover pressed into service as a dustcart. The money raised went to charity, Christian Aid one year and Save the Children the next. Participation was gratifyingly enthusiastic, but in spite of their indignation at the new rubbish spread by the next gale, they still dropped sweet-papers in the playground.

We liked to feel we were fostering self-reliance and consideration for others, though probably very little of it stuck. But of our three years' teaching experience, I think any good we did was through the Youth Club, simply because we felt ourselves it was worthwhile. We regarded it as ours, and so did the children. By the time we left the school, they had forgotten there had been a Club before "The J's", and were unfairly oblivious of the part played by other teachers in supervising it. Our pleas to Mr Beattie not to ban meetings after misdemeanours, and to allow the divine Scalpay maidens to attend, were transformed into epic battles in school folklore. Our personal involvement with the club was what counted —the wholeheartedness that we did not give to teaching. We have found exactly the same process in our hotel business. It is the level of emotional involvement in one's own efforts that transforms them into a worthwhile communication with others; trouble taken for the love of it blots out failures and excuses short-comings, it seems. We scarcely recognised our shabby furnishings and amateurish cookery in the glowing praise of our first guests: now our standards are much higher, but we are less single-minded, and our clients, I suspect, less pleased.

But to return to Sir E. Scott School in 1974. Two salient features emerged on our first day there. One was that almost the whole class register began with "M"—MacDonald, Macleod, Morrison. The other was that every naughty boy would have half a dozen brothers to plague you coming up the school. Both point to a dominant factor in Hebridean life: families are typically large and extended, and the ties of kinship are vital and intricate. "My cousin in Canada" may well be a third cousin twice removed, whose forebears left Harris over a hundred years ago, and who has never been seen on the island. A cousin he is, nevertheless. Islanders still have an exceptional memory for oral knowledge, and most people carry many-branching family trees in their heads, covering not only their own relationships but their neighbours' as well. It is almost as necessary to know other people's cousins as your own: otherwise you could inadvertently give offence, and in a small community it is important not to fall out with neighbours. This accounts in part for the delightful courtesy and discretion shown in conversation with newcomers to the island. The following conversation between an old gentleman of Harris and two foreign tourists is accredited and relevant:

"It is a lovely day today. Are you enchoying your holidays?"

"Yes, we like Harris very much."

"Well, well, it is not much of a place. But I am glad you are enchoying it. And where would you be from yourselves?"

"We are German."

A stunned silence from the old war veteran. And then:

"Well, they say Hitler was a very clever man." After all, they might have been Adolf's fourth cousins.

The need to establish strangers in the context of their relations is deep-seated. Islanders are at first rather wary of newcomers who settle here. For them, the sole and sad reason for leaving home and relatives is to find employment. Why on earth should anyone from the rich mainland leave parents and cousins and come to Harris, where jobs and housing are scarce? Surely such a person must be a black sheep at home, to have abrogated the duties of care for aged relatives and mutual assistance to younger ones, and fled to Harris. When we lived first at Leachkin, we were amused to notice that the decorous Sunday afternoon walk permitted to Church of Scotland families (but not to the stricter Free Churches) switched from eastwards up the Caw to out the West Side, so that we could be kept an eye on. We rudely put it down to sheer nosiness, but I think now it was an attempt to discern our roots. Once our families had been seen to visit us, so that people had a clearer picture of our background, these perambulations ceased. Nowadays, of course, more and more mainland families are settling in the islands. The standard explanation for these removals is now acceptable, and quite rightly occasions local pride: that the islands are a refuge from the violence, overcrowding and status-seeking of the cities.

One would think that the steady trickle of mainland refugees might cause conflict in a rigidly traditional society. In fact, I think we are remarkably well tolerated. Every incomer is a stranger and also someone's neighbour, and benefits from the ancient customs of hospitality and neighbourliness, long atrophied in industrial society. The crofter next door may well despise and dislike the newcomers, with their loud English talk and irreverent Sunday habits, but he will still help them find their feet. They will be brought buckets of potatoes, legs of mutton, chunks of salmon. If these attentions cease after a while, the incomer should review his own behaviour: he, too, is someone's neighbour, and should have cemented the ties by giving unobtrusive gifts and doing small services, and by trying not to tread on local corns. For the heavy-footed mainlander, this is very difficult. For a start, with the best will in the world, he is bound to desecrate the Sabbath. Island Presbyterianism is ferociously Calvinistic and relies on very literal reading of the Bible. The mainland Christian as much as the mainland atheist will find himself in confusion, for parts of Deuteronomy that never see daylight over the Minch are here brought into play. It is an abomination to the Lord for a woman to wear trousers. Conversely, the great festivals of Easter and Christmas are totally ignored here by the religious: the Bible has not given us firm dates for them, so why follow Popish tradition? Popery, one feels, is the unforgiveable sin encompassing all others, and as one grim old patient told a young Anglican doctor here, "The Church of England is chust next door to the Church of Rome." The most remarkable feature of island life is the strict observance of the Sabbath. Not only may no work be done, but no leisure activities are permissible except for reading the Bible and the *Christian Herald*. However, as it is a day of rest, it is respectable to spend the entire day, between the two long church services, in bed with drawn curtains. (The temptations of such recreation must, I am sure, occasionally further procreation, but no one has yet researched this.)

Even the islanders do not all live up to the rigours to which they are enjoined. They are also quite tolerant of incomers' aberrations. As long as one's breaches are not defiant, one will be treated with restraint. The pulpits and the letter pages of the *Stornoway Gazette* thunder every other week against the abominable practices and vile blasphemies of people like me, but in practice no one expects any more than that we be discreet in our abominations. The first time one hangs out washing on a Sunday, a mild rebuke will reach one at third or fourth hand: "they were saying that some of the old people do not like it." The second time, no one will say anything, but it will go down as a deadly insult. I think it is sometimes so intended: it always puzzles me that people who love the place enough to want to live here cannot conform on such a trivial issue. But human relationships are full of absurd stances: wars are indeed fought over which end an egg should be eaten from.

Very similar attitudes prevail in the matter of the Gaelic language. This is still the language of home for many people, perhaps most families, but contact with the mainland and television are steadily eroding it. Not surprisingly, the islanders are sad, though resigned. Occasionally, in print, they will rage against the arrogant incomers who are hastening its demise. But in fact, no one will force you to learn it or even listen to it. We have always found that if we go into a room or a shop where Gaelic is being spoken, people will immediately change to English, even amongst themselves, for fear that we should find them rude. I am sorry to admit our attempts to learn the language have been abortive: I feel we owe a debt to island courtesy in not having taken the trouble. There is great pathos in the delight our Gaelic-speaking friends have shown because our young daughter is fluent in their language. Yet no one considers it remarkable that her Gaelic-speaking contemporaries have to pick up English in infancy. Really, the islanders do not expect much of incomers, and their tolerance is commendable.

We would have found Harris life much more puzzling at first if we had not had kind local friends. The first person we met on our arrival was Mrs Peggy Macaskill, who held the keys of our rented house for the absent owner. She was full of kindness and useful advice. Often she would call us in as we passed her house for a cup of tea and her own delicious baking, and send us home laden with gifts—pancakes, scones and "maragan", the home-made black and white puddings that are an island speciality. Having arrived in Harris with no money, in fact in debt to the tune of one old Land-Rover, we were especially grateful for these tactful gifts. John Macaskill sub-let the croft on which our house stood, and soon became a familiar figure. He was a big, burly old man, who had to come through our narrow back door sideways, to his own great amusement. He was forever with his sheep, dosing, dipping, shearing, lambing, or just leaning on his crook watching them benignly. Though in his seventies, he would heave a pair of sparring rams apart, one in each fist, or toss a strayed ewe on his shoulder with a flick of his wrist. Often he stood deep in thought, with a lamb tucked under one arm, or inhaling blissfully the sweet scent of newly-cut hay packed into his little byre against the winter. He drove an old black van, in which his friends and family feared greatly for his safety, for if he saw a particularly interesting or a troubled sheep, he would stop dead or veer right or left the better to look at it, oblivious of traffic. The same disconcerting halts occurred if he spotted a likely-looking stone for the fine wall he was making at his house, for he was a talented mason, and in fact he and his sons were builders. But how could he distinguish good stones from bad at a glance, among all the rocks in Harris? We were very fond of John, and also in awe of him. His mixture of childlike enthusiasm and thoughtful observation made his conversation a delight. He died some years ago, but when we pass Leachkin I still expect to see him in his fore-and-aft cap, leaning on his crook. I never hear sung "He shall feed his flock like a shepherd" without thinking of John Macaskill, whose care for his flock was more illuminating than any number of theological commentaries.

When we first arrived in Harris, we ate what we could scrape up, on account of the unpaid-for Land-Rover. As spring and the first visiting relatives drew near, however, young married pride demanded some more respectable provisioning. We bought a small second-hand freezer, and looked around for things to put in it. Where was the butcher in Harris?

"Go and see the Macaulay Boys at 1, Ardhasaig," we were told, "the house with the trees at Caolas na Sgeir." Ardhasaig is next to Leachkin. 1, Ardhasaig is not the first in a street, but the first croft in the Ardhasaig township: the system of numbering sounds oddly urban to an outsider. As we neared the gate, a figure that might be a Macaulay Boy appeared shyly between the trees. I was not surprised that the Boy seemed to be older than us, as we had already discovered that island boys remain boys well into their forties, and into their nineties if they never marry. We were welcomed politely and asked how we liked Leachkin and the school and the weather. Being in a hurry to get back to filling my tiresome new freezer, I rudely (in retrospect) cut the pleasantries short by asking,

"Are you the butcher?"

"No. I am the butcher's brother. Calum is out with the van just now. Will you come in and wait for him? I'll make you a wee cup of tea."

I hastily demurred, and handed over an order for the actual butcher to deliver to us. On the way home, Andrew was plaintive. He would have liked to have tea with the butcher's brother, he said. We never went anywhere or made any friends. Why on earth hurry home? And anyway, I had been horribly rude.

So I had. I became very cross.

A few days later, the Land-Rover being off the road with seized brakes, we were walking back from work when an oncoming van stopped and out jumped both Macaulay boys, Calum and John Angus. They shook hands cordially and enquired after the Land-Rover. On hearing of its troubles, they promised help: they would see we got the spare parts: we would have them next day. And when would we come down for a ceilidh? We promised to call the following Saturday.

Next day, to our amazement, the Land-Rover parts duly arrived. Peter Mackinnon, the postman, a cousin by marriage of the Macaulays, had been called in to help, and had stripped the required pieces from an old vehicle of his own. Twelve years on, it is still the same story: if there's something you need, ask the Macaulay boys. If they don't have it, they won't rest till they find someone else who has. There have never been such neighbours, not only to us but to everyone they encounter.

That Saturday we went for our ceilidh, the first of many. A ceilidh does not mean the studio performance folk-concert suggested by television representations: it is simply a leisurely social call, with plenty of yarn-swapping and (of course) refreshments. John Angus's "wee cup of tea" is legendary, and puts many five-course dinners in the shade. In the coming months we learned his technique of hospitality. We would start making "must go" noises at about 10 o'clock.

"No, no, you'll just stay for a wee cup of tea! I'm just going to put the kettle on."

John Angus's kettle is trained to boil only when his guests make their next attempt to leave—about 10.30, perhaps. Then he disappears into the kitchen, to return with plates laden with goodies —bread and cheese, cakes, chocolate biscuits, or in extreme cases platters of salmon and salad. The consumption of this repast takes a good half hour. Sometime before midnight we try to leave again —and John Angus and Calum go hither and thither, fetching us things to take home, fruit, sweets, household goods, books and magazines. Their hospitality and generosity are astounding. Parting, we are always reproached with, "you didn't stay long enough!"

Nothing we can ever do could repay the Macaulays for their kindnesses. In those early days, it left us constantly perplexed, taxing our ingenuity to do little things in return that would please them. Their mother, a gentle, uncomplaining lady bent double with arthritis, liked scones rather than bread, but could no longer bake her own easily. I used to make some for her, and horrible they were—hard as rocks and half burnt: I can't bake like the Harris women. But they were as politely grateful as if they had been manna—and promptly set about showering us with yet more gifts, and time, and trouble.

I think I shall have a great deal more to say about the Macaulays in the following chapters.

3

Doing it Ourselves

As 1974 wore on, we settled in to our new friends and interests and our new home. Leachkin House was a grand place to be. It had been built by a wealthy dealer in tweeds, and inherited by his granddaughter, who was at that time living in Edinburgh. She wanted it lived in, to curb the creeping dampness which afflicts Hebridean buildings, and accordingly let us have it for a low rent. Two rooms were shut off, one of them containing what our landlady called "the bed that Bonnie Prince Charlie *didn't* sleep in"—an amazing construction with a headboard up to the picture-rail. The rest of the house was ours, including a large utility room, or rather utility suite, as it had a pantry, a laundry and a toilet off it, and a loft above. The possibility of this region as a carpenter's shop struck Andrew immediately. Soon it was full of lengths of timber, collected, cadged, and (when I would permit) bought.

We each kept a suspicious eye on the other's spending. Andrew would castigate me on the unnecessary cost in petrol of a shopping trip to Stornoway, and once there I would hover round him as soon as he got near a rack of chisels. Such vigilance was necessary. We knew that if we wanted to buy a large property in the next few years, we had to save everything we could.

Knowing the rigours ahead, we set ourselves a programme of frugality and self-reliance. We switched off the expensive central heating, for a start. Not that we had any intention of cheating our poor landlady out of her house-airing—we simply did not realise how generously low she had set the rent. Having been recently students, and for so long, we simply accepted this as our due. What swelled heads we had! Next, we surveyed our domestic machinery. There was no fridge and no washing machine. For fridge there was

40

a device in a far corner of the pantry called an ozocool, consisting of a cabinet of porous pottery, which had to be soaked and covered with a cotton wrapper, and then cooled the contents by evaporation. Andrew proclaimed sturdily that it worked very well: so it did, until the house temperature rose above 40°F, which occurred about Easter. After that, the cover went mouldy and so did the food inside. Washing was more entertaining. As there was a convenient stream running under the road by the house, we took the clothes out there for rinsing. As we waded knee deep in the freezing torrent, we would look up to see silent and astonished faces peering over the bridge above. Plainly, respectable personages like teachers should not do the wash in the manner of a Harris cailleach of 50 years ago. Some of the primary-school children made special Saturday excursions on their bikes just to stare at us. By the end of our first year, our towels and sheets were indescribably grubby. John Angus brought out from the recesses of his byre an ancient hand-turned washing machine, consisting of a zinc tub with a wooden lid. Andrew stuck an electric element in it, and it made a tolerable boiler. Unfortunately, if the clothes inside touched the wooden lid, they were indelibly dyed orange at once.

Though most of Harris has gone over to fridges and washing machines, many satisfying hand crafts are still performed daily as a matter of course. The uneven and rocky terrain makes it impossible to mechanise peat-cutting, potato-planting or scything, for example. Then all the crafts of the weaver can be, and often are, performed without machinery, through carding, spinning and dyeing to fulling the finished cloth. Most weavers only do the actual weaving at home, but many have the knowledge of the other skills as well. Old Mrs Macaulay used to sit twisting yarn for socks on a tear-shaped spindle as she talked, raising it with a gentle jerk and letting it spiral gently to the ground. I was fascinated, and Andrew made me a spindle to try my hand. Full of enthusiasm, I bought a sack of the single-ply yarn remnants on cardboard cones from one of the Stornoway weaving mills. This hairy, greasy stuff, when twisted into three plys, knitted up, and washed with washing soda, makes the rough, warm working gear of the islands, pull-overs, hats and socks.

My attempts with the spindle were not encouraging. The resulting yarn was either screwed up like a nest of worms or completely untwisted. A spinning wheel does the job more easily, so on our first visit to Aberdeen, I bore off an old wheel my parents had once been given. Mrs Macaulay assessed the missing parts, and John Angus and Andrew soon refurbished it. Twisting on this was easy and soothing. I soon fancied myself an expert, and wanted to try spinning from the fleece. The principle is the same, but the direction of the twist is reversed, and the degree of tension required to obtain an even thread is very sensitive. Mrs Macaulay patiently demonstrated carding the raw wool and rolling it with a little oil into long soft rolls, and spun these to an even yarn, both on the hand spindle and on the wheel. My own attempts were laughable —the rolls disappeared into compact fat sausages or broke into shreds. It would have needed many long winter evenings of practice to produce a usable result. Of course, this was how it used to be done, with the children set to carding and the women busy spinning or knitting by firelight. The men, I gather, sat in their dignity and smoked their pipes.

In the old days, still alive in the memories of the island's sprightly octogenarians, the cultivation of a majestic beard and the occupation of the only chair in the house seem to have been the chief tasks of "men folk". "Women folk" on the other hand, not only performed the household duties and bore large families: they spun, wove and knitted, cultivated the crops, milked the cows, baited fishing lines, fetched peats on their backs, cut and carried seaweed for fertiliser, and sometimes rowed the heavy wooden boats, though it was "man's work" to steer them. I once asked an ex-inhabitant of Scarp, as we strolled round that island, what on earth the men had done with their time.

"Well," he said, "every day they had a Parliament at the end of the mission-house, to agree what to do that day. Maybe they would decide on something, maybe not. They might just stay there and smoke and talk and then go home. But there was one job the men always did, because it was not decent for the women."

"What was that?"

"It was always the man who took the cow to the bull."

It was also always the man who cut peat while the women threw it on the bank to dry, and I soon discovered why: the cutter has merely to push the iron lightly with his foot and it glides through the soft wet peat; the unfortunate wife squelching in the bog below receives a weighty, collapsing slab, which she has to throw often above her own head-height to some considerable distance on the bank. Successive slabs must not land on each other. After one session, we reversed the roles and have kept that way ever since, which must seem comical to the traditionally-minded.

Peat is a big event of the island year. Only crofters have a right to cut it, usually on their township's common grazing, but people who do not cut all their quota are often prepared to let non-crofters take some. The Macaskills kindly let us have a bank, up on the shoulder of Clisham above Loch Seaforth. It was May, the views were superb, and we could see at once why everyone enjoys peats. We followed instructions and began by turfing the bank. The top surface, to about sixteen inches back from the cut face of the previous year is taken out with a spade and dropped turf side up onto the squelchy mess at the foot of the bank. This helps regeneration, and also gives the thrower something reasonably firm to stand on. A slash at right angles to the cut face is now made at one end, to help the first section of peat out. From then on, the taisgeir is employed. This is a narrow blade about 12 inches long, at right angles to a wooden handle. In Harris the blade is shorter: ours was made in Lewis, and old men shook their heads over it and advised us to lop a bit off it. However, Harris and Lewis have not managed to evolve different techniques, in spite of this disagreement: the cutter stands on top of the turfless strip, and with his foot pushes the blade straight down to take out a block about 18 inches long by three to four inches in profile. This wet, slippery slab, like a huge piece of chocolate fudge, falls off into the hands of the thrower who tosses it as far away as possible across the top of the bank. Other slabs are removed until the iron has cut a neat face vertical to the turf. The cutter retreats thus along the bank, and at the end of it returns to take the next section downwards, and perhaps a third one after that. By the end of the session, the thrower is running out of ground, and the wet peats may be stacked on the edge of the bank, one spanning two others underneath, so that air spaces are left.

At this stage, everyone looks nervously at the sky and prays for fine weather. If the soggy slabs do not have a few days of drying air and sun now, they never firm up satisfactorily at all, but disintegrate on the ground. That is why cutting is usually done between the end of April and mid-June, the driest part of the year. There is an old saying which runs "If you won't have peats by midsummer, you won't have peats at all."

After our first cutting, there were three weeks of unbroken

sunshine. When we went back to the bank, we wondered where our peats had gone. Close examination revealed tiny desiccated squares among the now well grown heather. The stuff had shrunk by half in all dimensions, for peat is about 90% water.

The next step is to set it damp side outwards in small "houses" —four peats leaning vertically together with one flat on the top to hold them there. After another drying period, anything from a couple of days to a couple of weeks, it is piled into small round stacks, with any still wet peats placed flat on the outside. When these are dry too, it can be piled into higher more conical stacks, protected from the rain by turves or plastic sheets, and left out for collection as required. However, in North Harris people take theirs home at this stage. Old fashioned hessian sacks are most prized for the purpose—they are easier to hoist on one's back than a plastic sack. Peat is less heavy for its bulk than coal, but carrying sack after sack of it to a waiting vehicle over rough ground is strenuous work. The bank we borrowed at first was uphill from the road, so we carried downhill—the most satisfactory way. Thereafter, most of our peat was cut on the downward slope, and we carried it uphill. This was made more difficult by our neighbour at peats, a tricksy man, who extended his bank between us and the road, so that we had to jump down into his quagmire with our heavy sacks and then up again. His action was regarded as very anti-social, so I had no qualms about jumping heavily on the edge of his cutting and kicking his peats into the bog. Andrew disassociated himself from these actions. I am unrepentant. There is a venerable island tradition of cutting throats over peats.

Once home, the peats are stacked for winter in a special way. A hollow oblong is marked out in peats placed slantwise, edge outwards. Inside this loose peats are jumbled. The better-looking peats are kept for the outer "wall", which continues upwards, sloping in slightly as it progresses. The slant is kept in one direction in most places, but one of our neighbours was a Scalpay man, and they do theirs herringbone fashion. Once the stack is nearing completion, the top is rounded over with a roof of flat peats. It is now perfectly weatherproof. People take great pride in the size and neatness of their peatstacks: in Lewis, where they are "mad on peat" and sometimes cut the banks twice each spring, the stacks

45

are sometimes bigger than the houses. They can never use it all up, but the tradition of the work is so pleasurable that addicts can't resist it.

Our first stack was not one of these monumental edifices. It looked about enough for a family of gnomes, such were the unexpected effects of shrinkage.

We picked up other useful skills from our local friends. Andrew learned how to make lobster pots. Suddenly, I was permitted to go to Stornoway for shopping: it was only there he could procure the 20 feet of Manila cane, the polypropylene twine and netting needle used for this job. The remaining ingredients, wood, rope, float and plastic rings for the "eyes" of the creel, could be found beachcombing. There were always plenty of wrecked creels on our rocky shore.

The base of the creel is a slatted wooden base about $18'' \times 27''$. Six holes drilled in this take the three hoops of cane, bent in a squarish profile, not pointed. Three lengthwise pieces of cane at the top and sides lashed to the hoops complete the frame, which is covered with netting, either ready made or knotted from black polypropylene twine. The apparent mysteries of net-making are not difficult to master once the principle is grasped. As much twine as will comfortably fit is wound on to the netting needle, and a scrap length of twine stretched taut at a convenient height. A series of triangular loops is made along this. Each side of the eventual square mesh should be about one and a half inches. A "mesh stick" such as an ordinary ruler can be used to keep the triangles all the same size. Now working back towards the beginning, the first row of knots is made. These are simply sheet bends, and once the knack of tying them with the netting needle has been mastered, they can be made rapidly and even-sized. At the end of the row change direction again, and so on to make a rectangular piece of netting about two feet wide and long enough to cover the hooped part of the creel. The scrap piece of twine which held the first row is now removed, and the netting is tied or stapled to the base. The ends of the creel are covered in a similar manner. To make the eye through which the lobster enters, a roughly circular hole is cut in the net at one side and the loose ends picked up and knotted with the needle. Two or three rows of netting are formed around the

circle and it is finished off with a plastic ring of five inches diameter. This is pulled inside the creel and tied to the canes opposite, and with any luck will have produced a nicely flared tunnel through which a lobster can easily crawl in, but not so easily escape. A suitable stone must now be tied to the bottom so that the creel will sink, and between this and the centre of the top should be made an arrangement of stout twine and slip-knots to hold the bait. The finishing touch is to cut a slit in one side and lace it up with string of a contrasting colour. This is where you will take your lobster out! The rope for hauling should be at least 30 feet long, or more for fishing in deep water. It is disappointing to heave a lobster pot over the side and watch it pull the entire rope and top float down into the murky depths because you haven't made the rope long enough.

After construction, the pots are blackened with paint or tar, to persuade lobsters to go in—they like dark crannies. Then the pot is filled with stones and sunk in the water for a few days: lobsters will not enter unsoaked pots, as these emit air bubbles and don't sink properly.

I spent a lot of time tanning sheepskins, trying to work out whether they were a useful source of income or not. In the end I decided they were not. I could ask between £5 and £10 at that time for a finished rug, and this represented hours of work. I could get the skins themselves for nothing during the autumn, which is the killing season. Most people dump the hides as they fetch very little anyway, and have to be salted and stored, smelly and oozing, until a consignment is wanted for some mainland firm.

To make a rug you must start with a freshly flayed hide, otherwise the wool will come out. Our landlady's utility room was soon redolent of fresh mutton fat: later, of rancid mutton fat. After an initial wash in warm soapy water, the flesh side has to be scraped of adherent flesh and fat. It is slippery work and greasy crumbs scatter in all directions. After rinsing and draining, which I did in the stream outside, the flesh side is pickled with a 4:1 mixture of alum and salt dissolved in water. Next day, the skin is stretched flat for tanning. Andrew made wooden frames for the purpose, about six feet by four with a zig-zag arrangement of netting twine to give the skin some support. About 20 short lengths of string were attached to the wool by slip-knots, and the skin was stretched taut by tying these to nails suitably positioned in the wooden perimeter. We used a chrome solution, consisting of eight ounces of chrome tanning powder to a gallon of water with the addition of two ounces of salt and a quarter pint of corn oil emulsified with washing-up liquid. This is brushed on daily until the bluish colour of the chrome can be seen in the skin on the wool side when the hairs are parted. The skin is left till all excess moisture has soaked into the leather—about 24 hours—then doused with water several times (out of doors!) to remove excess salt. Still on the frame, it now has to dry completely, which may take several days. Once it is dry, the unprepossessing curled up bits at the edges can be trimmed off with scissors, the skin side sandpapered, and the fleece side combed. This last is a very hairy job—I always did it sitting outside, with the wind behind me.

The work was satisfying, but laborious. After about 20, I had had enough. We sold a few and gave the rest away as Christmas presents. Some of the recipients were not entirely happy with the sheep wool that spread over their dark carpets, for try as I might I produced very few rugs guaranteed not to moult.

Much of our time and energy at Leachkin went into producing or catching food, and great fun we had playing at self-sufficiency. Our first requirement was a vegetable garden. As with most island houses our "garden" consisted of an enclosure fenced against sheep, with nothing growing in it but grass. However, a stream ran through it between rocky outcrops, and in summer this region was a natural rock-garden full of orchids and other flowers. Near the fence below the house were the remains of old lazy beds, and it was these we selected for cultivation. Lazy beds—no one knows where the term originates—are narrow raised strips about four feet wide and as long as the lie of the land permits, between which drainage ditches are dug. Each year that they are in production, they are well mulched with seaweed, and they are usually left fallow on alternate years. This is the ancient system of cultivation on all peaty ground in the islands. Nowadays, only those near the houses, if any, are used, but in the past, when the population supported themselves and their livestock on oats, potatoes and hay, they were everywhere. On a sunny day, the softened contours of these old ridges give a singular cast to the Hebridean landscape. They stretch up the hills to the bald summits, comb the tiniest offshore islets, and wriggle between the bare rocks of the Bays. The work involved must have been prodigious, for even when drained, peat will only produce well if it has a good dose of seaweed or dung added.

Andrew sweated to dig out the stubborn clumps of rush from the blocked up drains, and I followed, forking in the evil-smelling pile of festering seaweed I had been nurturing for weeks. The more rotten the better: fresh stuff, in the cold wet peat, becomes preserved and does not break down. Unfortunately, as we had gathered our seaweed in a school lunch break, near the playing field where all the rubbish fetched up, it was full of non-nutritious foreign bodies. I kept having to pick out old shoes, bottle tops, spent torch batteries, dolls' legs and so forth. By the time I had finished, I smelt pretty bad myself.

Having got our ground, as we hoped, fertile, we set about planting things. Andrew didn't know a cabbage from a lettuce, and I had never planted anything but candytuft and marigolds. We sought advice from books and knowledgeable friends.

"Globe artichokes will thrive in a frost-free situation," said the book.

"Well, you could try the potatoes," said local opinion.

"Maize or Indian corn may be easily grown outdoors in Britain," said the book.

"Kerr's Pink is a very good potato," said local opinion.

"In recent years courgettes and sweet peppers have gained great popularity," said the one.

"Well, you would be safest with Kerr's Pink," said the other.

So we tried everything. We had to have Kerr's Pinks, as it would obviously cause offence if we didn't. We also put in artichokes (both kinds), parsnips, turnips, swedes, courgettes, peas, beans (French and Broad), spinach, celery, kohl rabi, radishes, endive, lettuce, beetroot (red and yellow—what optimism!), leeks, onions, garlic and every known brassica. Everything came up in neat rows and as the summer nights lengthened I weeded them lovingly till midnight. Then things began to wilt, to turn strange colours, and to disappear. We suffered the ravages of caterpillars, cabbage root fly, aphids, eelworm, potato blight, scab, wart disease, celery rust and many, many more. What survived shot before maturity in the long light of July, or succumbed to gales in September. The Kerr's Pinks had lovely flowers and minuscule roots, whereas the parsley had immense gnarled roots and no top growth. The artichokes choked, and a mouse got into the box of carrots I was storing in ashes for the winter.

But we still had quite a lot to eat out of our garden—in the case of the cabbage tribe, more than Andrew cared for. By the next season we had learned some lessons, and our efforts were reasonably successful. Except for occasionally buying some tomatoes, we were self-sufficient in vegetables for the next few years, though our consumption was not very varied. We even had plenty to give away to friends. Andrew was always particularly pleased to donate outsize cabbages. He considers with Culpeper that "cabbages are extremely windy—yea, as windy meat as can be eaten, unless you eat bag-pipes or bellows."

With less windy meats we were kept well supplied by John Angus. Having discovered that we were omnivorous, and ravenous, he introduced us to some of the singular local dishes which might repel weaker stomachs. He brought us a sheep's head, horns off but eyes in, which is boiled as the basis for a delicious broth. He procured for me basins of stomachs, lights and suet to be used in the making of haggis, white puddings and the sweet fruit puddings. Finding we had a taste for offal, he brought us brains, hearts and livers. When I expressed an interest in cheese and butter making, he brought us a daily bucket of milk and instructions from his cousin on what to do with it. He got us a skinned cormorant, a traditional local delicacy. He introduced us to salt herring and salt conger, and threatened to get us a salt gannet, too: but warned us that you felt very sorry for the poor thing when you saw its big blue feet sticking out of the pot.

At this last item, our experimental zeal faded. We have never eaten a guga, the young gannets taken from Sula Sgeir by the men of Ness, and salted for eager consumption by Lewismen at home and abroad. I believe most of them go to Nova Scotia. How they export them I do not know. I expect they are parcelled up in brown paper by well-wishing cousins and sisters, with customs labels stating "one guga—unsolicited gift—value £4.75". What customs officer would suspect that the parcel held a salt gannet?

Though we baulked at gannet and felt it heartless to eat many cormorants, we had great culinary adventures as a result of all these free provisions. I insisted that it is extravagant and immoral to waste food. Andrew agreed with this principle, but I think he began to have doubts when he saw to what lengths of ingenuity I was willing to go. For instance, when I had suet over from a batch of haggis, I was not prepared to jettison it. I would try an old recipe for ginger pudding. Unfortunately, the stuff would not go through the mincer without gumming it up. I chopped it. It stuck to the knife, the table and the floor. The pieces were not very small, but still, it had worked for haggis, so why not for ginger pudding? I did wonder about the strong smell of sheep as the pudding boiled, for the recipe had in fact stipulated beef suet. The result was nauseous. It is hard to imagine what large chunks of mutton fat studding a ginger sponge taste like till you have tried. Even Andrew rejected a second helping.

Then there was the sheep's tripe. I hate tripe anyway, but had begged some out of thriftiness. It smelt very, very sheepy. Grimly,

I persevered with *Tripe à la Mode de Caen*. Simmer in a very low oven overnight, the recipe said. I put it all in my wedding-present le Creuset pot and went to bed, closing the door against the odour of sheep's entrails. By morning, a worse and more acrid odour had crept upstairs—burnt sheep's entrails. The kitchen was filled with black smoke and my best pot was ruined. I burst into tears, but later we both agreed we were glad not to have had to eat the stuff.

Having taken up a little desultory poaching, we were troubled by an excess of salmon. Andrew became ill-tempered on the subject. We filled the freezer, and gave up poaching, but well-meaning friends kept arriving with more and more "wee fish". In desperation, I turned to the *Penguin Book of Indian Cookery*. The recipe for Pork Vindaloo had a lot of vinegar in it—it might disguise the taste of salmon. I maintain the result was worse than the ginger pudding, but after 10 years Andrew cautiously classes it as "not really that bad, considering some of the other things." We also tried smoking salmon in a barrel over a fire of chips and sawdust, but the smoke must have been too hot; the result resembled salty cardboard.

Once we began to set lobster pots, we caught a few lobsters and a great variety of other creatures. Were any of them good to eat? Francophile cookery books assured us that sea urchins were a great delicacy, so one day we took two large ones home for lunch. But how did one eat them? And had they to be cooked first? We looked at them with misgivings; they were very beautiful, and entirely harmless. The small spines on their bases, on which they move around, waved gently. Better get it over as soon as possible. We dropped them into boiling water and gave them five minutes. They were very large ones, so arming ourselves with teaspoons and bread and butter, we sat down, as we supposed, to a hearty lunch. There was about a half teaspoonful of evil-tasting brown sludge in each —that was all. If we had eaten them raw, like the black-backs do, there would have been slime rather than sludge, and somewhat more of it. We varnished the shells and put them on the windowsill. After that, the sea urchins went back into the sea.

Another day we brought home a dozen enormous whelks. They oozed and eased their way over each other and up the side of the bucket, each dirty white shell supported on a dirty yellow foot.

Friends had assured us they were edible, but as we watched them, we began to feel mysteriously unhungry. We returned them to the water untested.

We got used to eating a certain amount of salt fish. It is traditional and popular in Harris, having been a necessity before the days of freezers. When the mackerel came in August, we salted down whatever we couldn't eat fresh, planning to use the rest over the winter, and keep the surplus for next year's lobster bait. The first few, from the top of the barrel, were quite good. As we got further down to older stock, they were indifferent, and a little later unpleasant and smeared with thick orange grease. By December, they were loathsome, but we ate them dutifully. One night after a particularly nasty specimen I was violently sick. We went off on holiday soon afterwards, and when we returned an unfortunate rat had fallen into the mackerel barrel and drowned in brine. After this we did not feel inclined to finish the contents.

When Andrew had made his first lobster pots, he used to set them hopefully off the rocks; but he soon got tired of catching nothing but sea urchins and whelks, and began prowling round the boats in Tarbert harbour. We could not afford a boat, but there was no question of doing without one. It was rather an unorthodox vessel—a little Avon inflatable, only 10 feet long. To save money, we did without bottom boards. Consequently, the floor was always wobbly and usually under water—rather like a floating paddling pool. We had no engine either, so that if there was much wind we had to row at incredible speed even to stay in the same place. However, it was a very suitable boat, as we could easily carry it around, or drag it up stony beaches. The tough rounded sides suffered no damage from hauling lobster pots in, it didn't matter if we went aground, and it was extremely stable. In a chop it was terrifying, but West Loch Tarbert in summer, unlike the open sea, has very little swell, even in a wind.

Once we had a boat, we could fish. The Macaulays advised us what to catch where. Close in to the rocky shore, one could get saithe and lythe at certain places. However, we usually snagged our tackle on the rocks and lost it. We were very impatient fishermen: if we didn't get a bite at once, we lost interest. Mackerel were much more rewarding. If a shoal was around, one simply dropped a weighted line behind the boat, and immediately they were on it, one on each hook. They are beautiful, lively fish, muscular and iridescent, with boldly-flared tails. We always snapped their necks to kill them as we took them off the hooks, but they continued to flap and quiver for up to half an hour, even if we beheaded and gutted them there and then. This sobering circumstance always stopped us fishing after about 40 fish, but you could get that many in 10 minutes on a good day. We grilled them very fresh, with a sprig of bog myrtle in the cavity, and they were delicious.

The fish that all our local friends praised as the finest summer fare were cuddies, small fish to be caught off piers and inshore rocks. No one could tell us what type of fish they were, only that they were small and exquisite in flavour. We presented various unknown fish from our catch for inspection—but no, these weren't cuddies. They might be very good to eat, but they would not—could not—match up to cuddies. Eventually, someone generously presented us with a bag of the favoured fish. When I took them out to fry, they looked very like young saithe—but surely not? We fried them in the prescribed manner: they were fresh and wholesome, but quite uninteresting in flavour—very like young saithe, in fact. To this day, I am secretly convinced that that is what they are. Perhaps in the past the friable bland flesh of these early summer fish was so welcome after a long winter of hard salted flesh that the traditional delight still clings to it. Certainly on fine summer evenings all the piers and selected rocks in Harris are full of men and boys with long bamboo rods, eagerly fishing for cuddies.

Our little boat was also an ideal vessel for salmon poaching. Being grey and silent, it could easily be slipped out in the summer twilight, when it, the pale green net and the grey floats were invisible to passing vehicles. There cannot be many Harris men who don't poach now and again, though very few do it on a commercial scale. Most people have more than enough salmon to eat after one or two fish, as it is very rich and oily, but it is difficult to resist going out again and again for the excitement of it. It is certainly as much a sport as legitimate rod fishing, but in poaching the interest lies in the secrecy of it and the attendant risk of being caught. Peace-loving, respectable, sober-living men are titillated by the possibility of themselves dashing across country, pursued by angry water bailiffs, or hauled into the Police Station at dawn, refusing to confess where the incriminating net is hidden, or apprehended on the highway with a bootful of fish. We were so entertained by this scenario that we almost wished it would happen, and besides, we soon grew tired of staying up all night to tend the net, so we insisted on doing our fishing in the morning, when all sensible poachers had gone home to bed. This worried our fishing partner dreadfully. I shall never forget one scorching morning in July, seeing him perspiring up the hill in a heavy tweed jacket, trying to look as if he had a hump back rather than 30lb of salmon underneath it. Unfortunately, and unknown to him, four fishy tails hung out behind.

Our pleasantest fishing was setting and hauling our lobster pots. From talking to other people and from gradual experience over our three summers at Leachkin, we learnt the best times and places to catch them. They are scarce till after they cast and regenerate their shells, and then as the water warms up in August and early September they seem to migrate inshore, possibly after the plankton

56

which begins to turn the water milky at that time of year. Lobsters, however, do not really like being exposed to the brightness of summer sun in shallow water over a pale bottom. They lurk at the edge of the rocks and tangle, and have the benefit of prey swimming in the warmer water over light sand and shingle nearby. So the best place to catch them is at the edge of the weed. In calm water inshore, it is quite easy to see where the dark weed-growth, looking brown or purple, gives way to deep turquoise bare sand. However, this brightness also gives the night-caught lobster a chance to escape as the sun gets higher in the sky, so that it is best to inspect pots as near dawn as possible. If we felt keen, we would go out before school, but really we did not mind if they escaped. We never sold them, and the 20 or 30 we caught each summer were enough to give our visitors a treat and to make presents for friends. What did infuriate us was that in our last summer a fisherman from further out the loch took to robbing our pots before dawn. That got us out of bed early for a time, but after a week or so we became so tired and disgruntled that we took our pots home and gave up.

Though we did not catch very many lobsters, we had immense enjoyment from these daily trips. In later summer, life swarms in the water. The often lobsterless pots were full of interesting things. As well as sea urchins and whelks, there were two types of starfish, the common kind (a voracious eater of lobster bait) and beautiful brittle stars, with thin curled arms fringed with crimson filaments. Whelks often turned out to be hermit crabs, peering apologetically out of doors, or staggering nervously away with their heavy houses on their backs. There were also gawky spider crabs and slow-moving squat lobsters, always too small to eat, which was rather a relief. Velvet crabs, with their furry backs and brilliant blue markings, were always spoiling for a fight, waving their pincers belligerently and dashing across the floor of the pot to attack an exposed hand. I was not nervous of handling lobsters, which can be rendered harmless if you grasp them round the back and elbows, but velvet crabs are another matter. Though small, they often delivered a nasty nip. I usually poked and shook them out. They swam beautifully, their blue hind paddles flashing as they descended. The other hazard to the fingers was stinging jellyfish, which often got wrapped round the ropes. It was then like hauling in a bunch of nettles. The live specimens are gorgeous to watch, richly tan-coloured and trailing five or six feet of milky white tentacles.

Quite often there were fish trapped in the pots, wriggling frantically to escape. We got a strange thin red pipe fish like an elongated sea-horse. Sometimes there were dog fish, which make excellent evil-smelling bait. We caught about a dozen lobsters off one. We once had a conger, which slid with a sinister grace into the boat, silent and sleek in its movements, but grinding and snapping its teeth between our boots. We stared at it with horrified fascination. A conger needs to be despatched by decapitation or crushing its head. If you don't kill it, it will bite. Sawing its head off with a knife was plainly impossible in a rubber boat. It opened its jaws to 180°, displaying rapier fangs, and I wondered about jumping overboard: I had once had a nasty bite from the severed head of a conger which had been officially dead for 24 hours. Fortunately, this one coiled itself round in a circle and shot back over the side. On another occasion we caught a red gurnard, a very pretty fish, like a mermaid's pet in a fairy tale, with large eyes and dragon-wing fins. They make good eating, so we were pleased to see it, but as I reached for it to break its neck, it gave a sad little grunt, and raised its dorsal fin hopelessly. We put it back in the sea at once.

We were rather silent on the way home after the gurnard, for it raised questions. We had felt sorry for it, I think, because it "talked". What of the other, voiceless fish, the lythe, mackerel, salmon and lobsters? Were they really any more alien and less deserving of pity?

After that, more things went back in the water, lobsters that were small or berried, or the occasional edible crab, too small to be worth the trouble of scraping out its flesh. Anyway, it was a great delight to watch our motley catch swimming for the bottom. Normally, there is little chance of seeing the free movements of such creatures in the water.

We always killed our lobsters by heating them in salty cold water, which I am fairly convinced is humane after observing them closely at all stages of the process. It must be done really slowly, taking about 20 minutes to reach 70°F, and remaining slow till the blue-black carapace begins to turn red. The creatures make no unnatural or distressed movements when killed in this way, unlike lobsters thrown into boiling water. Even so, actually catching them became less and less of a pleasure. When they were handled, they made hopeless, clumsy attempts to nip. In the puddles in the bottom of the boat, they tried vainly to swim backwards and escape. The light must have seared their dusk-loving eyes, and the heat of the sun soon made them froth at the mouth. We used to put them under the seat, covered with a cloth or seaweed and there they were peaceful. We reasoned that if we didn't catch them, someone else would, and then they were in for a rough time— stuffed into boxes to await transport to distant markets, and then as likely as not boiled alive in great cages at Billingsgate.

Before we had begun to catch and kill some of our own food, these considerations had been easy to ignore. Now they began to weigh on us, and we felt keenly the responsibility to deal well with what we caught, and in particular, not to waste life, any life, without good reason. This was impressed on us for ever by an incident in our last summer. We had been setting pots for weeks below the Macaulays' croft, and had caught nothing, so we shifted our operations to the far side of the loch. We left one pot behind, as there was no room for it in the boat. We felt we ought to go back for it, in case there was anything in it, but the place had been entirely barren. It was a fortnight till we reclaimed it. When I hauled it in, we saw a sad sight. A huge lobster, his body filling the whole space between the eyes of the creel, hung there dead. His massive pincers were spread wide, one over each tunnel of netting. He hung as if crucified. We looked at each other with silent guilt. It seemed appalling that this armoured giant, who must have lived many seasons to attain such a size, should die like that, stuck in a tawdry human trap. It could have been disease, or the presence of a nearby freshwater outlet that killed him, or starvation or confinement. There was no way of telling. Whatever it was, we could make no excuses. We had both felt strongly we should return to that last creel, but other pursuits had made us brush it aside. We had not taken the trouble to act responsibly. We felt like murderers, and deserved to.

The little lives and deaths of the lobster pots taught us a sobering rule: take only what you need, kill it cleanly, and be aware that you are a killer. In the West Loch we met a lone French yachtsman, who in his frail 20 foot craft, under sail alone, was heading for Iceland. "I catch le poisson, yes. But only one. I do not take for tomorrow." How right he was. There are not many like him. Often in a boat with our friends, we have seen fish after fish hauled in and left flapping and suffocating, while the line goes greedily out for more, and more, and more. The human faces are excited and laughing. The other mouths and eyes open in agony. The women scream at the wriggling prey, and the men have to unhook it, but down goes the line again. More fish than anyone can eat or give away.

We long ago gave up fishing with other people. Even if someone offers to gather me mussels, to save me time and bother, I usually refuse: for the half bucket I asked for will come back as two, torn off in clumps, large and tiny together. Even kind and generous people behave like that.

I think it was our fishing that first taught us to see that behind every human being, even the least offensive, lies a grim trail of waste, torment and death. We survive by pushing out or devouring other creatures: every one of us is a tyrant from cradle to grave. But the inevitability of suffering does not make the infliction of it innocent.

4

Wildlife

Though fishing gradually lost its attractions, boating did not. In our second season we bought another boat, telling ourselves we could easily sell it if we needed the money, which was indeed what later happened. This time it was a 13-foot clinker rowing boat, with an ancient ill-tempered Seagull engine. It had a mast, and with the addition of an unused lug-sail given by a friend, we could get along after a fashion when the wind was at more than 90°. Till we got the knack of stepping the removable mast we suffered public and humiliating dismastings. Islanders are very distrustful of sails, and long local memories hold grim tales of disaster in the pre-engine age. Many were the warnings we received of what would happen to us in our unballasted craft, if a freak gust, or a freak wave, or a freak current caught up with us. In a good summer breeze, we could charge merrily up the loch under our little tan sail, and we would see the traffic stopping on the road above to watch our certain doom.

We never, in fact, met with disaster, but on one September evening, it was presumed that we had. The telephone rang as we were getting ready for bed. It was John Angus.

"Hello Alison. Is that you?" He sounded slightly surprised.

I assured him it was.

"It is a very windy night tonight."

I was now surprised. It was a fine clear evening with a few gusts from the North. "It's fine down here. Is it bad at your end?"

"Oh well no, not too bad. It's a lovely night," he agreed, agreeably.

After perhaps five minutes of conversation, he asked: "And were you out in the boat this evening?"

61

"Yes."

"Oh well, were you?" John Angus cleared his throat in an embarrassed manner, and added, "Angus Alec said he saw you going past about six o'clock. He was phoning us."

After another few minutes of strained conversation, he asked, "Is the boat all right?"

"Yes, fine."

"Angus Alec said he looked out about 7.30 and it was upside down."

A hasty check from the front door revealed that it was indeed. I rushed back to the telephone.

"It is!"

"Oh well, it is lucky you weren't in it. We have been wondering since eight o'clock if you were trapped underneath it."

At that moment it did little for my confidence to realise that we could have been drowning for three hours before anyone came to rescue us, but hasty decision-making is not a Gaelic trait. Nevertheless, it was only five minutes before both Calum and John Angus were there, waist deep in the sea, and by midnight we had the boat dragged up on the shingle, and most of the gear salvaged.

Other than the night we didn't drown, we had no accidents. This is quite surprising really, as Andrew, who is normally very mild, undergoes a complete character change when he assumes control of a boat. Having crewed enthusiastically on ocean races in student days, he has dashing ideas of seamanship, even in a rubber dinghy. I had hardly set foot in a boat, except on a memorable family outing at the age of three, when the bung sprang out of a rowing boat we had hired, and the boat began to fill with water. No one on that occasion believed me when I lisped the bad news to them, from my squatting position near the said bunghole, so I was used to being disregarded at sea. Andrew left me in no doubt that he would keelhaul me if I didn't obey even the most idiotic commands instantly, and I became quite accustomed to rowing full speed into rocks and tangling the propeller of the malevolent Seagull in the ropes of lobster pots. In addition, having only a very blurred concept of right and left, I would sometimes suddenly swing the tiller from one to the other, and be completely perplexed about how to correct it. On one such memorable occasion I crashed my mother and several sacks of peat into the pier, to the great delight of all onlookers. Apart from the effect on my poor mother's nerves, no damage was done.

Really the West Loch was an excellent place for pottering in a small boat. The north side carries the road to Stornoway and a straggle of crofts, but the south shore is completely unpopulated, and gradually flares out under increasingly dreadful crags towards Luskentyre. Even in the little inflatable, we could quickly reach the wild bay of Stioclett. Here a low green point curved down to the loch, ending in tidal rocks. We could approach these with impunity in the rubber boat, and never tired of seeing the tangle flop lazily in the surf, while the gulls hopped up and down to avoid getting their feet wet. If we were quiet, we often saw otters. Andrew taught me to swim there in one of the rock pools, and as I floundered frantically in 18 inches of water, I could see a mother otter and her three cubs porpoising gracefully just offshore. They were there most of the summer, and did not seem perturbed by us.

On the short green turf ashore, there were the ruins of black houses, the windowless drystone dwellings of past generations. They could have been centuries old, but in fact they had been inhabited in living memory. Weather soon undoes them: the roofs were thatch, and once the fire goes out inside, they decay immediately. Beyond the houses is a long curving bay, of a type peculiar to the islands. Though sandy at low water, the upper part of the beach is steeply piled with huge round stones—mol—which block the boggy hinterland with its many streams, turning this area into a brackish loch. There are often herons here, and occasional stray swans and geese, driven to rest by bad weather. The water of the bay itself is superlatively calm and clear, and Andrew found it most rewarding snorkelling. Once he saw dozens of pairs of eyes peering up at him through the sand, probably buried crabs. There is nothing especially rare to be seen, but the clarity and colour over the pale bottom make the commonest weeds and fish a delight. I would not venture out of my depth, and to be honest, even in the shallows I was daunted by my surroundings, for the south end of the bay terminates in glowering cliffs, which seemed to watch our every move with disapproval, as if they had seen the black house dwellers off and meant to repel us too. That climbing honeysuckle and nesting ravens found shelter among the crags only emphasised our human intrusion. One day I stood painfully on the poisonous spine of a concealed weever fish, which confirmed my suspicions about the inhospitable nature of the place. But I still loved it.

The whole area is frightening and enchanting. Sometimes we sidled further along under the cliffs. Where the loch widens out and the inhabited north shore becomes distant and silent, what looked like a shallow indentation turned out to be a deep high-sided bay, where the sea made a desolate rattling suck against the stony beach. There was scarcely even a bird to ease the awesome solitude, only an unseen raven croaking high overhead. We pulled our dinghy up over the tumbled rocks, but we did not stay ashore long. There were a couple of bright white gulls bobbing on the deep green water below the cliffs as we edged out, and they were a relief. The summit of the crags above this desolate place is marked on the map as "sidhean"—a fairy hill. Some fairies. The Harris race must be grim and tough indeed: they can certainly cause a shiver down the spine. Perhaps it was a marine member of their tribe who, just round the corner, rasped long and loud, but without vibration, under the keel of our boat on another occasion. That unnerved us: after that we kept well out from the shore beyond Stioclett.

But it doesn't do to be too nervous of possible unearthly inhabitants. On one particularly luminous and magical evening, we were rowing silently home when I was petrified by a tremendous horse-like—water-horse-like—snort just behind me. I twisted round to face, not a kelpie, but a huge and benign-looking bull seal. His great grey nostrils exhaled fishy breath, his whiskers were thick as rat's tails, and his eyes were at least as big as saucers, but he was made of solid flesh, and friendly as a dog. He followed us leisurely half way home, dipping now and again so that only his whiskery nose was above the surface. We saw him several times over the next few weeks. Seals roam around, staying in localities they fancy for days, weeks or months as the mood takes them. We could often recognise individuals by their markings and head shape, but they never stayed for more than a month or so. Presumably it was not lack of fish that made them leave, as others always took their places. They lead a leisurely existence, fishing for an hour or so a day, and enjoying themselves the rest of the time in aquatic exercise and inquisitive observation. They are particularly interested in anything seal-coloured, sleek and silent. They were far bolder with the grey inflatable than with our other boat. Also, they like people in wetsuits: I once watched Andrew snorkelling offshore, unaware that two young seals were craning their necks to examine his black-booted feet each time they broke surface. They were only a yard or so from him, but so expertly do they swim that he neither saw nor felt them.

This happened at Isay, the little island lying against the summer sunset at the mouth of the loch. Once we acquired our second boat, we often went there to fish, swim and picnic. Like so many offshore islets, it is a microcosm of a Hebridean island. We put the boat in at a steep-sided bay terminating in a typical mol beach, walked across a tumbled ridge of rock and up a green hill, and ended up on a clifftop on the western side: but the towering gloom of such a landscape writ large is here scaled down to a comfortable size. The sandy bays where we swam are only about 20 feet across and the biggest cliff not more than 50 feet high. There is an impressive blow-hole on the north side, in which the sea roars and spouts, for the diminishing Atlantic swell makes a last effort on the back of Isay, and the salt spray continually driving over it makes it brown and bald. The sheltered side is lushly green, showing the remains of old lazy beds, though the island lacks fresh water and was not inhabited. It must have been pleasant enough work tending the crops there. The fertility of the soil on such islands is largely due to its constant manuring by sea birds. There is a gull colony on Isay, which spreads from the boulders by the shore up the sheltered south slope. We were delighted to discover this nesting area, as it was the first we had seen at close quarters. It contained mostly herring gulls, with a few black-headed, and some black-backs near the shore. These last indulged in a very flappy and noisy courtship, taking no notice at all of our arrival. The oystercatchers nesting on the shingle, on the other hand, circled low over the water, calling frantically. Their nesting hollows were lined with fragments of shells, carefully arranged dark against light to break up the visual area. The gulls, though, sometimes made no lining at all in their nest scrapes, but most added wisps of dried grass, a few making quite a comfortable warm cushion in the hollow. These choicest-looking nests were easiest to spot, and I think are probably made mostly in the centre of the colony, which is the safest part frequented by the strongest and cleverest birds. Young birds and dimwits have to make do with the outer edges, and seem to make a greater number of test scrapes before settling on a spot they hope will be secure.

Once the eggs were laid we never spent long in the colony and always kept slowly on the move, as the opportunist black-backs are ready to move in on unattended nests. We took a few eggs to eat, and very good they are. Local lore has it that if you take them in the first week of May and always leave at least one in the nest, the gulls will make up the deficiency with ample time to rear well-grown young. From observation I am sure this is true, but I have no heart for the theft nowadays.

We sighted our first chicks, scuttling for cover under the tussocks, and then left the colony alone till they were fledged. Any gull will attack a youngster straying into its territory, and black-backs in particular will eat them with relish even on neutral ground. Anyone who feels inclined to blame them for this should consider our own species. It is not, in general, considered polite in human society to eat other people's children. Nevertheless, it is thought quite proper for parents to promote their offspring's interests at the expense of other individuals, otherwise why does Africa starve while our own families grow to fat and bad teeth? The murderer's mum who maintains loyally that he is a lovely boy, and the parents who willingly accept a baboon's heart on the slight chance that their own precious infant may be saved, attract widespread sympathy and even praise. Yet we unthinkingly describe as "ruthless" the faithfully mated and parentally conscientious birds who in their desperately competitive world protect their families against intruders, with a possible free meal on the side.

Indeed, the parental care of these birds is touching to see. A pair of herring gulls nesting on the Macaulays' croft hatched a brood which included a chick with a deformed wing. It would never fly. Long after the other young had departed, they were still feeding the cripple, and one or other parent would escort it anxiously as it ran about the field. It was half into its second-year plumage when one day we found it dead. The parents hovered disconsolately overhead, without their usual warning cries. There is no NHS or family allowance for seagulls, but no human parents could have shown more selfless devotion. The student of animal behaviour may say that their responses were elicited by the infantile posture and vocalisations of the non-flying juvenile: but we are animals too, so what is to be said of our own behaviour when faced with a floppy-limbed crippled child who will never mature normally? If credit is given to us, it must be given to other species too, and much more to them, as they frequently struggle for a bare living in daily danger and hunger of which we are quite ignorant.

Any deliberate self-denial from an animal in the wild should be held in as much reverence as the highest human acts of charity. Even Saint Francis could beg his dinner: a seagull, on the whole, cannot. Wild creatures cannot afford to take time off. They cannot rest if they are old, sick or wounded—they must work to feed themselves and protect themselves from predators or succumb.

We became gradually aware of the insecurity of a wild creature's existence through the birds the schoolchildren brought Andrew after he had declared an interest in taxidermy. They brought dead ones thrown ashore by storms, which were stuffed in science lessons and perched on balance cases or hung from the ceiling, in a renaissance manner. Even a large bird makes a surprisingly light corpse. The bones are fragile and the feathers easily damaged by oil or wounds. The crop and stomach contents are often pathetically little: a sea bird in a storm has small chance to feed. We had some live rescues, too. These we took home to the peace and quiet of our back toilet. Our first was a black-back, too weak to raise his head. After he had rested, we pushed some herring down his throat. He pecked feebly and then swallowed it. He swallowed more and pecked less. He knew he was on to a good thing: black-backs are very intelligent. He regarded us with contempt and ate all the fish in the freezer, shaking it around with relish so that the walls were spattered with fragments of herring; the loo still smelt faintly of sea-bird and bad fish two years later. After a couple of days, we let him out into the garden. He swaggered all round the fence, then crouched in the corner nearest the loch, facing upwind. We took him in at night, and next day, on being taken out he made a short trial flight, then wisely returned for another meal and a night's shelter. On the third day, he took off perfectly, soared in a nonchalant circle to gain height, and flew off up the loch.

He had every chance of survival. Having summed us up as mugs, he suffered no stress from his confinement. Black-backs act intelligent and look intelligent. They have a very alert eye and a large cranium—which any myopic small-headed biologist will tell you means nothing at all. Our next patient had a demented look, and next to no skull except a large beak, with which he pecked us frantically and ineffectively, wasting strength and terrifying himself out of his wits. This was a young cormorant. We fed him, half by force, till he was strong enough to flap and walk properly, but as he did not get used to us, we felt it was best to release him at that point, in case his terrors killed him off. He swam off as fast as he could go, but that was not very fast, and we had misgivings about him.

Then some of the children found a dazed gannet staggering in the road near the school. He was tricky to handle, as his wings still seemed strong, and his beak forceful. But he could not take off, although we placed him on high ledges and various slopes. We tried to feed him, but he rejected the fish fiercely, and shook it from his beak when we tried to cram it in. We floated fish in a basin of water, but that was no use either. These birds are superb fliers, diving in a vertical spiral hundreds of feet to catch moving fish: it was a forlorn hope that an old basin with a few bits of dead haddock would tempt him. He hated us, and we hated to see him sunk to this squalid end. We had often watched with admiration a troop of healthy gannets corkscrewing one after the other on a shoal of fish, moving with such precision that half a second and half a yard separated each from the lethal beak of the next one down. We had seen them winging in easily in the early morning from St Kilda, 60 miles away, and back again in the afternoon as other birds fly between a housetop and a garden fence. We had decided to wring this one's neck for his own peace when he died. Andrew stuffed him with tears in his eyes. He was extremely beautiful, purest white with a butter-yellow head and pale blue beak and eye. He stuffed quite well, but the result was still a sad travesty of the living bird. That was the last piece of taxidermy Andrew ever did.

Afterwards, on an inland walk with John Angus, we saw another sad gannet perched on a rocky ledge. He told us what was wrong: the bird would be old and going blind, and so could fish no longer. He had found a quiet place to wait for death. "If I had my gun, I would put the poor thing out of its misery," said John Angus, but he had not, so we went away silently so that at least it would be undisturbed. Birds metabolise their food very quickly, and an already weak bird will starve to death mercifully fast, compared with larger animals.

A fisherman friend confirmed John Angus's verdict: constant high speed diving eventually so affects a gannet's eyesight that the old birds are first of all reduced to following fishing boats with the seagulls, in the hope of hand-outs, and then, unable to do even that, they give up and die. Our gannet must have been at that final stage. When we heard this, we were ashamed of our efforts to make him eat: better to have taken him to the water and wrung his neck in sight of the sea.

It is not only birds which suffer from lack of food and loss of physical strength. In February, at the end of a bad winter, one may see on the road to Hushinish a sight common enough in the Highlands, but always pathetic: the deer, normally so fleet and elusive, are down at the roadside, with hanging heads and gaunt flanks, waiting for any fodder the estate may have decided to allot them. Or just waiting: some years no one feeds them, but there must be a memory, or a hope, that human beings do not always mean guns. Once at the sight of our Land-Rover a stag raised his head hopefully and took a few tremulous steps towards us, but we heard later that there was no feeding in that season, and in fact no estate Land-Rover. Yet some memory must have stirred in the beast.

Often the sheep are in no better case. Every sheep provides its owner with a subsidy, which pays for winter feed. A ruthless owner who has no intention of feeding his flock can consequently profit considerably by overstocking and neglect. Sheep die of many diseases, and bad weather does not help, but if they succumb in large numbers the root cause is starvation. Such owners are entirely culpable. Bloated roadside corpses, sheep dead or half alive caught by the horns in fences of their owner's making, shivering beasts who have lost their fleeces through malnutrition, and lambing ewes with crow-pecked eyes where I know no shepherd has looked for days: these things make me sick with humanity. If weather and crows alone were to blame, everyone's sheep would suffer the same fate, but it is not so. Many people have few casualties even in a bad winter. For the others, weather and crows will only continue what laziness and greed begin.

Most people who go to live in the country from the towns are at some stage shocked by the bald facts of animal husbandry. Squeamishness or ignorance or both conceal from the town-dweller the source of his meat and leather. In the country he cannot hide from it. Beasts are chattels. If crofters or farmers act responsibly, as many do, their stock will be well cared for: if not, the life of their beasts is hell. If a straying sheep is knocked down on the road and left to die, or if an unattended cow dies during calving, decent people's sympathy will be with the owner, not the beast, because he has lost money on the hoof. Owners have all the rights, beasts none: they are property first, and living beings only secondarily. I remember being appalled as a girl by an account of a neighbour's losses given by a countrywoman who was herself very kindly to both man and beast. "Poor Jimmy!" she said. "He had 20 sheep up in that byre and they're all dead. He left them there penned over the weekend and forgot to go up and give them water, and in this heatwave they all died. Poor Jimmy, what a loss."

When the concept of farm stock as property is extended to wild species, the jargon is different, but the same absolute rights of ownership are implied. Wild animals become a "resource" to be "managed" or even "conserved" to fill human bellies or increase human bank balances. When we first lived in Harris we discovered that a grey seal "cull" was going on on some of the offshore islands in autumn. A series of letters Andrew sent to the Department of Agriculture and Fisheries and Nature Conservancy Council produced smooth answers: the seals might be taken only under licence, within terms of the Conservation of Seals Act 1970, for "prevention of damage to fisheries" or for "use of a population surplus of seals as a natural resource". The questions of whether seals damage fisheries and whether their population is in surplus had, it appeared, been settled definitively by the exhaustive re-searches of the Natural Environment Research Council. We knew perfectly well that all this bland verbosity covered for a squalid reality. The Harris Craft Guild (headed, I must say, primarily by incomers, not locals) with the backing of the Highlands and Islands Development Board, had got licences to kill moulted seal pups, so that their beautiful spotted skins could be used to make handbags and sporrans, and most popular of all, model baby seals, adorable trinkets for tourists. We had friends involved in this trade, and tried hard to understand and justify it, but could not. There was nothing, though, that we could do to stop it, except by saying what we thought, which offended people who found our opinions as incomprehensible as we did theirs. Nearly all our small Episcopal congregation, for instance, were "for" the cull: it was a resource, it could bring jobs and money to the island, the seals were over-crowded anyway, they ate too much fish while human populations starved. I said it was like SS officers making lampshades out of human skin. Someone suggested it would be less wasteful if we ate the carcases instead of leaving them to rot. I said I would as soon eat people. Of course, I convinced them of nothing but my own lack of Christianity. There is no common ground in such ethical arguments.

This was before Greenpeace sabotaged the Orkney culls. Public opinion, thanks to them, is changing. The bureaucrats of NERC have had to revise their definitive findings somewhat to suit the new situation. Publicity stirred up by radical conservation bodies, the media pictures of wide-eyed fluffy babies and the daring actions of their human defenders have inspired a widespread romantic desire to protect them. Many people now actually love seals—not toy trinkets they can take home on their key-rings, but the idea of wild free animals. It is like the transition from egg-collecting to bird-spotting as a popular pastime. The more species this attitude spreads to embrace, the better.

Our own dislike of the seal cull was motivated at first by a particular liking for seals: but the official bumph and bluff we discerned surrounding the seals is all too evident in official pronouncements on any subject it might be expedient to tamper with, whether it be badgers, oystercatchers or human embryos. After you have cared about something enough to read such stuff once, and it has proved not credible, an everlasting suspicion of bureaucratic integrity sets in. Governments appoint their own experts; of course these experts say what the bosses want to hear: that is their livelihood. They are hired and fired as script-writers are by film-directors.

But I must say something in praise of seals. They are the most enchanting of wild creatures because they reciprocate your interest. Seals in the water feel safe enough not to fear you. If you watch them, they watch you, with mild round eyes. They crane their necks and shoulders to get a better look. If you talk or sing to them, they will dip down silently and bob up again closer. If you go away, they will follow you, until distracted by some other amusement, such as rolling in the surf. Both sexes and all ages are curious about people and boats and dogs, and show every sign of enjoying a meditative existence. Very little is known about them. Our Harris grey seals, like others elsewhere, have been studied and tagged and counted and pestered on their breeding beaches, but individuals stay there only for about six weeks, so I doubt if one can conclude much from such research. What would an observer make of human beings, if he watched them only when they were copulating, giving birth, and suckling infants? For the seals, these activities are intensely packed into a few weeks of the year. The rest of the time they are at sea, and the only chance one has of observing them is by watching from shore or boat when they pop up, or by diving. As this situation is not convenient for tagging, counting or quantifying, the researchers usually ignore the seals' 10½-month holiday, except when they can "take" specimens "for scientific or educational purposes" under the Conservation of Seals Act 1970 sect. 10 (1)(a). They may find out what the seal last ate, though in fact even this analysis varies accordingly as the scientists are or are not government sponsored. They will never find out, though, what was going on in its head. Half an hour of watching live seals at leisure would have taught them more.

I saw my first seal at the age of three, on the holiday of the leaky boat. Ever since I have longed to see more. In Harris we have plenty of opportunity to do so, but the occasion never loses its freshness. I invariably stop in my tracks when I see a black domed head above the water. I wave and shout "hullo!", with a fatuous smile on my face. Andrew is no more proof against their charm than I am. Our small daughter regards our ecstasies coldly: she is a plant-lover and reserves such raptures for orchids.

I have mentioned the apparent enjoyment seals show as they laze in the water. The same delight in the pursuit of the moment can be seen in many animals. An otter sliding again and again down a seaweedy rock, a group of ravens looping the loop on a sunny afternoon, a sheep scratching its backside on a convenient telegraph pole—all these exhibit a satisfaction with life that is immediately comprehensible to us. We are in the same state ourselves when we are deep in our favourite hobbies, or lolling by the fireside after a hard day's work. The harshness and miseries of animal life, the hunger, cold, terror and pain, are only dimly imaginable to us, though they may excite our pity if we allow it: but the sight of an animal enjoying itself disarms us into fellow-feeling. The vitality of healthy creatures doing what they want to do is a great attractant.

During our three years at Leachkin, watching out for wildlife became a delight. We did not try to spot rarities, there was enough to enjoy in the daily life of starlings, gulls and seals. Gradually we became used to being in lonely places, without feeling the want of human noise and company. This is, I think, quite a step for the normal human brain. We are very familiar, on Harris, with the more usual response to solitary wild places: take a speedboat, possibly towing water-skiers, land on a beautiful deserted beach, leap ashore shrieking, light fires, throw off clothing. In a way it is a return to nature: the sounds and antics are certainly very reminiscent of the more exuberant of our monkey relatives. This symbolic rape of the wilderness is designed to show who is boss. Without such an assertion, who *is* boss? Certainly not a silent and cowed pink ape creeping across the sea in a nutshell, to land on a soil where his capabilities will not even extend to the knowledge of what to eat and how to catch it. The best such a creature can do is keep quiet and be humble. Even then he can never feel sure, in the silence, that the sea or the mountains will not gobble him up.

Wild nature is numinous. There can be very few people who, if they are quiet, will not sense it. Most of them dispel the oncoming holy terror by shouting or switching on noisy machinery they have brought for the purpose. What a boon the chainsaw is in a lonely forest, how reassuring the snarl of a motorbike on the fell tops! The alternative is to accept the dread meekly and to accustom oneself to a prickling scalp and slightly trembling knees.

The most alien and awesome place we visited was the Shiants —the enchanted islands, also known as na h'Eileanan Mora, Isles of the Sea, lying east of Scalpay. We visited them during a holiday with friends in a chartered yacht hired from Ullapool. On a glorious July evening, we decided on the spur of the moment to head west across the Minch. As the afterglow faded, the brief summer dusk hid the mainland, and the air was full of the soft throaty cries of Manx shearwaters, glimpsed only when they banked sharply showing the contrast of dark back and light belly. Dawn began almost as sunset finished, and as the sky brightened we saw it full of little birds flying eagerly towards the rising sun. They were puffins, streaming from their breeding burrows on the Shiants to their fishing grounds. The black basalt group loomed higher, and the puffins whirred thicker and faster in the golden air. Kittiwakes glided among them, casting mild dark glances at us, and shearwaters flipped on the frothy tops of shallow swells. As we nosed between Eilean Mhuire and Eilean an Tighe, exquisite music came and went faintly on the breeze. It could very well have been the song of sirens, it was so haunting and so attractive. I would have gladly driven on to the rocks to find its source, but fortunately I was not the skipper. A cautious approach to the many-ledged cliffs revealed unlikely singers. On every terrace were ranged thousands of guillemots and razorbills with half-fledged young, jumping and flapping their wings to greet landing mates or repel nosy neighbours. Could the delicious sounds emanate from these busy little birds? The razorbill's voice is described as "a weak whirring whistle and a protracted querulous growling". Perhaps the size of the choir, and the hum of many fast-moving wings reverberating under the overhangs of the cliff, could produce the angelic music. Or was it seals? I have never heard sounds that pleased me more. It was impossible not to keep thinking of Prospero's island,

> "Be not afraid. The isle is full of noises,
> Sounds and sweet airs that give delight and hurt not."

We continued up the channel to the only possible landing place, a steep mol beach on the neck between Eilean an Tighe and Eilean Garbh. The cliffs were great basalt columns, black and clean cut as a new creation. At their bases, vast cubes of rock 20 feet or more square lay tumbled like the pebbles on a lesser beach. On every ledge and in every crevice were nesting birds—kittiwakes, puffins, razorbills, guillemots, black guillemots, fulmars, shags and cormorants. Falls of lime-white droppings declared generations of birds. We anchored in the bay. The air was full of birds and the noise of birds. They zoomed or glided or flapped close to examine us, tame as penguins. A puffin darted beneath our bows and shot up with two sprats in his striped beak. Fulmars bobbed by the anchor chain, looking up at us with interest. As the day wore on, the hazy golden sunlight left the basalt stacks, and an inhospitable mist wreathed round the cliff tops and lingered beneath the natural arch of Eilean Garbh. Andrew and I took the small inflatable tender and slipped out onto the water, rowing very quietly or not at all. It was mirror calm. Immediately we were amongst rafts of birds of every kind. They eyed us curiously and paddled about six feet clear of us, but they were quite unafraid. There were no hasty take-offs. Auks floating, diving, bobbing and flapping dotted the silver water till it faded into the thickening mist. Then suddenly we were amongst seals—20 or 30 pairs of inquisitive eyes were fixed on us. News passed around and more and more heads broke surface. We edged nearer, they edged nearer. Fascination was mutual. There was a sudden deafening splash: our dinghy bobbed on the ripples and not a seal was to be seen. Then up popped a whiskered head snorting with satisfaction, and 30 more followed instantly. Everyone seemed pleased with the joke: they craned their necks, turned belly up, a few waved a flipper as they rolled, one dived silently beneath the dinghy and surfaced on the other side, rocking us slightly. Then they began to lose interest and drift away. We turned and paddled back below the cliffs. All we could say to each other was "Oh, aren't they lovely?" in an idiotic whisper. We were both shaking: the seals had been very many, very large and very close, and our boat very tiny. But while we were in their midst we had not been afraid at all.

On returning to our friends we were not completely coherent. Our wits were astray with the puffins and seals.

Andrew had misgivings about mooring all night in that place. The water was really too deep for our anchor chain. However, we were a night's sail from any alternative anchorage and no one had slept the previous night: besides, there was no wind and thick fog and our engine only worked occasionally, so we had little alternative. Our friends turned in. Darkness fell—real darkness because of the fog and black cliffs, even in summer. The air was full of the noise and movement of unseen birds. The anchor-chain grabbed and rasped unpleasantly. I risked mast-heading and refused to go below. Imperceptibly the intense and strange delight of the afternoon changed into an intense and strange dread, a conviction that we were not wanted here and must go. I had an overpowering sense of something hostile, though not evil, indeed good and protective, but not to us. "We can't stay here!" I told the skipper mutinously, with trembling conviction. An angel with a flaming sword could not have made me more sure of that. Andrew was not altogether convinced by metaphysical sensations, though he too was beginning to suffer from them: but fortunately the weather changed, and a fresh breeze suddenly began to chop the water and snatch the inadequate anchor. If it dragged, we would be on those terrible basalt cliffs, and the black-back we had seen there dining on puffin would be having us for breakfast. So we left. It was both foggy and windy and our masthead lights were not working. It was a nasty decision for Andrew as skipper to have to make, but I was extremely relieved.

This was not by any means the only time I have felt this way in an unpeopled place, but it was certainly the strongest such experience. After that it was impossible to relate such supernatural dread to mere physical danger or indigestion.

It is not surprising that the islanders who live in constant proximity to such places are traditionally famed for their psychic powers, in particular for the second sight: as Martin described it in 1716, "the singular Faculty of Seeing an otherwise invisible Object". Nowadays people are half-ashamed of the ability: they do not want to be regarded by the world as superstitious bumpkins or interesting aborigines. Once we got to know people in Harris, however, we heard so many instances of the singular Faculty that we too have come to take it for granted. Stories of the past, or of "a man in Lewis" can at first be taken with a pinch of salt: but when people one knows are concerned, it is not so easy to be dismissive. I will not quote the many experiences of local acquaintances, in case of causing embarrassment, but I can give some of my own.

The first happened within a year of arriving in Harris. A teacher we had become friendly with was off work with a broken ankle. Soon after seven on a clear Sunday morning, we saw a brilliant shooting star falling across the dawn sky. Immediately the perception of it fused in my mind with our friend, though I had no idea how or why. A week later almost to the hour, she died without warning. That would have been strange enough. But months later, we were walking along the road with her husband on a starry night, talking of other things: suddenly, he recalled that a week before his wife's death he had sat up in bed and seen a beautiful star falling past his window, and had thought it was for her. We told him of our similar sighting. I don't think he was very surprised: the "drug", the ball of light that signifies imminent death, is a well established local phenomenon.

More recently, at Scarista, I was digging foundations for a new building when I felt myself become restless and miserable. There was an unpleasant smell in the air. It became stronger and stronger, an overpowering odour of burning flesh. As it increased my tension became near unbearable. I dug and threw my spade aside and dug again. I was not surprised to learn later that a house had burned down at Seilebost, only I was puzzled that the sole inhabitant had been out at the time. Next day, though, I found the solution: his dog had been shut inside and had burned to death. I should mention that I had been seven miles upwind of the fire. This, too, is a typical sort of instance, as second sight and its peripheral manifestations often discern violent events from afar as they are actually happening. Most people, not being dog-lovers, would probably have missed that one.

I have quoted these particular examples because I can find no rational explanation for them. The coincidences involved were extraordinary, and besides, the sense of heightened awareness surrounding them was very intense: I knew I was not in my normal frame of mind as surely as I do when I stand up after drinking too much sherry. Very often forebodings and insights, whether later proved to be true or false, can be rationalised, because they do not carry this internal conviction. When that does occur, it is not really possible to confuse it with day to day perception.

Fortunately, such glimpses are not always of deaths. One day only a few weeks after we came to Harris, I was marking exercise books in the school staffroom when I suddenly became aware of what the art teacher was saying to someone else.

'It's really a pity. It's just falling down. There are sheep sheltering in it.'

"That's us!" I thought immediately, and blurted out rudely "What's that, Caroline?"

She was talking about the old manse at Scarista, near where she was living.

5

More a Liability than an Asset

Very excited, I told Andrew about the old manse. This must be the place we could convert into a hotel. Next time we were driving to the Sunday house-service in Leverburgh, we stopped on the road and eyed it. I was dismayed. It looked unutterably gaunt and dismal among its jagged stone walls and broken fences. It was dirty grey, so grey that we had passed it before without even noticing it against the wintry pallor of the hill behind.

"Now, that has possibilities," said Andrew, brightly.

I should perhaps explain that a "manse" is the Scottish term for the dwelling of a minister of the Church. In the past, such houses were always large and imposing, though plain. They were expected to house not only the minister and his family, but also passing travellers and large crowds of visitors at the twice-yearly Communions. They generally possessed extensive farm buildings and sat on the best agricultural land available. Ministers were well looked after. The Scarista manse was three-storeyed and T-shaped and obviously very roomy, thus suitable for our purposes. I was not impressed by its situation. It was set on the broad slope above Scarista beach. To east and west and on either side of the main road below were other buildings—the church, semi-derelict byres, old corrugated iron sheds, cottages neat and delapidated, lived in and empty, all straggling visibly and untidily across the whole hinterland of the two-mile-long bay. It did not suit my idea of romantic seclusion. It was not even obvious that from the house one could see the sands, though clearly the sea itself would be visible.

We parked the Land-Rover and walked across the sheep-bitten turf to the rising dunes which hid the beach from the road. Suddenly the vast expanse of Scarista bay was in front of us. It was a blustery grey day in February but the sands glowed and sang in the wind, golden, pink and silver. Inexorable Atlantic swells bore slowly towards them. As each green mile-long ridge of water breasted the shoreline it reared and hung stationary for an instant, and crashed, growling in the foaming shallows. Long wisps of spray tore loose from the threatening crests and mingled with the sand-devils above the tide line. Blowing sand stung our faces. Tatters of dry black wrack and broken shells scuttered towards us, chittering faintly against the massive roar of the water. Down the beach where the pale dry sand became wet and ochre were drifts of shells, a prodigal treasure of gleaming violet and yellow, pink, blue and silver. Some were as tiny as grains of sand, and the sand itself was made up of the shattered wrecks of shells. We crouched over their still and polished perfection till an angry wave bounded up and soaked our feet, then slurped ominously back down the steep slope of sand. On the dunes again, we looked around. Towards Tarbert, the mountains of North Harris marched out to the distant rocky island of Scarp. In front of them rose the steep end of Ben Luskentyre, and the low double hump of Taransay, with great white surf shooting up behind it. The other arm of the bay was the dark bulk of Chaipaval and Toe Head, stretched out in the turbulent sea like a monstrous dog on a hearthrug. In between was a wide light-swept horizon, with the tiny crown of Gaskeir central, and beyond that nothing but sky and water for 2,000 miles.

Turning back, the land looked mean. Scruffy fences divided faded grass from faded grass, apathetic sheep from depressed cows. The cottages and haphazard sheds looked dingy, and the old manse forlorn and hollow-eyed.

I kept relatively quiet about my misgivings, and we found out what we could about the decaying manse. It had been sold by the Church of Scotland seven years previously when a smaller modern manse was built, and bought by a gentleman who then delivered it under a trust to An Comunn Gaidhealach, the society which promotes Gaelic language and culture. They had had some plans for turning it into a summer school, but the undertaking proved too expensive, and they had done nothing at all to it even by way of maintenance: so there it stood with broken panes and slipping slates, deteriorating in the rain and wind. We wrote to An Comunn hopefully, asking to buy or lease the property. Replies were amiable, vague and Celtic. Yes, it was held in trust: yes, it was deteriorating: they might sell or they might not—it was up to the trustees. We inquired three times a year for three years. An Comunn sent us to the trustees and the trustees sent us to An Comunn. We fumed and fretted and saved up as much as we could. We enquired about other properties in Harris and Skye, but nothing we saw inspired us. Besides, prices seemed astronomical, £28,000! We had only £2500 after nearly three years' saving. There could be no question of a mortgage as we would have to give up teaching to work on any house we bought. We despaired and hoped, alternately.

All this time, we had not even been through the front door of the manse. We had peered guiltily through the windows on one occasion. There was a sick lamb bedded in the porch and a few healthier ones in the kitchen. Everything was broken, littered and dirty, and completely depressing. But one could, in fact, see the whole beautiful curve of Scarista bay.

Eventually, Andrew drove down there one summer evening with John Angus as moral support. They entered furtively by a broken window and prowled round the building. They came home elated.

"Well, Alison, that house will be yours," said John Angus decisively. "You'll get it yet."

I was sceptical, and not entirely sure I wanted it anyway: but Andrew was very animated about it, and took John Angus's intuition seriously. He drew out for me sketch plans of the lie of the house, and described all he had seen.

But there was silence from An Comunn and trustees alike. We went off on the sailing holiday I have already mentioned, and came home despondent. Everywhere but Harris was having a glorious summer. It rained every day. Our sturdy clinker boat seemed cloddish after the sporty Cutlass we had just been sailing. There was no house on the horizon. We had spent too much money on our holiday. We told ourselves we were sick of teaching, which was true, and of Harris, which was not. We would pack up and go.

Suddenly the *Stornoway Gazette* carried an interesting advertisement. "Stone-built mansion house in South Harris." Could it be? It was!

The old Land-Rover charged down the road at its top speed of 45 mph. We were almost too excited to speak, but unwilling to set our hopes high. The advertisement invited offers over £15,000, which might as well have read £150,000.

We climbed over the garden wall, as the front gate was firmly bedded in weeds, and picked our way through rubbish and nettles to the door. A black and white face appeared at the porch window: the house was by now a kennel, evidently. As the front door had no hinges and no lock, we lifted it free of its makeshift rope fastening and let the canine occupant out. However, he was more interested in company than in wandering, and took us all over the house, snuffing at the best rat-holes. I felt very sorry for him, locked up there alone for hours, perhaps days at a stretch. And if anyone bought the house, what would happen to him? Where would he be locked up next? I didn't notice much of the ground floor, except that it was full of agricultural litter and very dirty. From the first floor, the view was so magnificent that I cheered up. Andrew paced from room to room, measuring, stamping, and poking. Outside we could not comfortably make a circuit of the buildings, as the nettles were so tall and the ground treacherous with crumbling sheets of corrugated iron and bits of old bedstead. As Brown with landscapes, so Andrew with old buildings: he sees "capability of improvement" everywhere. But I kept noticing other houses getting in the way of the view and the ugly post and wire fences, and the road running between us and the sea: these things wouldn't be ours to improve. But I was becoming more than half enthusiastic. When we reached the small square of ground tucked between the arms of the "T" and the garden wall to the south west, I was wholly won over. This would be the herb garden. It would have geometric beds and a sundial. I have long since got over illusions about gardening in Harris, but at the time it was a potent force. We said goodbye to the sitting tenant and left him with regret.

We had the house valued. "More of a liability than an asset." Parents generously made up our savings to £5000, and we submitted this offer, the best we could afford.

Part Two

THE OLD MANSE

6

Settling In

On September 1st, we heard the Old Manse was ours. Immediately, everything was different. Already we saw our house white painted and neat, with a flourishing garden and trees and shrubs softening the line of the drive. Wrought iron gates? A fountain? An outdoor swimming pool? Peacocks? Nothing was too fantastic to consider. We wanted everyone to come and see this miracle. Those who did were inexpressibly shocked. The London friends who valiantly helped us with the initial clearing out were tactful, but silent. My mother was due to arrive in a couple of days, and they felt for her, and persevered. We were very pleased with our first clean up. The place *must* look better inside now—one could see that by surveying the pile of rubbish we had dragged out to the garden. There had been seed potatoes in the dining room, straw in the study, paper sacks in the hall, fleeces in the kitchen. Every room, inexplicably, had its few metres of barbed wire and pile of scrap timber. Outside, on the other hand, all the gateless gaps in the garden walls had been ingeniously fenced without recourse to wire at all—tottering barricades of rusty drainpipes, old bed ends, broken chairs, lengths of skirting board and glassless window-sashes impeded progress every 10 yards. There was a wrecked van in what is now the second dining room, and the corresponding wing on the other side had been stuffed full of hay, and boarded up with a door torn from its hinges in the kitchen, and sawn across the panels to cut it to size.

Once the grosser pieces of rubbish had been removed, we began to sweep up, or scrape up, the unpleasant detritus which was now revealed. Its composition did not bear close examination: it consisted mainly of very finely shredded wood and paper, mixed with soot and plaster, with an overlay of rabbit-skins and dog-

87

turds. There was, in fact, a very decisive canine odour about the place. There was another and more pungent aroma which we could not at first pin down, but soon we came to realise the origin of the expression "to smell a rat"; and not one rat but multitudes. Every door, it seemed, had been gnawed underneath to give rattish access.

We swept up till the remaining dust was so fine that its contents could not be recognised. We investigated the "private water supply". It consisted of a slimy cistern on the hillside in which a dead sheep floated. So we did not attempt to reconnect the plumbing. We brought a plastic container of water and some scrubbing brushes from Leachkin and scrubbed the drawing room floor and paintwork. The result was inadequate, but we considered it a great improvement, and invited a dozen or so friends to a sherry party there next day on the strength of it. We ushered them upstairs proudly ("Don't lean on the banister—mind that hole in the floor") and directed their attention to the extensive sea view. "This is the drawing room," we said. With a view like that, we thought this an obvious choice, but our guests seemed bemused. After a glass or so of sherry they began to see the funny side of it, and the occasion ended in great good humour.

After this euphoric beginning, we were left to more sombre reflection on our new possessions. The house was surrounded by glebe land, but our feu only extended to 1.3 acres, in a long narrow strip down to the main road. The church retained possession of the Glebe and of the old range of outbuildings behind the manse. This was to cause us much anguish because of its extremely unsightly rusty corrugated iron roof.

The house itself had about 19 rooms, but the six in the attic had insufficient headroom to comply with building regulations, and the two outlying single-storey wings at the front had had their internal access blocked up. They and the ground floor of the back wing were the most derelict parts: very derelict indeed. Water penetration from the skylights on the south west side had rotted floorboards, joists and lintels to a near liquid state. The many broken windows in this region had probably been beneficial, if anything, as the constantly moving air had dried at least some of the water pouring in from roof level. Any plaster that had not fallen had crusted with a leprous white scab on the sick hues of old pink and green limewash. "Hot water supply is from a Rayburn in the kitchen," said the particulars of sale. We kicked it gently and it disintegrated like a puffball in a brown cloud of ash and rust.

Upstairs at the front there were three rooms in relatively good order. The drawing room floor shook somewhat (and still does) but with a lot of scrubbing and a few coats of paint it would make a pleasant living room, with windows looking north-west to the sea and south-east to the rusty outbuildings. We would use the large room at the other end of that corridor as a temporary kitchen, and the small one in between as a bedroom. Down a short flight of stairs and up again into the back wing was the bathroom. It had an indescribably filthy WC and bath (perhaps it had functioned as a sheep-dip at one time) but the handbasin had been removed for someone else's use.

We arranged to leave Leachkin by November 30th, which gave us 12 weeks to make our new quarters habitable. The first priority was a water supply. Fortunately the main ran fairly close to the house, but we had to take a trench under the garden wall and in a zig-zag round to the "herb garden" to get it in at a convenient place, below the old bathroom. At first it was very easy to remove the required 30" depth in the deep sandy soil, but round the corner things became tricky. The ground was full of fallen masonry, and then of solid rock, and in the narrow path between the raised area of the herb garden and the house, the retaining wall collapsed burying me and my precious trench. I persevered with a pick-axe, and then with sledge hammer and cold chisel, having been allotted this unskilled job. I had to admit defeat. Andrew talked wistfully of blasting, but eventually decided it was inadvisable. We stood arguing among the ruins of the herb garden wall, straddling a plinthed network of ancient and stinking drains which I had unearthed just below ground level.

"You've put a pick through that one!" accused Andrew, pointing to an oozing hole in the terra-cotta.

"I didn't! It was broken already!"

"And there—and there—really! What on earth have you been doing?"

"Digging this bloody trench! Finish it yourself."

So he did. He very quickly came to the conclusion that 15 inches deep would be quite enough. We buried the pipe hastily before any inspector inspected it. We needn't have worried: other Harris water supplies coil brazenly over bare rock, as there is often no soil at all to bury them in. I am pleased to say that I was later justified in the matter of pick-axing drains. We discovered that this expedient had been used in a drastic attempt to clear blockages. The method is not to be recommended. It renders the surrounding ground noisome for years to come.

A shorter and shallower trench brought electricity in. The house was wired in a rudimentary way already, so we could now have lights as well as running water. We felt very civilised. We turned on our one tap and went from room to room switching lights on and off.

A few modifications were now required inside. The headmaster's wife donated a large box of half-used tins of paint and curtains and once the pink and violet hues beloved of the last tenants had been obliterated, we began to feel at home. Andrew put a sink in to our kitchen, having calculated that the water supply would be useful for the bathroom that would eventually be there. The water and waste pipes had to be got through a two-foot-thick stone wall, which took a very long time. We had not realised quite how solid old buildings are. We began to be less confident about the many extra doors and windows we were planning.

The bathroom window was broken, and we mended it unattractively with hardboard. The windows on the other three rooms were intact, but the shutters had been nailed up. Andrew freed them, as they are very useful in a stormy climate, and discovered the plaster behind reduced to damp rubble. He tried his hand at replastering. That was not as easy as we had thought either: I couldn't even mix it without producing lumps.

The Land-Rover plied to and fro with loads of furniture, tools and household goods. We were scrounging whatever we could and many people were kind to us. We collected a chair here, a rug there, pots and basins, cushions and fire irons. Almost every day John Angus would appear with something to add. "Would this be any good to you?" and if we asked if he didn't need it himself, "No, no, I was just going to throw it on the shore!"

Eventually we had everything but a bed. Beds seemed to be very expensive, so we bought a sheet of latex foam, which went at first on the floor, and later onto a homemade chipboard base. We are still sleeping on it. It is very good for sore backs and a great cure for malingering—it is so unyieldingly hard that it is nearly always pleasanter to get up than to lie in bed.

Just before moving day, we had the bright idea of inviting all our friends down, meals and beer provided, for a Saturday work-party at Scarista. It seemed like a sociable way to behave. We had heard and read of other do-it-yourself enthusiasts acting thus with success. They must have been made of tougher stuff than we are. About 15 men, women and children turned up. They all set to work with a will. Someone filled the holes we had made for light switches with polyfilla, another one used my whole supply of undercoat painting a single piece of furniture, and so on. They ate, drank and were merry, and talked incessantly. Then they began to sing songs. By 2 a.m. Andrew and I were sunk in monosyllabic exhaustion. It took a whole morning to clear up, and the best part of a week to recover.

On November 30th, we cleaned up at Leachkin and looked round it for the last time. We knew we would miss it, and the West Loch. There would be no boating off the vast surfy beach at Scarista. We felt rather bleak as the Land-Rover lurched up to the manse in the dark and rain. Once we had the fire lit we cheered up instantly. It was home now, after all.

The next few weeks saw some improvements in our living conditions. The luxury we most wanted was a hot water supply. Neighbours offered us the use of their bath, but we couldn't pester them every evening. We could manage to look clean enough for school with the help of an electric kettle, but we were more worried by cold than by dirt. The house was damp with the damp of years, and it was midwinter. We struggled out of damp clothes and shivered all night in a damp bed. We longed for hot baths. After some thought, Andrew retrieved the old hot water tank and fitted it with an electric element. By means of a stopcock, it could be filled direct from the rising main, heated up and tapped off into the bath. The only snag was that there was no way of telling when the tank had filled up until a fountain gushed out of the hole at the top. We got over this by sticking a wooden spoon, handle-down, in the hole: when it began to rise in the air, one switched off hurriedly. Sometimes we went away to do something else and forgot about it, only to be recalled by the clatter of the spoon shooting up and hitting the ceiling in a flood of icy water.

When Christmas came we found our cooking facilities rather limited. We had guests, and I attempted to cook a turkey in the ancient Baby Belling we had on loan. Even with a heavily-weighted chair under the oven handle, the door would not close. Fortunately, our neighbours at the old school-house over the road were away on holiday, so we were able to force an entry and instal the turkey in their oven. At dinner time Andrew struggled back up the drive in the wind and rain with the turkey clutched protectively to his chest.

A few months later matters improved in the kitchen. We still had peats at our old site in North Harris, and had gone up for a day to cut them. We went to the usual pool beneath a bridge to wash off our tools and boots before going home.

"Ugh!" I said, "Someone's dumped a cooker here. Very nice!"

Andrew bent down and squinted at it from all angles.

"Here, this looks OK!"

"What?"

"I'm sure it's in working order. Shall we take it?"

So we heaved it up the bank, and left it there while we scrambled up to the road to make sure there were no observers near: it would be too scandalous if some passing motorist recognised it as his second cousin's old cooker. The road was clear, at least until we had the thing poised to slide into the back of the Land-Rover. Suddenly an interested carload appeared round a bend, slowing down for a better look. We smiled in a carefree manner and continued our manoeuvres, then hopped in and drove home as fast as possible. It was certainly an exciting find, and after a few days drying out and the installation of one new electric element, it worked quite well.

After this wonderful discovery, we felt we were really coming up in the world. John Angus said the new cooker was "chust perfect".

He often cheered us up by assuring us of the chust perfectness of everything from the slightly shabby to the total wreck. Many an evening in our first winter, the Macaulays would wander through our filthy, empty, echoing ruin of a house, until John Angus was moved to say dismally, "Oh well, there's a lot of work here, eh?" and then, with unconvincing but warming enthusiasm, "but it'll be *chust perfect* when you're finished!"

Whereat Calum would hastily add, "Oh yes, yes, indeed it will —indeed it will!"

To this day, anything crazily defective is "chust perfect" in our vocabulary.

We had a few tussles with other inhabitants of the manse. The dog now lived in the old outbuildings, and seemed content to forsake his old territory, but the cows were more immovable. The open-ended single-storey wing on the south west had long been a favourite shelter for them. We heard mysterious clunks and reverberations in the night, which we eventually traced to this shed. We had to ask them to leave, as we had our boat there, not having sold it as yet: a careless bovine hoof could easily hole it irreparably. We tried to drive them up to the byres at the back, which looked just as comfortable to us, but they were not persuaded. They like the front garden, too. As I had brought plants from Leachkin which they were quick to find, I was not pleased to see them there. Also, we had a trench dug waiting for a telephone wire to be laid, and we were afraid of discovering some poor beast there with a broken leg. One Sunday morning just after Christmas, we went out to find all five cows in the garden, staring into this trench. We tugged the front gate as far open as it would go, which was an uncomfortable squeeze for a cow, and removed the barricades on the two side gates. Then began a comical dance round and round the garden, with the cows trotting delicately over and over the trench, while I ran in front waving a cabbage, and Andrew brought up the rear with a stick. They were nimbler and more cunning than they looked. They snatched the cabbage and avoided the stick. After about 20 minutes of whooping and mooing, one had got out into the field and then back in again, and another had taken refuge in the front porch. I don't remember how we eventually got them out on that occasion, but it was not the last. They were quick to learn that I could be relied on for handouts of cabbage, and soon every time I appeared at the front door, I would see a line of wet muzzles resting atop the wall, each surmounted by a pair of rolling dark eyes.

We had many encounters with the rats who regarded our house as their house. We would not really have minded them, if they had not humiliated us in front of visitors. Mrs Macaskill, who had been so kind to us in Tarbert days, came to visit us. "Poor Alison!" she kept saying, dismayed by the chaos around. I assured her the house was just what we wanted, and proudly showed her my kitchen, specially scrubbed for the occasion. Just then a cheeky young rat poked his head out of a hole in the skirting. Poor Mrs Macaskill screamed aloud.

My mother came for Christmas, and we lodged her in our bedroom: we shifted ourselves to one at the back, which we suspected of being rat-infested. Not a rat did we hear. My mother, on the other hand, sat up all night with the light on, while rats danced a hornpipe on the hardboard of the ceiling.

Andrew's aunt came to stay, and on finding a cracked egg in the backyard (we had hens by then) she brought it up to the egg rack in the kitchen. A little later she went in there to find a large rat finishing off the meal he had doubtless begun in the yard. We all rushed at him, but he slipped off downstairs as circumspectly as he had come.

At Christmas, I bought one of those very hard, spicy salamis, a great luxury to us at that time. I hung it picturesquely from a nail in the kitchen, and shaved off a few slices when we had friends in, oiling the cut end. It was lasting very well. Then one morning when I went in to get breakfast, I noticed a trail of plaster-white footprints on the dark-stained wood floor. They issued from the hole in the wall where the plumbing pipes came in, proceeded insolently across the floor, thence to the seat of a chair—the back of a chair—horrors! My precious salami dangled just above! With trembling fingers I inspected it. Toothmarks.

What to do? Well, I trimmed it carefully, and made sure I consumed the next couple of slices personally, and I said nothing to anyone about it for a long time, not even to Andrew. But after that I did not hang edibles ornamentally from hooks.

The rats still came to see if I might have slipped up from time to time. One windy night I was kept awake by something banging insistently. Blearily, I got breakfast. As I pushed an empty milk carton into the swing top litter bin, a large rat leapt frantically up the inside. This was the source of the nocturnal banging: he had run up the water pipes, jumped on the lid of the empty bin and fallen in.

"What on earth will we do with him?" I asked Andrew, pointing to the shaking bin.

"I could hit him on the head," he suggested, doubtfully.

"Of course you can't do that! It's not fair. He's terrified."

Andrew took off the lid and looked in. The rat cowered, thinking his hour had come.

"We'll take the bin outside while we have breakfast," he decided.

This seemed like a good idea: the rat might escape, we hoped secretly. But he didn't. After breakfast he was still there, leaping just short of the top of the bin.

"Oh, let's just turn the bin on its side," I said.

"Don't be daft! He'll be back in the house at once. We've got to get rid of him."

"All right. Take him up the hill and let him go."

"We haven't time. We're late for school."

"I'll take him, then."

At this Andrew rushed off up the hill, muttering rudely that it would take me all day to get up there. He let the rat out at the first fence, and I have no doubt he was home before we were that day.

As soon as we started planting our ground we were troubled with other raiders. We fenced our ground in January, with an ugly post and wire affair. Any alternative fencing was much too costly, and continuing the old stone walls of the garden would take far too long. We sank rabbit netting along the bottom, and planted a hedge of Olearia Macrodonta four feet inside the boundary. The rest of the field in front of the house was dotted with young trees of every imaginable variety. If they could do it at Poolewe, I said, we could do it at Scarista. So in went pinus contorta, birch, hawthorn, rowan, elder, hebe, griselinia, eucalyptus, beech, sweet chestnut, horse chestnut, walnut, elder, willow, rhododendron, hornbeam, hazel, whitebeam, pyrus malus, ash, broom, oak,

Leyland cypress—in fact, just about every tree or shrub ever known to grow in the Northern Hemisphere. By March we had planted about 2000, quaking at the expense in money and time, but reasoning that if we wanted the place to look cared for by the time we set up in business, we had to start at once. I might as well admit now that of the 2000, perhaps 20 have survived. They are all Olearia Macrodonta. The prize specimens have grown to a little over three feet. Most of the trouble can be traced to our windswept, saltblown position, but initially the chief enemies were the Raiders. They were a pair of enormously fat wedders (adult castrated rams) who officially grazed the glebe. They quivered with flesh, like Arabian Nights eunuchs. They looked too heavy to walk, let alone jump. Yet these beasts could leap nimbly three feet in the air and land on our garden wall. Thence it was an easy waddle to the new tasty plantings. We would rush after them shouting and hurling stones, grab them and bundle them unceremoniously back over the wall, turn the garden hose on them, fire an airgun over their heads, but they were undeterred. We thought our harassments were successful, as the spring wore on, for we stopped seeing them around. Yet things continued to be eaten. One morning we happened to get up very early—and there they were. It appeared that they had their breakfast and left before eight o'clock. Then our neighbour Janet Miles reported that every day she saw them jumping over our wall just after we had left for work. Sure enough —looking back from the school bus as it climbed the hill, we saw first one and then the other appear on the wall, watching coolly till the bus had gone. They worked a five-day week like us: their depredations ceased at weekends. Fortunately they were sent off up the hill for the summer, and by the next winter we had installed a barbed wire barricade below the top of the wall, sticking out at right angles to forestall jumping sheep. The raiders troubled us no longer, but the next spring we noticed they had a new interest. They were now in the field to our left. The field on our right had much better grass which was being saved for hay. So they would heave themselves through the fence at the roadside, walk along the road below our house, and squeeze through the roadside fence of the preferred field: then back again at half past three. Why half past three? We wondered. Then we noticed that their owner usually drove up from his house in Leverburgh to do his rounds of the Glebe at about 3.45.

From all this we concluded that sheep either have a most remarkable biological clock, or else they are much, much brainier than they look. These two must have ended up as mutton the next winter, for we didn't see them in following years. They must have made very greasy broth.

There was one sort of animal pest which we were ourselves responsible for introducing. I was very keen to keep some livestock of our own. It seemed a waste to have an acre and a half of ground and nothing to enjoy it. I suggested a cow, and John Angus promptly offered us one for a housewarming present. Andrew put his foot down and has never relented.

"If you have a cow," he said, "what would you do with the calves?"

"Eat them."

He snorted. "Nonsense! In 10 years' time you'd have a herd of bulls, and they'd all be inside sitting by the fire."

So that was that.

Hens, however, were permitted. I costed out carefully how much they would eat, how many eggs they would produce, and what their carcases would be worth at the end of a year's laying: there were directions for all these sums in the book I had bought on poultry keeping. This was fine in principle, but in practice our hens have never lived up to it: in particular they are very vociferous against carcase-value.

At first we shared our hens with John and Margaret Blatchford, who lived at the old school house over the road. In return they shared their bees with us. The bees died in their second winter, but the hens flourished, to the continuing detriment of our garden.

We persuaded the Glebe tenant to remove his hay from our shed, and retrieved the sawn-off door for later re-use. John and Andrew prepared these quarters for our expected pullets with paternal care. There were carefully smoothed wide perches—none of your old broomsticks, which cramp a hen's toes. There were three nest boxes snugly fitted into an old open fireplace at one end. There was a feeding trough made of guttering—new plastic, not scrap iron which might be contaminated with lead paint. The floor was scraped down to the old quarry tiles and thickly covered in straw. A rope was hung from the rafters with a bundle of cabbage leaves at the end to provide entertainment. A temporary fence was erected outside round half the yard, in case the pullets would wander off and get lost before they were used to their new surroundings.

Into this luxurious home, some 14 foot square, came 10 very small and scruffy Light Sussex/Brown Leghorn point-of-lays. They arrived on the ferry in two cardboard boxes. Here and there a beak or an eye peeped through an airhole. We all assembled for the unpacking by torchlight. Out they bundled, cheeping sleepily. We placed them on the perches in the recommended manner, which seemed to cause great alarm. They hung on with their great scaly feet, craning forward to peer at the floor a dizzy three feet below. One or two fell off. We replaced them and left the house in darkness. When we listened at the door the noises had already subsided.

During the next few weeks we wasted a great deal of valuable time getting to know our hens. At first we had to coax them out of the house with a handful of grain, but we soon wished we hadn't bothered. We were doing a great deal of digging for a variety of reasons—tree-planting, vegetable garden, soakaways, drains. Wherever we dug, they converged, with the triumphant fruity cooing of hens who have found their heart's desire. Our ground is full of thick, soft cream-coloured grubs, which live on the roots of wild (and cultivated) parsnips. These are ambrosia to hens. Their voices rose to an emotional vibrato: they hopped on the spade and on our boots: they scratched fountains of earth back into the holes we had dug. I have used the past tense, but they are still at it. Wherever we dig, we have hens helping us. The front garden is by now nearly hen-proof, but one's enjoyment in gardening there is spoilt by the huddle of excluded hens cackling disconsolately outside the gate.

Our first vegetable garden was a patch in the field in front of the house which had been cultivated for potatoes the previous year. The walled back garden was ploughed up that year, and we planted potatoes there to clear the ground. I would bribe the hens into the yard with a cup of grain, and then sneak round to the front to pick up my gardening tools very quietly. But I never escaped notice for very long. I would soon be aware of companionable clucks and chuckles, and there they would be, busily scratching up the seeds I had just planted. Eventually we had to put a temporary fence (yet another temporary fence) round the patch till the vegetables had grown sturdy enough to survive. But it is very entertaining to watch hens gardening: I have seen one pick up every single pea in a 30-foot drill, test it for edibility, and then drop it; then on to the next with a querulous squawk, as much as to say "I bet this one's just the same!"

Some hens are much of a muchness, and others are strongly individual. These latter inevitably acquire names. In our first batch we had Pioneer, Gutsy and Idiot. Pioneer, who is still with us, is an upright and conscientious hen, who always takes the initiative in foraging new ground, never pecks anyone, and lays regularly; but she talks to herself anxiously a great deal. Gutsy, who died of a gastric crisis some years ago, was gutsy. She it was who tested the peas. She had a floppy comb under which she squinted with a quizzical expression. She especially liked our picnic lunches in the summer, but she was not ill-mannered like her successor Big Feet, who would zoom in on a sandwich with harpy-like precision, and be off with it while your hand was still half way to your mouth. Idiot was a problem. She had a very small comb and a demented eye. She crowed like a cock and then glared round crazily to see who made the noise. When the others moulted, she pecked them viciously and drove them from their food. One day I found her pecking a hole in Gutsy's back, and chased her screeching round the garden with a crowbar. After that she was madder than ever and staggered around shrieking something very like "Repent, the end is nigh!". She succumbed to lunacy and bronchitis in the end.

Apart from Idiot and a few who followed her example at the time, we have never had problems with pecking among our hens, nor have we ever seen the strict peck-order which is supposed to be so characteristic of barnyard fowls. When I put breakfast in the trough in the morning, everyone jumps in it feet first without regard to rank. Perhaps it is because we have plenty of space, or because we have never had a cockerel, or because every year we bring in a new batch of point-of-lays. Certainly there are disagreements between the established hens and the newcomers.

When we brought in our second lot of pullets, the older generation left the house in a body and sat out in the rain all day. Later introductions were not so traumatic. New pullets dart in, and seize titbits from ponderous older birds, and the old ones peck them for it: but the same thing happens again 10 minutes later. The young birds are impudently undeterred, and the old ones outraged but ineffective. Birds of the same year group will spar quite fiercely with each other, but there do not seem to be consistent winners or losers. I cannot believe that after watching our hens for eight years I have missed what Konrad Lorenz, whose judgement I greatly respect, calls "a very definite order, in which each bird is afraid of those that are above her in rank". If our birds are not so orderly, perhaps it is because they are not Teutonic.

Our rewards have not been all that the poultry handbook promised, but if one leaves aside the subject of gardening, our hens have done well for us. We are never without eggs, and we need never be embarrassed by wasted food—hens like a varied diet and will try anything from curried beans to Stilton. There is no problem with party dregs either—give our hens a quart of mulled wine for breakfast and they are happy all day. They are conversational, too. The air is always full of their bickering and exclamations. In the winter I can't imagine why I ever complain against them. It will be a different story in the spring, though, when the bulbs come up —further than intended, assisted by large scaly feet.

7

Plots

Life at Scarista was nothing like as relaxed as these bucolic observations might indicate. From the day we knew the house was ours, we were working at it doggedly: working so hard at each task as it came up that fortunately we had little time to brood on what was still to be done. That was reserved for Sundays, when we did our paperwork and planning: we would wander from room to room, appalled at the amount of work to be done, bickering over the smallest details. For the other six days, we laboured wholeheartedly. As soon as we got in from school, we changed into our filthy old clothes and worked till bedtime.

By April, we were dismayed at how slowly things were going. At this rate it would be 10 years till we were finished. Our energy after school was limited: often we were so tired that we made mistakes and ended up doing the job twice. We pinned our hopes on Saturdays, but they were often disastrous. All that was needed to throw us, in our state of permanent exhaustion, was a friendly caller or so coming to see how we were getting on. After the visitors had left, it was impossible to get back into gear.

Obviously if we wanted to be in business by the next summer or even the one after, we had to give up teaching. We argued bitterly over when we should resign. I was for doing it at once, if not sooner. Andrew was more cautious, and felt we should continue earning for some months, so that we should have some fat to live off, and also to maintain an appearance of sobriety and respectability: we were badgering every grant-awarding body we could think of, and would obviously require a large bank loan for a time, so it seemed prudent to be teachers rather than dropouts until this was all arranged. In the event we did not resign till September 1977, a year after we bought the manse.

Knowing we intended eventually to set up a hotel, we had found out years before what assistance was available for tourism projects from the most obvious source, the Highlands and Islands Development Board. They give no assistance towards purchase of old buildings, but a 35% grant and 15% fixed interest loan towards building works and a 50% grant for equipment. This was good, but not enough, if we wanted to get into business quickly. Local Authority money was available for a housing loan, followed by an improvement grant, provided the property was plumbed, wired, insulated and daylighted to their required standard. We decided it would be preferable to pursue this and call on the HIDB for help with converting and equipping to hotel standard.

At the same time, we approached the Historic Buildings Council, as the house is listed Grade B. Three jolly representatives came up from Edinburgh to see us. They admired the house, enthusing over its plain late-Georgian frontage, its original shutters, doors and window casings, its old cast iron fireplaces, its superb box locks. We were very pleased: we had been rather cast down by our local building inspector suggesting gloomily that all the back wing was fit for was demolition. The Historic gentlemen didn't like the back as much as the front ("so Victorian—quite different proportions") but at least they did not seem inclined to do away with it. They offered us a 50% grant, but the cost of implementing their meticulous proposals would have been prohibitive, and eventually we turned it down.

While we were still waiting for a reply from the HIDB (this is always an on-going process) we began to hear nasty rumours on the Local Authority side. If we applied for change of use to a hotel, we would need a building warrant; if we got a building warrant we would have to carry out not only the work we intended, but everything else that regulations demand of a hotel. We might need a concrete staircase—single-sex toilets—a fully hygienic institutional kitchen—sealed-off attics. Again, the cost would be prohibitive and, in addition, our rates would be enormous and our house wrecked internally. We were bewildered. We were intending to cater for eight to 10 people, and only in the summer. Why couldn't they live in the sort of house we had in mind? Why did other similar establishments not have concrete staircases and half a dozen toilets? The answer, it seemed, was that they were established already. But why had they not had to conform to start with? Ah, they had not applied for building warrants. But the HIDB wanted a building warrant: how could we get any money from them if we didn't have one? Well, we would have to abide by regulations, then.

That was the official line. We had not until now thought of doing other than abide by regulations. But the rules of the game seemed to be quite irrelevant to the sort of business we wanted to set up, and the game itself very like Monopoly: land on the right square and collect £200, land on the wrong one and go to jail. Then we heard some kindlier counsel on the unofficial line: carry on until you are stopped. It is the best piece of advice we ever had. It became our motto.

Extreme circumspection was now the order of the day. It was revealed to us that regulations are mainly a matter of terminology. If we were not a hotel we would not need permission for change of use or a building warrant. Therefore we would not be a hotel, but a superior seasonal guest house. We called ourselves Scarista House, and took care not to allow the word "hotel" to appear on any official papers, or even to cross our lips for the next year or so.

We paid back our Local Authority loan and turned down their grant. We informed the HIDB firmly that we had been told we definitely did not need a building warrant for our type of project. They seemed to believe it, and as negotiations with them proceeded, we found that we would anyway do much better taking assistance only from them than in any other way: this was because our own labour on the building project could be costed as part of our 50% contribution.

These sleights seem innocent enough now, but at the time they were intrigue of Machiavellian proportions. As we had no money to spare, and would not have any for several years, we were comically apprehensive of being found out in our attempts to bend the rules. Not only did we not call ourselves a hotel, but for the two years after we opened, we did not dare advertise locally, or put up signs at the gate, and for the first year, we did not even accept non-residents for meals. It made things hard going.

While we were still repairing the structure, before the conversion stage, the subject was sufficiently worrying to make us wonder if we ought to abandon the scheme altogether. If we declared ourselves a hotel, the revenue from eight guests would never pay for the work we would have to undertake. On the other hand, if we were rumoured to be a guest house, visitors would be rightly annoyed at being charged hotel prices. And we had never intended to be a guest house: we had in mind gracious public rooms, bedrooms with private bathrooms, and interesting, even exotic food. We did have doubts about the morality of this: did we really want to devote our lives to selling luxuries to people who had more money than was good for them? Sometimes we decided yes and sometimes no, but even when the answer was no, we were quite certain we did not want to offer any other sort of tourist accommodation. If we were not going to be a fairly luxurious hotel, we would be something completely different, like a poultry farm or an old folks' home.

Another reason for doubt was our realisation that initially, at least, we would have to be unlicensed. In Scotland most property is not freehold, it is sold on a feu, and every feu presupposes a feudal superior, who may or may not be the seller. The superior may retain certain feudal rights—not *droit de seigneur*, but others equally irksome. In our case, our superior was the Church of Scotland. Our feu disposition contained a lengthy list of restrictions. These are more or less standard to properties feued by the Church, and are designed to protect the decency of that indecently rich organisation. For instance, we must not use the place as "a meeting place, meeting house or institution for any religious denomination or for religious purposes, or for betting, gambling or gaming, or for any purpose which would create a noise or nuisance. . . . and the sale or keeping for sale of intoxicating liquors in or upon the feu or any part thereof and the buildings erected or to be erected thereon is specifically prohibited."

Naturally we resented all this stuff and nonsense. The Church Trustees in Edinburgh had long ago pocketed the cash for the crumbling building they did not want. If anyone now tried to turn it into a mosque or a casino, we felt it should be up to the neighbours to complain, as only they would actually be bothered by a "noise or nuisance" emanating from it. There is, of course, a safeguard for neighbours in that planning permission has to be sought and publicly advertised for such a conversion, at which stage anyone is free to object: but feudal superiors, particularly godly ones, are not prepared to take their chance in this way along with the common herd. As it happened, we did not intend to lease the place to the Moonies or even turn it into a brothel, but we did want to be able to offer guests wine with their meals. We had bought the manse with misgivings on this matter, but as we had no intention of running a public bar we thought a partial relaxation of the no-liquor clause might not be seen as unreasonable. However, as it turned out, we were greatly overestimating the sweetness of reason among the Trustees to the Church.

Being green, we were rather offended by their first refusal, but had an alternative plan, which would not be lucrative for us, but would at least keep our guests happy. This was the system used in some College common rooms and many of the country houses which take paying guests for their sporting estates. In such places there is a drinks cupboard or a drinks trolley, and people sign a book as they help themselves, and are billed for the total at the end of their stay. Unfortunately, we were too frank about this plan. The respectable lawyer we spoke to in Stornoway hastened to tell us that we would need a Club licence even to do this. I mentioned a couple of expensive Hebridean sporting paradises by name. What about them? They must have Club licences, he assured us, very definitely.

We went away puzzled and worried. We were not sufficiently cynical to disbelieve him—but we had doubts. A few more years of studying the intricacies of the Licensing Act converted these doubts to certainties. The places I had mentioned might well need Club licences to serve liquor, but "need" is not "have", of course. What they did have, and what we lacked, was the awesome respectability conferred by size, wealth and titled owners. For the most part, these powerful stimuli trigger the same reaction in legal and official persons as a bristling mane and a low growl do in puppies: they fall on their backs and widdle themselves.

We had a third plan up our sleeves, and in desperation sought advice on this one. How would it be, if we treated our guests to an aperitif and a carafe of wine with dinner? No good, the law told us gleefully. It could be presumed that our charges included a concealed sum to pay for the liquor, or that we were using it as an advertisement or bribe—horrid and ungentlemanly thought! If we were taken to court, it would be up to us to prove that this was not the case, and that would be virtually impossible.

So much for being innocent until proved guilty.

In fact, if we had kept away from lawyers and officials and quietly pursued either of these plans, I am sure we would have had no trouble: by the time any action would have been formulated against us, we would ourselves have achieved a measure of respectability and growling status, and no one would have felt like interfering. "Carry on until you're stopped" would have been as good advice here as in other particulars. But we had blown our plans to too many people, and lost our nerve. The only course left open to us was to warn people to bring their own drinks—and even then, we were grudgingly told that in the event of a police raid we could be presumed to have sold the stuff to our clients. For a year or so we actually expected that police raid, but fortunately policemen have better things to do.

A legion of worries proceeded from the licence question. Would anyone come to a totally unknown hotel which couldn't be called a hotel and was suspected of temperance? Would they expect plaques with "Thou God seest me" in the dining room? Would the abstemious atmosphere encourage people who *liked* such places? How would they get on with fellow guests who had brought a cheap case of whisky from Tesco and swilled it with abandon? Could anyone eat a six course dinner without an alcoholic digestif? Would anyone believe the food was worth eating if they couldn't buy a decent bottle of wine to accompany it? What about people coming off the plane, as there was not much but "Blue Nun" in Stornoway?

In spite of intermittent cold feet, we decided to carry on with our project. It was our only chance to do what we had been planning for years, and really dropping it was unthinkable. It would have left a hole in our lives. But in the event, all our anxieties about the licence business were fully justified. It continued to plague us more than rats or woodworm or wet rot, and that is saying a lot.

8

A Spot of Filler

As soon as we bought the old manse, we heard three unpleasant tales about it.

"Miss! Miss! It's haunted. It's that near the graveyard. Gus says he wouldn't walk past it at night, not for anything."

"Oh no, I wouldn't go near it. You're not going to *stay* there, are you, Miss?"

This was easy enough to discount. In fact, in spite of its grim exterior, the house always had a happy and welcoming feel as soon as one entered, even at its most derelict. For some time we had a sneezing presence, which would creep up on either of us while we were in alone, and sneeze loudly at knee-level; but it was harmless, even jocular: the ghost of a rat with hay-fever.

But there were more serious rumours: that the chimneys had fallen in on each other, and that the roof was full of dry rot. We got our brush up the chimneys, without much impediment, but the soot was mixed with substantial bits of masonry. However, by sweeping very gingerly and infrequently, we have so far managed to preserve the chimneys, and most of the smoke does appear to come out of the top. Disaster is imminent, but all may yet be well. The dry rot was not so easily dealt with. Neither of us had ever seen it. We knew it was supposed to have a characteristic odour, and certainly parts of our house smelt quite indescribable. The old kitchen was particularly aromatic. I think it was probably a combination of ancient soot and rat piss, but being inexperienced we put it down to worse causes. On removing a patch of the matchboard wall-lining, we discovered a spectacular growth like a furry black spider's web of giant proportions. It proceeded from a damp-blackened wooden lintel, into which a screwdriver sank

108

like a knife into butter. The exposed masonry glistened evilly wet and brown. Dry rot!

In fact it was manifestly wet rot. Everything around was dripping. We are now pretty certain that dry rot does not occur in Harris: the air is saturated to a level that this organism cannot tolerate. What islanders call dry rot is woodworm, with its dry, powdery symptoms. At the time, though, we were deceived. How much more of the stuff was there? Would it proliferate hideously when we put in central heating? And as for the woodworm which had been peacefully eating the place for 150 years, wouldn't they like the added warmth too?

We made a panic decision to call in Rentokil, and it was a bad one. It was the only job we didn't do ourselves, but we perfectly well could have, by hiring spray equipment. Naturally the Rentokil representative assured us we couldn't do it anything like as well as professionals, but only mugs listen to that sort of advice. We were mugs on this occasion. Fortunately, we did not have access to any other experts during the rest of our building programme.

The de-woodworming was very expensive, and was to be even more expensive if the roof timbers weren't laid bare for ease of access. Mug-like, we decided to knock all the old plaster out of the attics. Anyway, we told ourselves, it would show us if anything else was wrong. There might be rusty slate nails denoting slipping slates, or rotten rafters which would need replacing.

Knocking the lath and plaster out of what was at that time seven fair-sized rooms was a formidable undertaking. Weakly, we looked round for help. A large party of friends got together on a Saturday and set to with hammers and crowbars and hatchets, and wild enthusiasm. Through the haze of choking dust, we began to notice the soundness of the timbers and the solidity of the plaster. But there wasn't much we could do. We had promised a dozen people they could smash the place up, and they were doing so with verve.

Getting rid of the broken up plaster was a test of ingenuity. Andrew removed the small sash window in the front attic and rigged up a makeshift chute made of matchboarding stripped out of the kitchen. This was angled over the roof of the porch to reach the ground. We picked out the laths to make the wreckage more compact—they kept us in kindling for years. The plaster was shovelled into buckets and tossed down the chute, then barrowed through the garden and shovelled out into the Land-Rover. Each load was then taken to a low cliff at the roadside a mile or so away and shovelled (again) into the sea. Like building the pyramids, this work was extremely labour intensive. However, unlike Pharaoh, we have little talent for organising people, and after the wrecking party we preferred to do most tasks ourselves, or with just one or two helpers. The clearing up operations took weeks, during which we breathed and ate plaster dust. I was still picking up chunks of plaster from the garden six months later: and Andrew's father spent most of his holiday removing many thousands of lath nails from the exposed rafters.

Once the haze had cleared, we could see that the roof was remarkably sound. Scottish houses are sarked—that is, planked—between the slates and the rafters. To bear this extra load, rafters are correspondingly massive. In the Georgian front wing, these timbers were particularly weighty, and of such dense, dark red pine that the adze marks showed as glossy as on oak: none of your modern balsa-weight hairy white stuff! Andrew was ecstatic about the quality of the wood and the interesting carpentry revealed.

Woodworm had certainly had a feast, but without making much impression on the thicker timbers. Floorboards had suffered most, particularly where leaks had swelled the grain, leaving it spongy and toothsome when it dried out. The sawn pine laths at the front, but not the split ones of willow at the back, had gone the same way, and so had the sarking under the south-west facing skylights. Apart from that, the worst damage was to the rafter ends below leaking roof valleys, and to joist ends, particularly below windows on the south-west side. In the front wing the wall plate was exposed, ventilated and sound, but in the back it had been closed in with masonry to prevent draughts entering the roof, and had consequently rotted.

Once the plaster was removed (but a few square yards would have done) the cause of most of the structural damage on the lower floors became dramatically clear. Three innocuous looking skylights on the exposed south west side had been leaking, and had poured destruction from attic to ground level. The sarking and wall plate had gone, and below that, the floorboards, joists, lintels and window sashes on both lower floors. In fact the thoroughness of the devastation was quite an advantage: it was possible to cut out wells through all three floors at the damaged points, which made it much easier to hoist up and install the new concrete lintels for the windows. Elsewhere, when an isolated lintel needed replacing beneath an intact ceiling, this was a very tricky manoeuvre.

We set to work on the south west wall about Christmas. As well as taking up the floorboards and sawing out the joist ends, we removed all the interior wall linings on that side—a mixture of plaster, hardboard and tongued and grooved matchboard. This meant there was now nothing to hold the windows in place. Andrew wedged them up precariously. They all needed replacement sashes or at least panes, which they gradually got over the next year. Of course, when one blew in and smashed in a gale, it was a repaired specimen. The old kitchen area was without wall lining for 15 months, so we were lucky not to have more such breakages.

The observant reader may have noticed that I have left the sawn-off joists flopping in mid-air. This is just what I would have done, but fortunately Andrew had more wit, and forearmed himself by importing a bundle of Acrojacks, which soon became prized possessions. These are sliding steel tubes with a flat plate at top and bottom, which can be extended by means of a lever to support ceilings or anything else at that height. They are invaluable for propping up anything that might fall on your head. They held the loose joists until Andrew had bolted on new ends, and lent support to masonry until new lintels were slid into place.

In fact, the new lintels did not slide into place. They were thrust and heaved and hammered with much cursing and barking of knuckles. The masonry had settled comfortably round the old rotten wood lintels, and when these were jiggled free, the irregular hole had to be squared off with a cold chisel and measured. Then a wooden mould of the same dimensions had to be made, which was filled with concrete and left to cure for a week or so. Inevitably, when taken out of the shuttering and swung up to the hole, some piece of masonry would still be fouling it. As the lintel weighed a couple of hundredweight and was dangling just above our heads, last minute adjustments were nerve-racking. Every lintel was a long and arduous job, and we ended up leaving at least one that should have been replaced. A crack in the outside rendering assures us that it is still rotting away.

While these operations were going on, we took advantage of the mess to remove the old fireplaces from the two bedrooms in that wing. They were late Victorian, to my mind very ugly, with tiles in lurid shades of green and steel hoods with random flourishes on, painted pink. So many people told me they were beautiful that I tried to remove them intact, but my hands must have faltered and I am glad to say the venom-green tiles shattered under their own weight as soon as I began levering their ensemble off the wall.

Below one of these bedrooms was a warren of sculleries and pantries which we intended to knock together into a new kitchen. I wanted an Aga, but it seemed a long hope, in view of their price. By good luck, the *Stornoway Gazette* about that time carried an ad. for a "solid fuel Aga, £40 o.n.o.". There was only one problem: an Aga weighs a pretty solid ton, and is too bulky to get into the back of a Land-Rover. We borrowed a lorry for the occasion, and fortunately the sellers had a friend with a fork lift truck, so from fork lift to lorry it went, and safely back to Scarista. We could have done with the fork lift again, but in its absence made do with a sloping ramp of rubble and turves, of which materials we always had plenty at that time. Using three crowbars and the combined might of all male neighbours, the stove was slid off the lorry and into the back porch, very carefully, as being old and fragile, it threatened to collapse under its own weight. It was a long time till we had a kitchen to put it in, but Andrew took the opportunity to adapt the bedroom chimney above for its use.

Then we lost interest in indoor tasks. The weather was improving towards the Easter holidays, and there were plenty of things to do outside. In fact, I had already spent many hours struggling in wind, rain and frost to afforest and vegetate our grounds. Having a thick layer of blubber, I was better equipped to withstand winter weather than Andrew, and anyway I could not be let loose on any of the structural work, except by helping with a heave now and again, or clearing up. Andrew's next priority was to reslate where necessary, which is the coldest job imaginable, but fortunately we had an exceptionally warm, sunny spring and summer—much too dry for newly planted shrubs which had already suffered salt-burn, but excellent for roofing.

I think at first we had a vague intention of reslating the whole house. However, an experimental attempt on the front porch soon put paid to that. Our slates are Ballachulish, which are always small, starting at about 16″ long above the gutter and decreasing to perhaps 8″ at the ridge. These slates were often re-trimmed and used again, with a decrease in size each time. On the porch they went from about 10″ long to 5″. By the time they had been stripped and re-trimmed by us, they were like fish scales. As this small roof is hipped, it is complicated to slate anyway, and has three ridges, a horizontal one with two angles running down from it. The job took about 10 times as long as we had expected. The only other area that got done before we opened was the front wing above the porch, which needed new lead in the valleys to protect the repaired rafters underneath. By this stage we were being less careful to re-use every possible slate, and discarded some of the more minute, so this time work went rather better. Anyway, Andrew was in no hurry to finish it. He had a wonderful view to look at, and complete peace and quiet. He got up to his perch by means of an extension ladder propped on one of these lightweight DIY scaffolding towers. There was absolutely no chance of me pestering him up there—I never got higher than the first floor windows. I could not even be heard when I shouted up for advice on what type of carrots to plant or to remonstrate with him for putting cement on our only carpet. Oddly enough, he could hear me when I yelled "Food!" but for the rest of the day he was his own master. When he came down he was very jaunty about the dangerous state of the rest of the front roof.

"The slates are cemented together to stop them rattling. Just wait till the nails start rusting! It'll all come off in one 10-ton slab and brain anyone who happens to be passing."

We are still waiting for this exciting event.

Slating is interesting work. The irregularities of the old hand-riven slates make them far more exacting to apply than modern machine-cut or synthetic versions. The craft requires special tools (always a recommendation to Andrew) including that vicious implement, the zax. This is like a heavy narrow-bladed cleaver with a two-inch curved spike at the back. The blade is used to chop the edges of the slate to the required size and shape, and the spike to punch a hole for the nail. This satisfying task could be done at ground level, so I did it. It is a very good aggression releaser. I was sorry when I had trimmed, measured and stacked every slate from the jumbled heap we had salvaged from a re-roofing operation in Tarbert. It was less enjoyable moving the unused slates to another site when roof work was over for the time being. Wherever they are stored, they seem to get in the way. They have just been moved for the fifth time. As Andrew can't resist begging or buying Ballachulish slates when they are on offer, the pile keeps growing. He is saving them up for all the re-roofing he is going to do some day.

After the roof, we tackled the windows. They were a mixed

bag, exhibiting every degree of craftsmanship from excellent to appalling. Some had had replacement panes fitted using cement and 1½″ nails. Many panes were broken and much wood was rotten. In places the putty had perished to such an extent that a north-westerly blizzard during our first Christmas had deposited a small snow-drift on the opposite side of our sitting room. For the worst affected windows on the south-west Andrew made completely new four-pane sash and case windows, which he greatly enjoyed. Where possible, though, we patched up. It was a job where division of labour paid off. Andrew would remove the sashes, make any joinery repairs, plane them to fit, and put in new weights. The original plan had been for him then to burn off the paint with the Calor gas blowlamp, which terrified me: but after his first effort, we went out visiting and came home to find the treated frame blazing and crackling. After that he was no longer trusted with the blowlamp, and I took it over, with trepidation. I burned off encumbering layers of paint and hardened putty round broken panes, replaced glass, and repainted. Most of my work could be done outside as the weather was glorious. Indeed, it was so fine that one Saturday we removed all seven windows from the front of the house, and propped them in the garden for repair work. These are Georgian 12-paned sashes with delicate astragals, and though they were in better shape than those in the back wing, work on them was fiddly. By late in the evening they were still not quite finished, but as it was calm and warm, we left them overnight, intending to do a few secret Sabbath touch-ups in the shelter of the garden wall, and reinstate them on Monday. On Sunday the church bus and attendant cars passed slowly by at 11.30 a.m., the congregation staring at the windowless house with interest. At midday, a spiral of white cloud appeared on the horizon, and in 10 minutes a sudden summer gale was whirling and flapping through every room. When the congregation passed again at 1.30, all the windows were blatantly and scandalously back in place.

Work on the windows included making new apertures. At the planning stage, I was particularly keen on extra windows here and French doors there. Andrew was less enthusiastic, and eventually we agreed on two new windows on the first floor at the back, which would be situated above existing windows and would improve the external appearance, as well as lighting two en suite bathrooms. We would also make a hatch between kitchen and dining room, and enlarge a small window in the kitchen to take a glazed double door into the herb garden. This seemed a modest enough programme. We started with the enlargement job. As there was already room there to swing a seven-pound hammer, it was deceptively easy at first. The cement and rubble beneath the sill came away cleanly. Underneath that was the masonry proper—roughly-faced blocks inside and out, with an infill of rubble and dull-sounding, slightly sticky lime mortar, which absorbs shock and cannot be chipped or reduced to a powder. The outside rendering is a layer an inch thick of similar consistency. In places it seemed to be falling off the walls: but not in the right places. It clung to the masonry in a muffling blanket, resisting impact. Out came the 14-pound hammer—the three-foot crowbar—the five-foot crowbar. It took several days to get down to ground level. Admittedly this was my work—doubtless Andrew would get on much better. He would have to, as I had temporarily lost the use of my wrist through too much hammering: it has never quite recovered.

Andrew was condescending. He started the much more difficult hatch through what had been the original back wall of the Georgian building. There was no hole here at all. The first task was to mark corresponding positions on either side of the wall and knock off the old plaster. This revealed the masonry, which had to be taken out separately on the two faces of the wall. After the layer in the dining room had been removed, a concrete lintel had to be put in place to support the wall before the kitchen side was attacked. Of course the settlement of years had tied the blocks on either side firmly together. There was no room to use a heavy hammer, and it was a case of chipping laboriously with a selection of chisels and short hammers. It took almost a week to excavate, and in spite of the two lintels, a sinister crack began to open in the dining room plaster. In the end the dimensions of the hatch were decided by an enormous block with only its edge protruding into the required space. Removing the whole of it would have made a gap twice as big as we wanted: and who knew what else would have to go to get it out? We could end up removing the whole wall. Consequently the hatch has never been tall enough to take a hock bottle.

It was the same problem with the first window aperture. Andrew had managed to remove about three-quarters of the outer layer of masonry without incident, when he discovered that the corner of a half-ton block stuck up into the remaining section. It is almost impossible to split rock when it is embedded in traditional shock-absorbing lime mortar, so the only solution was to remove the whole thing, and remake the gap with smaller stones. He hacked out as much of the surrounding rubble as possible, exposing all the edges of the obstructive block. We surveyed it from ground level. It could be roped around, but we didn't much care for the prospect of hauling it on top of ourselves. Eventually we tied it to the bumper of the Land-Rover and reversed hard, on the principle of tooth extraction through door slamming. We rolled it across the yard on a crowbar to a place where the soil was deep enough to bury it, and it is now under the coal bunker. That window took all of two weeks by the time the gap was made up to the right stage again. We realised we could not afford the time for any more of this, and the remaining window appeared only on the plans. The resulting windowless bathroom was at last temporarily wall-papered—it could be tiled once the window embrasure had been made the following year. It is still papered and the tiles eventually found their way onto the kitchen walls.

During the first year of renovations I spent a great deal of the time digging. I could safely be left to do this sort of work, which could not be said of my efforts with more skilled tasks. So while Andrew was running spiders' webs of pipes all over the house or matching up existing joinery details, I was usually digging. I dug the garden, the trenches for drains, the soakaways. To deter damp and rats, I dug a wide rubble-filled ditch round the house at ground level, later topped with gravel to make it one with the path. But most of the time I dug the drive. Andrew measured and straight-edged and levelled, and set up networks of string to keep me right, and I dug out anything between six and 14 inches of turves and soil, from the road to the garden gate and then parallel to the garden wall. At intervals Andrew checked up to make sure I was dumping the tons of earth only in permitted places. Large rocks had to be taken to the back door, where we would later need infill for the kitchen floor. Turves and soil were to fill in unwanted ruts and holes left by delivery lorries and the removal of rubbish, or piled at a point where we intended to start a shrubbery. This barrowing was all uphill—dumping on the downhill slope of the field was strictly forbidden. I dug and barrowed and dumped, and on the return journey filled the barrow with bottoming—broken stone about three inches across—tamping it down with a crowbar to a minimum depth of six inches (Andrew checked frequently). After several weeks of work and 10 tons of bottoming, we were visited one Saturday by a father and son we knew who were holidaying nearby. They viewed my work patronisingly—they would finish the drive for me that very day—and the car park too. Seizing the best barrow, the best spade, the only pick and the best shovel, they charged off. I was left with the small narrow-wheeled garden barrow and a minute heart-shaped shovel with a cracked handle. Disconsolately, I glowered at our friends as they rapidly skinned the turf round the corner of the wall, with a total disregard for camber or gradient. On went a thin scatter of bottoming— three inches at most! As for dumping, off they went downhill and threw up a huge pile of turves in the middle of our field. I was speechless. Spluttering with rage, I sought out Andrew. He was defensive: it was very kind of them to help, and they were getting on very quickly.

"Not much wonder! What about the six inches of bottoming?"

"Well, we're running out of bottoming anyway. We can't afford any more."

"Why the hell didn't you tell *me* that?"

Andrew looked very uncomfortable and told me not to shout in case I offended our friends.

This is quite the most outstanding example of male chauvinism I have ever encountered. Our friends, as promised, finished both drive and car park that day. They have been full of ruts and holes ever since—with the top gravel spilling off into the grass and large puddles where the all-important levelling strips were ignored— indeed, swept away: I saw it with my own eyes. Also we have a structure of dumped turves rather like a long-barrow half way down the field. I have planted pampas grass on it, but it looks very strange. Still, I suppose if we had waited for me to finish in accordance with the rules, the first guests would have dropped off a six-inch ledge of bottoming into a muddy hole as they came round the corner.

The next step in roadmaking was to top the broken stone bottoming with a powdery substance which rain and pressure would turn to a binding glue. At first we used hoggin, a sort of greyish subsoil composed of rotten stone, found above glaciated bedrock. We made frequent trips to a disused working a few miles along the road, shovelling it into and out of the Land-Rover. After the first 50 yards or so, our mine was running out, and time as usual was short, so we had a load of quarry-dust delivered, and the loan of a mechanical pressing plate to squash it into the surface. It was inexpressibly dirty stuff, rather like coal dust in its appearance and habits. There was not quite enough of it, so the surface was never really properly bonded. There was never quite enough of anything—basically there was not quite enough money.

The gravel for the top surface was rather scanty too. As we passed the quarry near Tarbert one day, we had seen a heap of attractive chippings, mainly white, from a quartz vein in the grey gneiss. We booked this at once—it would echo the intended white and grey exterior of the house perfectly. For a long time it sat in a heap at the top of the drive, while I recovered from my discouragement at roadmaking. Eventually by spreading it rather thinly I stretched it to cover all the garden paths and the length of drive visible from the road, blending it off into the commoner grey stuff at the corner. Sweating over this dusty job, I provided welcome entertainment for the fencing gang sunbathing on the dunes opposite. They were taking part in a job creation scheme—described locally as "on the creation", or more cynically, "on the recreation".

Painting the house to match the drive was a cosmetic operation to which we looked forward greatly. The dingy grey walls with the rendering patched, cracked and missing were a constant reproach. Disused gutter brackets and abandoned fixings for clothes ropes and cables added to the appearance of neglect. We had absorbed subliminally from Blue Circle products advertisements that Sandtex protects lighthouses for up to 15 years. Fortunately, we did not realise then that it can only withstand the Scarista climate for three at the most: if we had known we would be painting our way round the building for the third time in 1984, we might have settled for limewash. Anyway, we bought some paint and read the instructions. Apparently there were about half a dozen operations necessary before we could apply the desired coat of dapper white with grey window facings. First of all we wire-brushed the walls to remove lichen and moss. In our windswept climate very little of this stuff takes hold, but we were conscientious nevertheless, and covered every inch. We lost a great deal of skin from our knuckles. Next day we washed the whole building with an expensive patent solution which smelt suspiciously like cheap domestic bleach. It acted similarly, too: our clothes developed white spots and the remaining skin disappeared from our hands. Next we repaired the many broken areas of the rough-cast with the recommended mix. This was more artistic work—rather like icing a Christmas cake. Then these new surfaces had to be treated with stabilising solution, a most obnoxious, sticky, runny yellow liquid which felt and smelt like cough mixture, but with the additional unpleasantness of immediate and immovable bonding to the skin. Our hands, arms and faces first turned sticky yellow and then gradually blackened with dust. The penultimate stage was an undercoat of Snowcem. The only way of applying paint to roughcast is with a banister brush, or rather with 20 or 30 banister brushes. We searched every shop in Tarbert for more brushes, even turning up old stock in pre-decimal prices. When Tarbert was exhausted, we bullied all our friends into surrendering theirs. John Angus produced from his byre some very ancient specimens which might have become curios if they had not been rapidly worn flat against our walls. Even so, we had to make a special trip to Stornoway to buy all the banister brushes in Lewis before we could start the Sandtex coat.

At last it was all done, and it looked wonderful. It had taken us three times as long as expected and cost twice as much in paint and banister brushes. We made the small economy of not buying a new front door. Andrew sawed the rat-eaten bottom off the old one, and fitted a new bottom section. "You just put a spot of filler in that crack before you paint it," he advised, hopefully. Andrew has great faith in filler. I applied it as directed and it cracked out immediately. Still, it looks better than rat's toothmarks. Painted shiny dark blue it did not look the same door at all as the dirty, green hingeless object that had barred our first entry to the house.

The same blue paint did wonders for cheap plastic gutters and downpipes, which were a considerable saving over authentic cast iron. Anyway, I distrusted cast iron: the section above the back door at Leachkin had crashed onto the doorstep one day just after I had gone inside.

By this time we had left teaching, and were casting around for every penny. Even our potatoes were carefully sorted into the edible (which we sold through a shopkeeper in Tarbert) and the inedible (which we ate). We also sold eggs and any surplus vegetables through the same kindly merchant, who I am sure did not actually want runtish lettuces and deformed turnips, but paid us well for them nonetheless.

It is wonderful how being without income focuses the mind. We knew now that no further options were open: we had to be a hotel, we had to be open by the following summer, and we had to have bookings by then. There were nine months between stopping teaching and opening day, and a vast amount of work still to get through.

9

A Long Slog

We worked a very strict regime. From Monday to Saturday the days were broken into two-hour slots with ¼-hour breaks in between, ¾-hour at lunchtime. Lunch was always bread and cheese and supper usually some unholy mixture of eggs and cabbage. I stopped work half an hour earlier than Andrew in the evening to make our meal. On Saturday evenings, I had the doubtful privilege of knocking off at 6.30 to do the weekly wash. This was always quite a business, as everything in and around the house produced its own sort of grime—earth, plaster, cement or paint. In fact as far as outer clothes went, we wore the same jeans and jerseys till they were so caked with cement and full of holes that they had to be thrown out. This way we at last worked through all the surplus garments of our student days, except for evening dress. It was always a great relief to throw another outfit away, as our wardrobe was not roomy—it consisted of a cardboard box each.

We looked forward immensely to Sundays. The Sabbath rest consisted of doing the housework and catching up on the letters, forms, plans and orders that had not got done between supper and bedtime during the previous six days. But our greatest treat of the week was to take out our large yellow work chart on Saturday evening after supper, and tot up the number of hours we had worked in the week. We kept this record as an encouragement, and also to satisfy the Highland Board of the value of our labour as a contribution to the project, without which we could not claim a grant. We filled it in with scrupulous honesty. If I visited the loo and collapsed in there with exhaustion for five minutes, I deducted that time from my daily total: likewise telephone calls and conversations with the postman. I am amazed at how honest I once was.

The rot set in when I overheard a visiting Highland Board official say to Andrew, "Of course, when you write down your labour contribution, remember that your wife's work is only worth half the rate . . ." Half? After that I doubled and trebled hours with malevolent satisfaction. In fact if my statistics were to be believed I must have worked about 36 hours some days.

It was quite difficult to persuade people that we were doing anything but having a nice holiday. There was one infallible way of testing our industry.

"Do you get up very early?" people would ask.

No, we did not get up till 9 o'clock.

Ah. Then we were obviously lazy. We could see it in their eyes. The fact that we worked punishingly till 10 at night meant nothing: it would have been more virtuous to get up at six and sit all day with folded hands, apparently. But the early morning is no use to either of us. In my opinion it should never have been invented.

By the time we were working full time on the house, it was regrettably clear that, though the outside was becoming quite presentable, the inside was more or less as it had always been. What of the plasterboarding, partitioning, plumbing, wiring, decorating and curtains? We both prefer being outside to being in, particularly me. Andrew had in fact done a steady quota of inside jobs. I kept putting them off: I hadn't decided the colour schemes —I couldn't choose paint till the curtain fabrics came—paint was dear in Stornoway, I would buy it in Aberdeen at Christmas—and so on. Then I was very insistent that the garden had to be planted out before I retired indoors: so I spent much of January out in a sleety wind putting in the herbaceous plants we had brought from my mother's at Christmas. Andrew's parents had valiantly cleared a wide border all round the front garden the previous summer, so there was a lot of space to fill. In March, still in a sleety wind, I sneaked outside again guiltily, with several dozen packets of seeds clenched in my teeth to prevent them blowing away. These filled the gaps in the border. Then there was the vegetable garden at the back—no good having guests without vegetables to feed them on: and somebody gave me strawberry plants—these had to go in where the previous year's vegetable patch had been; and then I couldn't resist some raspberry canes and currant bushes to keep them company. The herb garden had to be attended to, as well. It had been stripped the previous year of its grass, and dug over—with difficulty, as during some renovation in the past it had obviously been used as a dump for broken slates. I had rebuilt its retaining wall and put in two pleasing flights of rustic steps, but had neglected to make any sort of wheelbarrow access: so all the rubbish had to be carried away in buckets, and all the gravel for the many paths between the small geometric beds brought up the same way. It was a long job, but looked very neat and delightful. A stoneware sundial made by our friend Edi Thompson, was the finishing touch—or not quite final: there was still the planting to do. I crouched over the dusty little beds, attempting to confine each type of seed to its own area—very difficult, as a perpetual whirlwind blew there between the high walls till April, by which time I was incarcerated with the paint pots. For at last even I was forced to admit that redecorating the stairs was more important than weeding the asparagus.

We had planned the final internal layout very minutely at an early stage, even down to the furnishings and lampshades. We had spent many Sunday afternoons wandering from bare masonry to unhinged door with tile and fabric samples, vainly trying to assess the finished effect. This was necessary because practically everything we wanted to buy had to be ordered from the mainland, and we had to assume a long delivery period and time to rectify mistakes. In the event we were still often kept waiting for materials. We spent an unbelievable amount of valuable time at the end of the telephone chasing up orders. Either stuff simply did not arrive, or else it arrived broken, in a smaller size, or in short measure (never, we noticed, in a larger size or too much of it). As nearly all firms demanded prepayment it was then up to us to sort things out. Often we gave up, defeated by the escalating cost in money, time and energy of endless phone calls and letters. We discovered that all traders have office staff rigorously trained in the technique of customer deflection. Below are the responses to a typical furious phone call:

1) I will put you through to Mr X.

2) I'm sorry, Mr X is not here at the moment. I'll get him to ring you when he comes in.

And at a later stage in the day, when Mr X has not rung back, and has been angrily rung up again:

3) I'm afraid Mr X has gone home/is off sick/is on holiday for the next three weeks/has left our employment.

There are some variations on this pattern. There is "I'm afraid we haven't received your order" and "I'm afraid you will have to ring head office—we're folding up this branch at the moment." Fortunately, we had made our plans and done most of the ordering in ignorance of these complications. It was always a relief to see the red MacBraynes lorry grinding up our drive with something we had long been expecting: a relief, that is, until we had finished unloading it, stacking the materials, and checking them against the order. Then, disbelief! Yet again, we would be 20 lengths of 2 by 1 short, or there would be plywood instead of chipboard, or some such horror.

As every room in the house was destined for major refurbishment, deliveries posed another problem, that of storage. Everything had to be shifted around as work progressed. One backbreaking pile of 167 sheets of plasterboard we moved four times. The timber for studding and other rough work could not be got under cover at all, as it was too long. It sat out in the yard, wrapped in ineffective plastic sheeting, getting so wet that when you banged a nail in, you got squirted in the eye. When we moved the remnants of it in order to finish off the car park, we discovered, too late, a large clutch of addled eggs and a squawking pullet, cosily installed under the steamy black plastic. The smell of rotten eggs did not improve the timber's working qualities.

Once we had paid for the goods and submitted the orders (which I hope I have made clear was not the same as receiving the goods we had paid for) we were more or less obliged to carry out all the work we had planned. There is no point in paying for three bathroom suites (even if you only receive 2½) and only installing one bathroom. This was just as well, as it meant we had to stick to fairly optimistic plans of what we could do even when time was running frighteningly short. Our more preposterous schemes had mostly been weeded out before we ordered: hence we never did actually send for the chips for the pseudo-Roman "cave canem" mosaic we had intended to lay on the front porch floor. In the event it was just as well—it was bad enough taking up and relaying the jigsaw of old stone flags there to allow the installation of a ventilating pipe underneath. These pipes were the only way we could get air under the ground floor at the front: as there was grass growing up between the floorboards in the hall, airflow was obviously necessary, together with laboriously scooping out barrowloads of soil from between the joists.

This scheme itself replaced a more time-consuming, more expensive, but undoubtedly more rat-proof one, of laying concrete floors throughout. We stuck to that for the back wing, and it was even more expensive and time-consuming than we had thought. At the end of the back wing was a porch, concreted already, and the old kitchen, also concreted, under a revolting layer of rotten lino tiles. This was to be a utility room cum workshop. Between it and the dining room hatch was a series of three small rooms and a wide dog-legged corridor leading to a door into the hall. All this area we knocked into one, to make the new kitchen. It was a particularly insalubrious part of the house. Three chipped and cracked sinks with ornately gridded overflows and wrought iron supports harboured the filth of years. Further dirt-encrusted fancy brackets held collapsing shelves from which hung shreds of mouse-eaten Fablon. The doors had been extensively chewed by rodent incisors. Opposite the door into the hall was a cupboard known for years as the Rat Cupboard, until it became the Wine Cellar, which harboured about as many rats then as it does bottles of wine now. The wall surfaces throughout were livid pink and green distemper, eczematous and clammily damp. Our feet sank through the rotting floorboards, into a wet pit where the south west wall had channelled the rain, and chunks of damp ceiling dropped on our heads like dung. We stripped out everything except the more adherent areas of the ceiling—sinks, shelves, partition walls, plaster, floorboards and the waters under the floorboards, together with barrowloads of earth and rats' nests, and the bones of many a Grandfather Rat. Once the floor area was cleared to a depth of 9 inches, we had to fill it in again with hardcore before concreting. We brought in all the masonry we had knocked out of the various apertures, and smashed it up with hammers to get it down to size. It was a convenient if strenuous way of disposing of unwanted stone. We have a small electric cement mixer which we regard with more affection than any other piece of equipment. This was set up on blocks outside the back door so that there was room to tip the contents into a barrow. I mixed 1 bucket cement, 2 buckets of water, 2½ buckets sand and 4 buckets gravel per load. Andrew barrowed it away and tamped it level over the new floor area. It was the most backbreaking job of the whole conversion.

The kitchen floor was far from finished: indeed it went on and on. We had decided we wanted the ratproof qualities of concrete coupled with the warmth and spring of a wood floor, so the eventual plan was for concrete, then a damp-proof membrane, then 1½" expanded polystyrene sheeting, then chipboard, then vinyl-faced cork tiles. The result is certainly warm and springy, but unfortunately seepage of water from the French windows on the south west and from over-enthusiastic washers up has made the chipboard rot and swell along the joints in two places, causing the cork tiles to lift. When the chipboard went down, we left areas to fill with concrete as plinths for the new cool pantry and the Aga. Unscrupulous local builders do not always take this precaution with solid fuel stoves: we know of two houses where stoves have been installed directly on the joists, with a discreet skim of concrete round the base to fool the building inspector. Of course results were disastrous, though at least there was some excitement for the Tarbert Auxiliary Fire Brigade. Anyway, we were more cautious. I also installed a facing of concrete blocks to go behind the stove, but the whole lot peeled off on top of me. I left in a huff and Andrew plastered it instead. It was the winter after our first season before we got the cork tiles down in the kitchen and the quarry tiles in the back porch, pantry and utility room. I spent a lot of the first summer hovering nervously near the kitchen door, in case any of the ladies who were interested in the cooking would come in and see the filthy chipboard floor.

If the kitchen floor took ages, refurbishing the dining room took ages and ages. One window with its casing, panelling and shutters was collapsed, the floor was shocking, and the fireplace not only hideous but broken. Most of the old plaster had been replaced with hardboard, now very sagging and rotten, on creaky studding depending from crumbling wooden pegs pushed into the masonry. It would have been quicker to rip the lot out and start again, but too expensive, so we patched up. We soon learned that modern timber is not only poor quality but also much skimpier than old. The new floorboards were thin, hairy, floppy things which required padding against the joists to bring them up to the correct level. The resulting botch-up still creaks abominably. One year Andrew had squeaky shoes and between that and the floorboards I am surprised people could eat their dinners. The remaking of the window was more of a success. By good luck, we had happened to notice that someone along the road who was doing up his croft house had discarded by the roadside three more or less Georgian style 12-pane sash windows, only slightly rotten, and a bath not much the worse for wear. We got the lot for £35. These sashes were narrower than the aperture in the dining room, so this had to be built up to the right size. Then Andrew painstakingly cut down and remade the panels above and below and the handsome moulded surrounds, and re-hung the shutters. With the by now proverbial spot of filler in the joints, it looked quite authentic. Andrew was inspired by this success to make a matching moulded surround for the new hatch and give it double panelled doors. As usual, I heard how very much better he would do that sort of job if he had a few more moulding planes, but I thought the effect very satisfactory anyway, as I hastened to tell him.

The next task was to remake the fireplace. The surround was in quite distinguished looking varnished pine, and we removed this carefully, expecting, and getting, further collapse of hardboard and studding, together with soot and rats' nests. So that wall had to be re-done with heavier strapping and plasterboard. The demolition of the hideous fireplace (green tiles painted brick red) was positively pleasurable, but the hearth slab remained intact in spite of all our pounding and bashing. In the end, we built up a new concrete slab on top of it, to carry an old steel fender. In our temporary kitchen there was an attractive arched cast iron fireplace, which we heaved downstairs to replace the green and red abomination. Unfortunately this too had been painted, in this case mauve. Under the mauve it was blue, and under that cream, and beneath the cream another two layers of indescribable gunge. It took many pints of paint stripper and many hours of labour with a wire brush and screwdriver to remove all five layers: and then it was too small for the pine surround. However, a fillet of wood all round stained and varnished to match made up the deficiency. When the cast iron was blackleaded, the effect was fine. It was enhanced by the addition of an overmantel mirror found in a friend's coalshed. This was initially a filthy and depressing object, with cracking and curling veneer and gaps where bits of the inlaid floral pattern had dropped out. It looked hopeless, and was not in fact a valuable piece, but once the veneer was relaid and patched up and the whole French polished it was quite imposing. The thought of seeing it in position even inspired me to decorate the room, but this job was so distasteful that I put off painting the rest of the house for another six weeks. I was working through a particularly sticky gallon of white gloss paint that had to be stood in a bucket of hot water to make it fluid at all.

After the dining room, which took a whole month, we reviewed the work ahead. That room had really only been a repair job. What remained to be done was more serious: the installation, plumbing and drainage of four bathrooms and the partitioning and tiling of two of them; a complete hot water and central heating system; the total electrical wiring of the back wing and the power wiring of the front; roof insulation; framing and plasterboarding of the attics and kitchen/utility region; total redecoration; an endless list of patching up plasterwork and joinery; furniture repairs and re-upholstery, and finally, laying carpets and installing furniture. We had already taken our first booking for June 14th. We had about 16 weeks left. This realisation was oddly exhilarating. There was a sporting chance we wouldn't make it. We would be like certain hotels in Majorca at that time in the news, where holidaymakers arrived to find the rooms not yet built.

For the next few weeks we were light-hearted. I opened a door that was off its hinges and it collapsed. How funny if it happened to a guest! We dug up the evil-smelling old drains to connect in the new ones, and roared with laughter when by some vagary a strong draught of foul-smelling air surged through the WC up the sitter's backside. Could we save this effect for June 14th? Best of all were the hotel bookings which were steadily coming in. We would squat in the semi-permanent hole in the hall floor, and ask in a genteel telephone voice if the unsuspecting customer would like a private bathroom, and then collapse in hysterics at the end of the call at the thought of the allocated bedroom lacking not only a bathroom but also the greater part of its plaster and floorboards.

We were amazed and amused that bookings were coming in at all. Our attempts at publicity had been very haphazard. We had no idea what to charge or how to advertise, and homework on the subject consisted in writing to various pleasant-sounding hotels advertised in an old copy of *Country Life*. A collation of their brochures and tariffs gave us some ideas for ours. The brochure format we decided on was cheap yet dignified, at least so we hoped: a sheet of white card with two folds, opening out to show the text and a sketch of the beach. Closed, it had a view of the house on the front and a map of Harris on the back. I did the drawings and Andrew the map and lettering (Roman: he won't touch anything else). It is decidedly unprofessional, but we have stuck to the design: the black and white symmetry of the house and the general slightly tatty impression of home-madeness are characteristic of our whole operation, and any-one who didn't like the brochure probably wouldn't like the reality.

As we were starting with only four bedrooms we did not need to attract large numbers of customers. We were, in fact, rarely full in the first season. Looking back it is surprising anyone came at all. Some were recommended by friends, and the remainder came because other places were full, or from our advertisement (a modest one) in *Country Life*. We simply did not have the cash to advertise much. We argued hotly over our precious ad. It could only occupy six centimetres of single column. We dared not call ourselves a hotel, for reasons I have mentioned before. It couldn't carry a drawing, as the National Graphical Association would not permit our own artwork to be used. Andrew insisted on perfect grammar —none of your sloppy advertising language. I insisted on a thick black edge to make it stand out from the page. We did not realise how lucky we were when it actually attracted customers. We long ago gave up advertising: it has never done more than pay for itself except in that first year. Whether it was the refined syntax, the funereal edging, or telepathic concentration that did the trick that time, we have never discovered.

10

The Eleventh Hour

In early January, we had gone to Aberdeen with a shopping list covering everything from beds to picnic flasks. For 10 days we scoured auction rooms, antique shops, and discount centres, and by the end everything had been ticked. Our choice of purchases, looking back, was quite extraordinary. We got an old washing machine for £8 in an auction, and bought new hoses separately. We didn't bother with a fridge or vacuum cleaner, reckoning we could survive for a few months without them. On the other hand, we spent vast amounts on Coalport china and Mappin and Webb cutlery, making up the core we had gathered as wedding presents. We bought an old loose-covered suite for £20 for the drawing room, and complemented it with a Chinese rug at £800. We did without a new frying pan, and bought (as the receipt states) two dragons and one elephant to make the hall look homely. Our system was not as crazy as it sounds. We tried to view every room as if we were guests entering the establishment for the first time. The place must not look institutional, but gracious and comfortable. There must be interesting pictures, ornaments, books and mirrors: these would both please in themselves and distract attention from the general level of shabbiness. Guests were not going to be bothered if we took a handbrush to sweep the stairs and used old sheets instead of mattress covers, as long as they saw plenty of expensive curtain fabrics and antique chairs and silver teapots. There is no doubt that the ruse worked, when the time came to put it into practice.

Everything we bought in Aberdeen was stuffed into my mother's house. Fortunately she is the only occupant, or she would not have been left with much space. She had already donated large quantities of furniture, rugs, crockery and ironmongery which had equipped our holiday cottage when I was a child, and all this was waiting for removal in her attic. We took over her lounge and a bedroom or so with our new purchases, and crammed a bulky sofa into her sitting room, giving her our kind permission to sit on it until the removal van arrived in April.

Back in Harris, we had been accumulating possibly useful items for years. John Angus, of course, had been a chief contributor. He had collected for us cooking pots and lemon squeezers, armchairs and blankets, asparagus dishes and blacksmith's bellows. He was constantly reviewing not only his own possessions, but all the reject furniture and equipment of his many friends and acquaintances, for things that would be of use to us. Then when Andrew's parents came to stay, their small car was stuffed with an unbelievable quantity of plants, furniture and bric-a-brac from Cornish relatives. We ourselves had developed an acute eye for the half-buried bit of rubbish with possibilities. In addition to the overmantel mirror from the Blatchfords' coalshed, we salvaged a wrecked brass bed from the old school-house garden, and a broken dining chair from the tip where we dumped our plaster rubbish. The latter matched reasonably with three other chairs which were smuggled to us by a well-wisher from the lorry collecting for the local Jubilee bonfire. All these things were in desperate disrepair, but they were free: only our time was required to make them presentable.

Time! It was running out rapidly. The removal at Easter was fun. We enjoyed seeing all the things we had bought, and piling them into the dining room along with the salvage from the rubbish tips. But afterwards we were dismayed. There was so much of it, and a lot of it was disgustingly dirty and broken. It had been all very well saying two years or even a year ago, "It just needs a new leg and re-upholstering" or "This table top is fine if we make a new base", but it was a different matter with only eight weeks left. The high spirits of the previous month or so disappeared. We were in a state of permanent, sweating, cornered dread, and exhausted to shaking point.

My mother was with us to help sew curtains. I kept cutting them wrong. The hems drooped and the seams bulged. My mother's finger wore out and she asked for a thimble. I couldn't think what she meant. My brain was reduced to a sewing machine. It took me three days to realise I could borrow a thimble from a neighbour. Andrew fixed the last joints on the immensely complicated plumbing system he had devised, and filled it up. Water poured through the utility room ceiling. We both burst into tears. It took hours before mental coherence returned sufficiently to track the trouble down to just one missed joint behind the hot water cylinder. The initiation of the central heating was a virtual replay of the same scene, except that having survived the previous shock, we did not so much sob as snivel over this one. But I remember soon after that standing with one foot in a bucket of wallpaper paste, howling in loud earnest. I had jumped down into it off the edge of the bath in the course of papering a bathroom. I hated that bathroom anyway. It had suddenly appeared in my pleasant first floor kitchen, and I was now relegated to the dingy back regions, with new pots and pans and a new cooker, but no cupboards or work surfaces. I think the first evening I prepared a meal there, crouched on the floor chopping vegetables, was secretly the most miserable moment of that whole wretched time. The old kitchen was filled with sunset light, and the new one seemed dark as a prison. Suddenly I realised that on every spring and summer evening for the foreseeable future, here I would be, unable to breathe the air or look at the sea for even a few minutes. At that moment, the life of a hotelier had no attractions.

Then we began to be plagued by curious visitors. Friends and acquaintances and people we had never met before came to see how we were getting on. Some were shocked and sympathetic and others maliciously amused, but really their reactions were unimportant. In that desperate race against time, every half hour away from work was a disaster, and the effort of making conversation was enough to bring on mental prostration. Andrew could produce no words at all, and I would babble complete nonsense. If the visitors stayed more than a few minutes, the unusual experience of sitting down sent us to sleep. Sometimes the callers were would-be guests, directed hither by other hotels who had a vague idea that something was happening at Scarista. A few stick vividly in the memory. There was one peculiarly unpleasant couple with a loathsome little girl—I think of them as South-African style

English—who ranged over the whole house sneering at everything, and told us they would never under any circumstances frequent an unlicensed hotel. The child got wet paint on her little handies and had a blue-faced screaming fit. I recovered sufficiently from lowered morale to observe tartly that we would never under any circumstances allow small children to stay. Andrew looked shocked at my forwardness: we had a lot to learn yet about Keeping Guests in their Place. But on the bright side, there was a charming American couple who arrived late in the evening, sure they would find a bed, and on finding only bare floorboards, took time off from their accommodation-hunting to share a bottle of Southern Comfort with us in a toast to our success. Their good will cheered us up considerably, even though the Southern Comfort put paid to work for the rest of the evening.

Our American well-wishers were the exception. For the most part, though friends regarded us with embarrassed pity, solid citizens who passed by were scandalised at our effrontery: to think they might have been beguiled into booking a holiday at Scarista! They went away puffing and shaking their heads. They could be forgiven: a photograph of the Library taken three weeks before opening day shows bare plaster walls, a gaping hole where the fireplace ought to be, a pile of timber where the bookshelves are now and the floor covered in masonry rubble. It was the last room to be tackled. Andrew had used and enjoyed it as a workshop, and on eviction he suffered the same pangs as I did over the kitchen. Indeed, the pile of boards in the photograph represented his last stand: it was the Japanese oak and parana pine for the shelves. He ripped these inch-thick boards down with a hand-saw in odd moments, lipping the pine with oak to make the front surfaces more attractive: then over two days, a whole wall became a massive seven-foot-high bookcase of five bays. I had taken the precaution of leaving that wall unpapered and unpainted: we wasted no effort by that stage. The fireplace was an adaptation like the one in the dining room, using another cast-iron back from a bedroom. It got done in about a quarter of the time, even though the throat had to be remade in this case. From this reconstruction I recollect one of those ludicrous sexist remarks which I so prize. The telephone engineer came in to instal a coin-box.

"Ah!" he remarked approvingly. "Andrew's making a good job of that fireplace."

"I'm doing it, actually," I said.

His tone changed abruptly. "That'll never be any use. The throat's much too wide."

Suffering from the island convention that forbids women to use foul language to men, I said nothing: but Andrew heard all about it later in extremely colourful terms.

Meanwhile Andrew was probably sitting at the sewing machine trying to correct my ill-fated efforts at putting gussets in a piece of cloth required to recover the rolled back of a Victorian sofa. I had been at it, off and on, for two years. I found it quite impossible to work out the shape of the gussets and equally impossible to sew in my numerous wrongly-shaped attempts. I have no warmth towards sewing machines and mine is particularly ill-tempered. Eventually, when I had recovered all the other pieces of furniture which required only scissors and hammer and tacks, I had to confess to total failure with the sofa. Andrew was astonished. He completed the sewing job in about 10 minutes, without so much as breaking a thread.

With about a week to go, we had still not quite finished decorating—or at least, I hadn't. Andrew was in a state of acute anguish about it, but he had plenty of other things to do, completing the joinery for the basin fitments in bedrooms and bathrooms, and finishing off the wiring. We had been used to working with inspection lamps until the nights got light enough to do without, so that wiring could be the last job before walls and floors were finally sealed up and painted. I applied mile after mile of woodchip paper around the tufts of wire sticking out of the walls, and followed with a coat of emulsion. As soon as that was dry, on went the light fittings and power sockets. As the floorboards were banged down, I shuffled along behind on my knees, with a large pot of filler, optimistically trying to stop gaps half an inch wide. It was hopeless, of course: even when backed with crumpled paper, the filler dropped out as soon as the new paint set on top of it. Andrew regards the deficiency as mine: he maintains that cellulose filler is very good stuff. Last time I decorated I disregarded his advice and used putty instead, which was the old practice, and it is much more successful.

The standard of my decorating is particularly poor. Every corner in the house harbours creased and misapplied woodchip paper. No botcher should be without this useful material, which is especially favoured in Harris, because it covers old damp-ridden plaster and badly applied modern plasterboard, and conceals the joins where successive generations have butted hardboard to lath and plaster and plasterboard to hardboard. Moreover, it glues firmly to the wall everything underneath that might otherwise disintegrate. Best of all, from my point of view, it doesn't matter how dirty and paste-smeared it becomes in the course of application, because a couple of coats of emulsion will hide all. Wonderful stuff!

As the days and hours grew fewer, we set our sights gradually lower. Only one room was booked for the first night: so we reasoned that if that room and the stairs and public rooms were ready, we could creep around getting the others completed over the following two days, as they filled up.

"So long as the paint's touch-dry—that's all you need. If we keep the windows open they'll never smell it," I assured Andrew, encouragingly.

We bundled all the odds and ends of paper and paint up to the attic, and bore the many tea-chests of books and ornaments, mirrors and pictures down. Our neighbour Margaret Blatchford gave up two days to dusting the books and placing them on the shelves. We chased round distractedly with things to put on mantelpieces and things to hang on walls. The problem about walls held together with woodchip paper is that even that miracle material will not bear weight. As soon as we selected a place for a picture and banged in a nail, there would be a slow tearing sound, and a sinister trickling of rotten plaster.

"You can only hang stuff on battens!" Andrew said wearily, for the twentieth time.

"But there's not one in the middle."

"You'll have to put it to one side, then."

"We can't have a dirty great picture stuck at one side of the mantelpiece!"

"Well, you can't have it at all."

We had become too terror-struck to be methodical. When pictures fell off the wall, we scuttled off to unpack chests of dusty

137

glass and china. Feeling too shaky to wash it by hand, we put all our best crystal into the newly-arrived dishwasher, chipping every single piece. Shaking with horror, we turned our attention to fixing the last curtain poles: as usual there was nothing to fix them to, until Andrew took up the attic floor and painfully stuffed a block of wood down inside the plaster. I screwed at the wrong time from below and the block fell down the cavity with a hollow clatter. I went off in despair to make the last pair of curtains, and when I hung them, one was a full six inches shorter than the other. We fitted the bedroom carpets, and found them permanently creased with lying in a heap for two months: we shuffled and jumped and banged, but the creases stayed. We turned our attention to the stair carpet, and discovered I had ordered about twice as much as required, at horrific expense.

With 24 hours to go, none of the bed linen had arrived from the mainland, in spite of many pleading phone calls. In a panic, I telephoned a shop in Stornoway, to send an emergency parcel of pillows and quilt covers on the bus. That afternoon, the missing goods turned up closely followed by the box from Stornoway, which contained all the wrong things and a large bill. I unpacked it all on the front lawn, darting aside feverishly to pull up weeds, between curses. There was no large enough and clean enough area to unpack inside: furniture was on the move, out of the dining room and attics where it had been stored. As we staggered and panted upstairs beneath vast items of Edwardian mahogany, we wished we had stuck to modern cardboard and hardboard furniture. Flakes of new paint littered the new carpets. Out came the paint pots again. And some of the furniture was not exactly complete. There was a dining table top which required anchoring to an alien pedestal—it remained a shaky job all season, though most people were too nice to mention it. One of the bedrooms, to be occupied in approximately 42 hours' time, had no drawer space, by an oversight. A frantic search through the attic unearthed an old painted desk, from which Andrew with lightning cuts of the saw removed all but the stack of three drawers. I applied a quick coat of paint and disappeared into one or other of the wardrobes with a bale of silk and a pot of Copydex, to put a clean lining on the incredibly filthy interiors. My parents had bought a vast suite of walnut bedroom furniture for 10s.0d. in 1952, to furnish all the bedrooms of our cottage. It now did wonders for three out of our four. The two small wings of the gigantic wardrobe did two rooms, with the washstand in one and the dressing table in the other. The mirror door from the central piece of wardrobe, with handsome swags of carved fruit, made a nice feature between two beds, and in another room, the cylindrical marble-topped commode stood between two others.

Meanwhile our neighbours had come to our rescue. The late sunset of June 13th saw a polisher at every window. A pile of dusters accumulated as the grime of years was removed from the more visible areas of furniture. Outside in the car park David Miles and his son shovelled like demons to spread the huge mound of gravel there neatly over the whole area. They all worked hard and went away charitably without requiring refreshments or conversation. We carried on sweeping up and packing things away till we were too tired to see straight, and fell into bed.

Next morning we stepped out of our filthy attic into a house unnaturally clean and luxurious. Carpets . . . furniture . . . curtains . . . ornaments. It was certainly not our house. We wandered around in a daze, trying to remember what still had to be done. I went out to pick flowers from our meagre stock in the garden. Janet Miles and Margaret appeared with a large bunch of red poppies for the hall. The brilliant blooms gave us courage: things seemed to hang together again after that.

We made up beds and set fires and brushed the stairs half a dozen times, as the dark brown pile felted in the manner of new carpets on to the cream surround. I put off starting cooking till 5.30: I knew if I began too early I would lose my nerve.

We scrubbed our permanently grubby hands and faces and donned unaccustomed and uncomfortable clothes, and waited uneasily, like children in party garb debarred from playing outside. At last a dark blue car appeared at the end of the drive. Andrew looked grim.

"Here they are!" he said.

Part Three

SCARISTA HOUSE

11

A New Career

Colonel and Mrs Burdett were not, in fact, at all terrifying. On the contrary, we could not have wished for more genial first guests. Nevertheless, the first evening was not easy for us, and must have been exhausting for them. Bursting with pride, we showed them their room and the public rooms and the public telephone and the way to the beach. Like eager sheepdogs, we hustled them from place to place and barked far too much. When they had eventually managed to shut their bedroom door on us, we had a confab: when would we break the astonishing news that they were our first customers? We decided to spring it on them before dinner. When they appeared, we would offer them a celebratory drink to mark the occasion. Perhaps champagne? We had been given some as a present by my brother—to drink for breakfast, he had directed decadently, but that had hardly suited our lifestyle.

Half an hour before dinner, we put the champagne in the freezer, arrayed ourselves in even cleaner and more uncomfortable clothes, and lay in wait in the library. Things did not really go according to plan. Our guests smiled kindly, but did not seem surprised they were the first. And they were teetotal. I went back to the kitchen to attend to the vegetables, feeling strangely constricted about the throat. Later Andrew put the champagne away again.

"Never mind, we'll drink it ourselves sometime," he said.

Dinner was anxious for us, and can scarcely have been less anxious for the two unfortunates in the empty, silent dining room. We kept creeping to the hatch to listen for the sound of cutlery: when that went quiet, Andrew could go through to offer the next course. As I passed dishes through to him, I could see brilliant sunshine sparkling on the sea and flooding the dining room, and I imagined how our guests must be enjoying the view. In retrospect, they must surely have felt so overfussed as to be incapable of enjoying anything.

It turned out that Colonel Burdett could not eat puddings. This news, conveyed to me from the dining room, turned my heart to lead. There was apricot ice cream with meringue in it, which I regarded at the time as the greatest delicacy on earth.

Over coffee, we pestered our poor guests further with sociable chit-chat, to such effect that it was well after midnight by the time we had cleared up and put another coat of paint on the adapted desk-drawers. I should think our victims must have been glad to escape to bed. Fortunately for them, two more couples arrived the next day, so they did not have our undivided attention for the rest of their holiday: and as five out of six guests for the next four days ate pudding, and three of them accepted a glass of sherry, we recovered our spirits somewhat, and became slightly less painful company.

We did not admit it even to each other—we did not dare admit it—but of course we started with entirely the wrong idea about our guests. Having for so long lived, worked and breathed Scarista House, it was to us the sole end of existence. We had spent years deciding what "the guests" would like and every thought and effort had gone into ensuring that they got it. We presented our finished offering with immense pride and enthusiasm, and the least hint of coolness in the recipients was a dreadful snub. We could not see, I suppose, that all these services which we regarded as gestures of our own overflowing goodwill would be regarded simply as bought goods by our customers. Oddly enough, we did not really consider what we got in exchange: money. Money was unreal. We hadn't had any to spend, except on schemes to please guests, for a very long time. What we took in for the first season was immediately swallowed up in next week's grocery bills. It had no spending power.

It was surprising, really, that so many of our early customers were kind in their acceptance of what we had to offer. In many respects, the place was gruesome. The odd rickety table and creaky floorboard scarcely signifies, but there was no booze, no television, often no fellow-guests, and worst of all, nowhere to get away from us. If they descended into the library, we were there: if they went up into the drawing room, we were there also. If they popped up to the bedroom during breakfast, I would be anxiously changing the sheets yet again. If they took a deckchair into the garden, I would weed around them. If they lurked in the hall, Andrew would appear at the kitchen door in case they wanted anything. They couldn't even have privacy in their cars. We had no cattle grid, so Andrew was always on the look out for guests coming or going, in order to run down and open the gate with a friendly smile. It must be disconcerting to come to the Outer Hebrides for peace and quiet, only to find you are never alone and can't get to the beach without climbing barbed wire fences. The fences had never bothered us, but our guests were up to three times our age and many of the ladies wore skirts: we had not considered these things.

For the first few weeks, as soon as the guests had escaped in the morning (as it must have seemed to them) or as soon as we got rid of them (as it seemed to us) we would get out tools and paint and continue frenziedly with the repairs and renovations which had not quite been completed by June 14th. There were endless frustrating adjustments to be made to roller blinds that did not roll, to WCs that rocked, to doors that jammed. There were second coats of paint here and there, and curtain hems that had only been tacked or pinned. Then there was the kitchen, with its unspeakable floor and doorless cupboards. The attic where we slept had been plaster-boarded, but the joints in the board were untaped and unfilled: the other attics had not even been plasterboarded. Andrew got as far as plumbing in our bath, the old cast iron one heaved up from the original bathroom. This was a great relief, as previously we had had to creep down to use one on the first floor after everyone was in bed. After this major improvement, we lost impetus, and attics and back regions remained exactly as they were till the end of the season. In fact, in the case of the attics, they are far from finished even yet.

Once the guests' quarters were tolerable, we found it a full time job keeping them that way, even though there were often only two or three rooms occupied. During breakfast, whichever of us had a spare moment would dash upstairs to make or change beds and whip away used tea trays. Once breakfast was over, I would clear up in the dining room and kitchen and attend to the washing. Andrew did the cleaning, arrayed in a best pullover and jeans kept for the purpose, in case he should be seen by any guests. As soon as he had finished and showed signs of drifting back to his oily tools, I was after him with an armful of dirtier garments. The dust of housework made him sneeze incessantly. It was bad enough when we only had the handbrush, but once we moved on to my sister-in-law's cast-off vacuum cleaner his sneezes grew even louder and longer. I was very suspicious.

"How come you never sneeze with plaster dust or fibreglass, and can't stand a morning's housework?" I wanted to know. The only answer was an incoherent sneeze.

Anyway, the alternative to cleaning the guests' rooms was the kitchen work, which included making bread and chasing up orders on the telephone. Faced with this choice, Andrew stuck to vacuuming, with streaming eyes.

By lunchtime we would feel we had almost licked the day's work. Then someone would return looking for a snack, very surprised to find that the Western Isles are virtually devoid of pubs and cafés. My imagination does not run riot at lunchtime. We eat bread and cheese. Most guests did not regard this as attractive, and anyway the bread might not be ready, and the cheese might not have arrived. "Just a little soup," they would plead, shivering in the keen July air. It was our fault, I suppose. We always turned off the heating and threw the doors open the minute people went out, not only to save fuel, but also to prevent our own collapse from heat exhaustion. But to a southerner or an American, an indoor temperature of 55°F and a stiff sea breeze out of doors do not constitute summer heat. Groaning, I would hastily chop vegetables, and use some of the precious cream intended for dinner time to make the resultant purée palatable. If we had been warned that people intended coming back, we would short-circuit the demand for soup by turning up the heating and producing a salad. In fact, lunch is a meal we have never come to terms with. We have tried making breakfast bigger and better, and lunch more expensive and more meagre. We have put tins of homemade shortbread in the bedrooms, and turned a blind eye to people nicking rolls from the breakfast table, but we have still not succeeded in weaning everyone off a mid-day repast. Not that long ago someone even asked for sausage and mash. It was not forthcoming.

Back in 1978 I might have gone as far as to produce that sausage and mash on request, but it would not have been without a considerable amount of bad language even then. Lunchtime was our only chance to take a short break ourselves to discuss business, and possibly to sit out in the sun and air for half an hour. By about two, it would become obvious that the day's work was not over after all. Laundry washed and unwashed would be piling up, requiring starching, pegging out, taking in, and ironing. Andrew did most of this. He prized his position at the rotary ironer—he could sit down. As we were not yet used to walking about in tight shoes in an overheated house all day, sitting down was a most desirable state. He liked hanging out washing, too, as it meant a breath of fresh air. This blatant disregard of local standards of male decency caused quite a stir. Cars would slow down on the road while their incredulous occupants stared up at Andrew and the washing line. They could not have been more shocked if he had got himself up in women's underwear.

Meanwhile I would attempt to clear the weeds and pests from the much too ambitious and by now neglected vegetable garden. Pests wasted a lot of my thought and time. I sat and stared at maggots and caterpillars, slugs and aphids, and wondered what to do about them. Our old stone walls are full of snails, which are charming to watch. But they eat lettuces, also marigolds, nasturtiums, broad beans and peas. One evening, wrathfully, I scattered half a packet of slug pellets round my few remaining lettuces. Next morning 32 snails lay in pathetic liquefaction. After that, the lettuces had to take their chance. Once they get bigger and tougher snails don't like them, anyway. As for cabbage white caterpillars, I thought I had found a solution. I collected a hundred or so in the skirt of my apron and spread them out before the hens, expecting they would be instantly executed. But not at all. The hens recoiled with terrified looks and squawks of indignation. I held out a particularly fat caterpillar to Pioneer, but she turned and fled. Gutsy picked one up cautiously, and spat it out again. The whole flock stood at a distance, complaining vociferously, while I went through the miserable job of grinding a hundred caterpillars to death. However, I had planted brassicas in such quantities that even after the caterpillars and root fly had had their pick, there were more than enough left for us: unfortunately, the pests, like us, preferred calabrese and cauliflower to straightforward cabbage.

By five o'clock gardening would have to stop as new guests would be arriving, requiring tea and conversation. Then it was time to start dinner. I retreated to the kitchen, with an armful of muddy vegetables, while Andrew set tables, wrote menus, served dinner, cleared up and set breakfast. It was a rare evening when we got to bed before midnight: more often it was between one and two in the morning.

The evenings never went quite as I had imagined they would. I had seen myself, in my mind's eye, walking round the dining room at the end of the meal to join in gracious conversation with the guests. Two dress-lengths in a bag in the attic signified my intention of making suitable attire. In fact, of course, I finished every meal frayed, greasy, and crimson in the face. For the first few weeks I would splash my face with cold water, put on a clean shirt, and take the coffee up to the drawing room, where Andrew would join me, and we would force the guests to make small talk. Sometimes it worked, but more often it was very painful for all concerned. After a day in the open and a heavy dinner, most people prefer to lapse into somnolence over coffee. They can always turn their chairs or interpose a book to defend themselves against fellow guests, but against determined hosts there is no defence. If they were quiet I thought the meal had been inedible: my face would revert to crimson as I wondered inwardly if the pastry had been burned or the Hollandaise curdled. Then some kindly person would say "That was a delicious flan" or "The Hollandaise was perfect". Did I simper and look gratified? No. I would blurt out "I thought the pastry was burnt" or "It was pretty curdled." Andrew would stiffen and turn pale green. Nowadays he and the staff only let me out of the kitchen after a tough briefing on what not to say to guests about dinner, but it is pretty much of a strain for everyone.

After a month or so of this sort of thing we rather lost confidence. Andrew (who would be wearing a clean shirt anyway) would deposit the coffee upstairs and withdraw to the safety of the kitchen, which would be in a state of upheaval—both sinks full of fish-heads and vegetable peelings, every flat surface piled with dirty dishes, and stacks of saucepans on the floor. When we had cleared sufficient space at the table, we would sit down and eat whatever was left. Sometimes it was a bit of everything, sometimes it was six helpings of soup or eight helpings of pudding. Whatever it was, we ate it with great relish. Here were all the luxuries we had dreamt of for years—sticky meringues, oozy Brie, real coffee, rare roast beef. The greatest treat of all was at breakfast time—bacon rinds! We did not actually salvage these from the guests' plates, I hasten to add: I trimmed them off and cooked them separately for us. However, I cannot deny that on many occasions untouched crispy duck skin and roast potatoes sent back from the table ended up on our plates, not in the hen pail: and we were certainly not above draining the dregs of the guests' wine bottles. With all this, we thought we were living very well.

We were, in fact, very serious about the food, in the Michelin sense. As we were inexperienced and dealing with small numbers of guests, we had decided to have a no-choice dinner menu. By allowing a choice we would be sacrificing freshness, as to keep to any sort of budget we would be forced to reuse the same dishes or ingredients over several days. At first we declared an alternative of an omelette or salad to the main course, but this looked so unimaginative on the menu that we dropped it after one season. I simply could not bear to see the same word on the menu day after day, even it if was only "omelette". I often feel the same way now even about "cheeses" which appears every day. Andrew writes the menus by hand one for each table, and I try not to look at them. Everything is cruelly unequivocal in black and white. "Potage Parmentier". Who is to say that it *is* "Potage Parmentier"? I have only once been to France, and do not frequent French restaurants. The recipe books disagree, and the results of all taste overwhelmingly of cream. I can't get my hands on that much cream and anyway the cream we do get tastes either of disinfectant or decay. Better call it "Potato Soup". No, that's too bald. "Cream of Potato Soup"? But then there isn't much cream in it—and a classic cream contains egg yolks—and so on. Besides my misgivings about foreign nomenclature, I found it very difficult to describe things until I knew how they were going to turn out, or even if they were going to turn out. If I suspected that I was going to blacken the caramel for the fourth time, or that the profiteroles were not rising, or that there was not enough spinach to go round, I was reluctant to commit these items to paper. As dinner time, usually 7.30 at that date, approached, Andrew would begin to follow me round the kitchen, pen in hand.

"Do you know the menu yet?"

"No!"

"Do you know *any* of it yet?"

"No!"

"You must know some of it. What's in that pot?"

"Stew."

"What sort of stew?"

"It's got mushrooms and wine in and that bloody Italian plonk has made it a foul shade of beetroot red."

"What are you going to call it?"

"How do I know? Bloody Italian plonk stew."

"Oh come *on*. It's quarter past seven."

A threatening wave of the carving knife would get rid of him for five minutes but probably no more. When I eventually divulged, between gritted teeth, my decisions on the various courses, he would be bound to make further trouble.

"Stuffed tomatoes?" he would query, suspiciously. "How many are they getting each?"

"One."

"Stuffed tomato," he would write.

"You can't put that! It sounds like some horrible Wimpy bar. No. 23, a stuffed tomatoburger in a sesame seed roll with French Fries and Crispy Onion Rings."

But on looking through our old menus, I see that he did put that, not once but several times, and not only "Stuffed Tomato", but "Baked Potato" and "Pork Chop". Occasionally there is a diffident "s" tacked on at some distance, as in "Fresh Fruit Tartlet s", presumably reflecting a furious diatribe from me.

Sometimes the roles of pedant and aesthete were reversed. For example, at twenty-five past seven:

"You can't have chocolate mousse. You've got haddock mousse for the second course."

"They don't taste the same. The fish is a heavy gelatinised sludge and the chocolate is very sticky."

"Can I call it a soufflé?"

"Of course it's not a soufflé. It's got no gelatine in it and it's runny."

"Well, can I call the fish a soufflé?"

"It's got no egg yolks in it. Call it a mould if you like."

"Fish *mould*?" He sounded very doubtful. "Fish cream perhaps?"

"It's got no cream in it."

"Chocolate cream?"

"It's got no cream in it either. The cream's sour again."

"Well, we can't have mousse twice. It'll have to be a cream."

"I'll have to put the sour cream in it, then" and before he could protest, mousse and sour cream would be stirred into an evil-tasting mess, but at least reduced to a cream-like consistency, sacrificed on the altar of accuracy.

The perpetual threat of sourness which hung over and still hangs over the cream is one of my chief bugbears, but it is not the only staple that is difficult to obtain. In fact, difficulties of supply here are formidable, and it took several years to get our ingredients anything like tolerable. Stornoway has the same sort of shops as any other not very prosperous little town, but it is 55 miles away over a mountain road—a full day's trip for us, and therefore usually an impossibility in the summer. Tarbert has the usual village shops, with fresh fruit and vegetables twice a week (in theory) but because of transport problems, stocks are small and prices high: and even driving to Tarbert and back takes the best part of a morning. There are vans which bring fresh fish round the island, but you take what you get, haddock or herring or whatever is going. To obtain shellfish, you have to know the fishermen, and you have to buy in a quantity that makes it worth their while, a whole box of prawns or a whole sack of scallops. For the first few seasons, I depended heavily on telephone shopping from Stornoway—expensive and unreliable, as shopkeepers might well be too busy to get the box of goods to the bus station on time, or their own stocks might fail to arrive on the ferry. The bus passes our door twice a week, on Tuesdays and Fridays at 8 o'clock. It was always an anxious time. Would the butcher's boys have dumped the 2olb of meat on the tomatoes this week? Would the fruit shop have forgotten my order yet again? As often as not the answer was "yes". For simpler groceries, one of the Stornoway Cash-and-Carries has a van passing on Wednesday, but again, successful deliveries are subject to their having obtained the goods from their mainland suppliers, at whose mercy they are. We might get no toilet rolls, or only New Zealand butter, or tea bags instead of tea. Once instead of poultry mash I got a sack of instant mashed potato: it took me a long time to recover from the shame of having that delivered at our gate.

During the first season we were always struggling with supplies. I found that I had stocked up far too heavily on dry goods—red kidney beans for example: we ate the last of 28lb this autumn, and I don't think a single bean was consumed by a guest. We had not established secondary and tertiary contacts for fruit and vegetables and shellfish so if the first one failed, as often happens here, we were stuck with frozen peas and last week's whiting. Our own vegetables—Harris vegetables in general—were not in production till late July, and we had not reckoned with such a long hungry gap. Our own soft fruit did not grow at all, and I am ashamed to say I had frequent recourse to tins for fruit ice creams and cold soufflés. In fact, a combination of inexperience and desperation tempted me to make use of many unpleasant ingredients which are now totally proscribed: frozen puff pastry, tinned French beans, Danish bacon, battery chickens and ducks, shop jam, and bottles which could be converted into something optimistically described as "hors d'oeuvre". If we were near a shop, we bought sliced bread for toast to save effort: it took me a good ten years to learn to slice homemade bread proficiently. We used coffee bags for breakfast, and fruit juice out of packets. (I was interested to note, incidentally, that the Dorchester, or perhaps it was the Connaught, was still reported as using coffee bags for breakfast in 1981, and that in 1984, that most famous and applauded Lake District restaurant of them all used packet juice—no less than 5 varieties. Why doesn't he make it up to 57? At his prices he can probably afford to.)

In fact, our food was far from satisfactory. We made great efforts, but I was conscious all the time of an undercurrent of guilty uneasiness, not at honest mistakes, but at shortcuts and deceptions. To this day, leafing through old menus makes me hot with embarrassment. It is not only the recollected horrors of unsatisfactory results: I can remember vividly who sat down to eat them, so thoroughly is the summer of 1978 imprinted. 24th of June—soggy courgettes, and I tried to glaze rehydrated dried chestnuts, and everyone left them. Not much wonder. And we had let a friend bring a party to dinner, and were terribly worried in case the dreaded officials found out. 27th of June—baskets of peas. The handles fell off but AT LEAST THEY WERE FRESH PEAS. Mr Babington Smith had two helpings of orange fool and next morning Andrew did not hear him order a boiled egg for breakfast and he never got one. 4th of July—Timbale of Chicken—oh horrible, reused left-overs, and heavy as school rice pudding. 30th July— that was the salmon that was so bad we knocked a pound off the price of dinner, and they said they hadn't noticed anything wrong with it anyway. 4th of August—coffee meringues—the cream curdled and the meringues disintegrated in a pool of coffee coloured whey. 23rd of September—Fried Plaice—I actually refried plaice from lunchtime, I really did: and I used minced up cooked venison in the Moussaka. How could I? Well, I did. 24th of September— our end of season party. Andrew's aunt got food-poisoning from the chaudfroid of chicken. Filthy stuff, gelatine.

The food was winning the right sort of recognition, though. We had been very nervous about it at first, but we knew how we wanted it to be: balanced, fresh, cooked to the instant, homely in the best sense. It makes me miserable to keep things warm, make dishes ahead, or re-use ingredients. Of course, on occasion I fell into all these errors, and still occasionally do. Then the concern that everything should be just ready can miscarry: nearly every day on this system there is likely to be a hard potato, a half-frozen ice-cream, or a fish still clinging rawly to its backbone. All the same, by the end of the first season, we were confident that the food could succeed. I was gaining experience about timing, we were building up a network of suppliers, and I had learnt what not to attempt: fiddly, feminine, time-consuming things like quenelles and papillotes, with which I would lose patience long before the battle was won. I like food I can crunch and chew: frothy, fluffy concoctions are not for me, and if I attempt them the result is likely to be of the texture of institutional suet dumpling. It was, in a way, daunting to realise all the things I could not do. But to hearten us, we knew that a few staunch supporters had already recommended us to the Good Food Guide, which proved to be most important to our future success.

People seemed pleased with other things as well as the food. The anxious attention to detail that had gone into the years of planning seemed to be paying off. Many guests commented that it was like staying or dining with friends. In particular, people seemed gratified that they had access to all our books and were trusted not to steal them. We have so many that we would be unlikely to notice if they did. All the same, we were quite surprised and very pleased that the majority of guests treated the hotel as they would the home of a friend. We were touched to see visitors walking upstairs boots in hand rather than dirty the carpet, or leaving their napkins unopened so that we would be spared the trouble of laundering them.

Of course, not all guest behaviour was impeccable. I shall return to some of the more colourful exceptions in a later chapter. In the meantime, I admit that the extraordinary antics of certain wealthy clients had made us begin to doubt whether we wanted to be wealthy after all: so that when we had failed to make our fortune at the end of the first season, we were not nearly as upset as we might have been. At least we had a full six weeks without an overdraft.

12

Monster

By the middle of October, the guests had withered away and the gales had set in. We spent the next six months in deep depression. My depression was deeper than Andrew's, but his was not negligible. We had planned and worked for five years towards the completion of our project, and now it was done, there was no challenge left. Nothing seemed worth doing.

There was, in reality, plenty to do. We had to obtain a fire certificate, which is compulsory for any establishment taking more than six guests. The fire officer's first account of what we would be required to do was appalling: either a concrete staircase, or a wired glass screen with a fire door on each landing. The results of such barbaric treatment in fine old houses can be seen in many hotels and public buildings. We were determined we would not do this. I insisted hotly that we would rather go out of business. Andrew, with greater tact, discovered that all that is required for a first-floor situation is that the escape route should be protected from the spread of fire. That is to say, one is not concerned with the guest who sets up a conflagration in his own room, but only with preventing the fire from spreading to the corridors and staircases. We could therefore do without wired glass screening if we made the doors of every bedroom and public room fire-resistant and self-closing—a more expensive and time consuming task, but much less unattractive. The typical institutional self-closer is very ugly, of course, but there is a more discreet type consisting of a spring and chain anchored between the doorpost and hinge. This is totally invisible when the door is closed, but much more difficult to fit. Asbestos sheeting is ugly material, and I greatly resented covering our pleasant panelled doors with it. We minimised the damage by applying the sheet on the inside. In the public rooms, Andrew then concocted a mock-up six-panelled frame which he placed over the asbestos. After a few coats of paint, this presented quite a convincing appearance, but it was a fiddly job, and the bedroom doors are still awaiting the same treatment.

We had other things to catch up on after the fire precautions work. The attics and kitchen region would have been deemed uninhabitable by most people; but the house had run perfectly well all the previous summer, while we inhabited the uninhabitable, so that there was little incentive to do anything about it. However, we did complete the work we had planned in the kitchen wing, tiling the floors throughout and where necessary the kitchen walls. Andrew made cupboard doors very cheaply out of knotty pine tongue-and-groove panelling, with a simple cross-member top and bottom at the back and wooden knobs. The result was very pleasing, and the wood has mellowed over the years to a dark honey colour.

The attics were less inspiring. The rooms were full of junk thrust up there because we could not make an immediate decision on it when we were furnishing the house: very broken pieces of furniture, hideous ornaments, spotty mirrors, pictures with cracked glass, tattered rugs, mildewed cushions. There were boxes full of university lecture notes and trunks full of oddments of curtain and dress fabrics, and all the other attic denizens that might come in handy some time and never do. Everything I threw out Andrew retrieved, and vice versa. Tempers and time were lost in quantity. Eventually we compacted most of the stuff into two rooms, and began to work our way round the others. Our so-called "bedroom" had already been plasterboarded, but all the raw edges and nail heads were visible, and required to be filled. As I proved quite incapable of cutting accurately the odd sizes and angles of plasterboard needed to follow the lines of the roof, I took over the filling. The results were a disaster and a lasting reproach. The gap between sheets of plasterboard should be carefully filled with a special plaster, then joined with a continuous length of paper tape. When this is hard, it is coated with a smoother finish plaster, polished with a damp sponge before it is completely dry. A skim of finish is then applied over the whole wall. A proficient worker can achieve a very good effect, and Andrew has since become quite skilled at it. But I made a horrible mess. When I applied the filler, too runny or too lumpy, I was of the opinion that the tape would hide it. When I stuck on the tape, creased, squint and torn, I felt sure the finish plaster would cover it. When it came to finishing, I thought perhaps it would look better after it was painted. Once it was painted, it became obvious that nothing further could be done. To this day the walls look like something applied by a careless novice in a casualty department.

We spent far too much time that winter indoors contemplating our unsatisfactory workmanship, and worrying about the season past and to come. We took to listening to the radio news twice a day. None of these pursuits is wholesome. A good dose of wet and wind or a shot of frost are the best possible cures for depression, but as there was no work to be done in the garden at that time of year, there seemed to be no reason to go out. But a reason soon occurred which over the years has caused us to clock up countless hours trudging hills and beaches in hurricane, blizzard and downpour. One evening, we were shivering in the library over a meagre fire, conserving central heating oil and peat, when the telephone rang. It was John Angus. After the usual preamble about the weather, he came to the point. Would we like a dog, a very nice young black labrador?

We did not want a dog, because of the inhibitions dogs place on travelling abroad and sailing. We intended to do a lot of these things once we had amassed sufficient cash.

John Angus told us a sad story. The dog was homeless, in fact had been destined for the bullet: his master was moving into town and could neither take him nor find a new owner for him. John Angus had taken him in, and was looking for a home for him.

"And if I don't find one, I'll keep him. He's a lovely dog. But if you want I can bring him down for you to see, and if you don't like him I'll just bring him away again."

So that was agreed. John Angus, Calum, and Jet arrived. Jet went through his paces: sit, heel and come. After that he sat beside me apologetically, scrounging biscuits while we had tea.

"Now don't feel you have to keep him, Alison," said John

Angus. "I'll just take him away again. I'll find another home for him. I sent one like him to Glasgow not long back."

Glasgow! Sent to Glasgow on a rope—possibly in a crate—on the ferry—in the train.

"Oh no, we'll take him!" we both said.

We could not keep him that night, because the porch floor was only half tiled. He could sleep there once it was finished. So we arranged to pick up our new friend on Sunday evening. When we kept the appointment, we were very impressed that Jet trotted out to our car and got in without being asked.

"He *knows* he's ours now!" exclaimed Andrew, looking besotted.

What we realised afterwards was that Jet got into any and every car, given the chance. It was not many weeks later that we looked out of the window to see him sitting up in the front seat of a visiting VW Beetle between its two human occupants, with his beaming black face sticking out through the open sun roof. But on that February evening we put his willingness to travel down to canine sagacity. We gave him a good dinner, which he can hardly have needed, as no one, biped or quadruped, ever leaves the Macaulays hungry. However, he wagged his tail politely and ate it up. We settled him on a bed of blankets in the newly tiled back porch, where he would get warmth from the works of the freezer. He looked humbly grateful, curled up there.

"Don't you think the freezer humming will keep him awake?" I asked.

"Of course not! I bet he's been living in some horrible old shed."

He certainly smelt like it.

"We really need the room in the porch, though. I'll make him a kennel soon."

And in this happy delusion we went to bed.

So John Angus played kind uncle to yet another hopeless and homeless animal. He is a clearing house for the unwanted, useless, sickly and elderly: not only dogs and cats, but a varied selection of other creatures from a lamb severely afflicted with warts to a fierce nanny goat. He always knows who is likely to want a pet, and if the creature is too unprepossessing, it ends its days at Caolas-na-Sgeire.

But back to Jet. He was about eight months old, black and shiny as an aubergine, with large flat feet, rather short legs, and an enormous broad head. We thought he would grow into his head and feet, but he never has, quite. Occasionally people ask if there is Staffordshire bull terrier in his ancestry, but this is a slander.

I had always imagined that Labradors are the most obedient and devoted of all dogs. Labradors belonging to friends seemed possessed of the patience and meekness of saints, their moist eyes turned up to Master with the fervour of a Baroque altar-piece. Jet lived up to the stereotype for about the first week. He was very easy to house train and very downcast at his errors, and utterly

crestfallen when reprimanded for putting his front feet on the table to help himself from our plates. He retrieved a ball or stick and gave it up on command. He walked to heel. He came at once when we called his name. He tried to take an interest in his daily training sessions, when he was instructed in "stay" and "come". But after a week or so, he had failed to be satisfied with "stay" and "come". What on earth is the point of staying while Master walks out of sight, just so that you can then follow when he calls "come"? Surely it is better to go along with him, or even to run ahead of him and trip him up? And why spend half an hour a day staying and coming over the same boring 20 yards? Why not go rabbiting instead?

We tried the Woodhousian accent, we tried a reward of doggy

chocolate drops. Jet gave us odd looks. Why is he talking in that funny voice? Doesn't he know I like Cadbury's drops better? We tried morsels of fried liver. He came for those very quickly, but without staying even for a second. Andrew kept his daily attempts up for a good six weeks, and then admitted humiliation and defeat —the first of many. Nothing is more demoralising than a dog who yawns at you scornfully on the word "stay", and turns his back with an exaggerated groan on the word "come".

"At least he comes when you shout his name," said Andrew, defensively. Not for long. We took him out every afternoon for a run on the dunes—half an hour. Jet did not think half an hour was enough. He would come when he was called until we reached our usual turning place: then we could shout ourselves hoarse and purple for 20 minutes till he was ready to go home. Andrew beat him as hard as he could, ending up with a sore arm as well as a sore throat, but it made no difference. In the end we decided he got 45 minutes walk minimum. He has gradually extended it to an hour and 10 minutes.

At first he also had morning games after his training session. We would throw a rubber ring or a stick, and he would bring it back with great enthusiasm and drop it to be thrown again. Then playing with our young neighbour Reuben Miles set him thinking: it was much more fun to run off with the ring and be chased for it, ending up in a good tug of war. So after that one or other of us spent half an hour every morning tearing in tight circles round the field, while Jet bounced on ahead, flashing his negroid teeth and the whites of his eyes. The ring stretched till it snapped and he chewed it into fragments with great satisfaction. His Granny in Aberdeen sent another—and another—and they went the same way in no time. He ran down to Reuben's house and stole his football, but that ended up in pieces in a couple of days. We bought both of them another one in Stornoway, and Jet's was in little pieces before we had even finished our shopping. After that we relied on sticks, and got a lot of exercise chasing them.

We borrowed several volumes on the care and training of dogs from the library van, and they all confirmed our failures. The delinquencies were ours. Any dog, it appeared, and most particu- larly a Labrador, could be trained by firm, consistent handling in the basics of canine behaviour: to come, sit, stay and walk to heel, not to beg at table, and to know his place.

The trouble was that Jet did know his place—as Our Leader. At first he was gentle and tactful, but when we were too obtuse, he was forced to take a firmer line. He directed all our activities personally. At meal times he would sniff the air to see what was on offer, and if it was something he liked, he would fix me with a basilisk eye till my nerve cracked and I handed it over. If Andrew and I so much as touched each other, he would thrust us apart, offering his great whiskered face as the only seemly object for caresses. When we went for a walk, it had to be on the dunes: what is the point in walking by the sea? There are no rabbits in it. He would push our legs from under us, and whine till we headed up the beach. No sitting down to look at the view either: we would be trampled under four heavy feet, to the accompaniment of squeaks and growls. If we wanted to do any outside work other than rabbiting, it had to be done while he was having a nap: otherwise he would show his dislike of our efforts by physical obstruction—trampling on the flowerbed, jumping up and down on new concrete, and sitting on our tools. The cattle grid has never been quite as good as it might be because of Jet's part in its installation. When we drove anywhere, Jet was first in the car, and he sang loudly all the way to our destination, with his back half in the back seat and his front paws on my shoulders.

All in all, we were no longer our own masters. But as our liberties were gradually eroded, we took some comfort from the thought of the coming boating season. We had no boat of our own, but we had been left in charge of a sturdy day-boat belonging to a friend, who lived most of the time away.

"At least," we said, "Labradors like boats. He'll be no trouble in a boat."

Had we not seen a small fleet of Mirror dinghies on the Isis, each competently crewed by a golden Labrador? Had we not observed one of the same breed skippering a Folkboat at Falmouth? Were they not seadogs in origin, used to hauling longboats ashore in freezing surf?

The boat sat in our yard up on its trailer that winter. In odd moments I climbed up to scrape the wooden parts and revarnish them. Jet sat below on the gravel with his toes turned out, howling loudly. He did not like to be left out of anything, and in particular he did not like me to be on a higher level than he was. Dogs are sensitive to the etiquette of status: they do not like creatures low in the domestic hierarchy to grow suddenly taller. I was definitely at the bottom of the social heap as far as Jet was concerned. Andrew hoisted him into the boat to mollify him, but he did not like that either. He jumped up on the engine housing, looked down six feet into the yard, and got vertigo. His howls redoubled.

"I hope he really will like boating," I said, anxiously.

Andrew got *Plover* back on her moorings, and one fine spring day we set off to get her ready for forthcoming summer trips for guests. We took the rubber dinghy out and started pumping it up on the shore. Jet was amazed. He jumped backwards and forwards across it and bounced on the swelling sides. Then he became offended with it. It went on growing and became too hard to trample. He grabbed the foot-pump, got accidentally kicked, and deliberately shouted at. He sat down on the seaweed covered rocks, squeaking crossly. He enjoyed carrying the dinghy to the water— there was ample opportunity to entangle himself in the painter and our feet. Andrew got in and took the oars and Jet clambered in, too. By the time I had pushed off and jumped aboard, he had decided he did not like life afloat, and was half way over the side. Andrew grabbed him and thrust him onto my lap, and by winding all my arms and legs round him I managed to keep him inboard during the five minute row to the big boat. He obviously regarded *Plover* as some sort of island, for he scrambled over the side with scarcely a leg up.

"He doesn't seem to mind the big boat. He'll be all right now," we said to each other, encouragingly.

But we were wrong. He got up on the engine housing as before, but now there was worse than a six foot drop. There was water all around. For half an hour or so we tidied lockers and pumped bilges, and all that time Jet perched atop the engine like a circus elephant, shivering and howling, with his tail between his legs. We rowed back to the shore feeling rather desperate. Half way there Jet lunged out of my arms. Once overboard he swam frantically for a raft of seaweed. His front paws scrabbled for it, and it sank.

With a look of horror and a dismal squeak he turned back towards us. What had happened to terra firma? He swam all the way to the beach, looking to right and left for the first boulders, and once he had found one, he perched on it and jumped from rock to rock. He did not at all like the way we were laughing at him. He hurled his wet bulk at us, and then rushed up the beach and started chasing someone's hens. It took a lot of running and shouting to get him back, and by that time several grim-faced old ladies were standing at their doors watching this disgraceful example of incomer behaviour.

"He may like the boat better if we actually take him somewhere in it—to an island with rabbits," I suggested.

So when the first trip of the season was arranged, we set off with all our guests, packed lunch for everyone, and Jet. Andrew took the boat from her mooring, and brought it to the pier, where the rest of us embarked. Jet was bundled in before he knew what was happening, and I pushed off quickly in case he would jump out again. With the engine running, his perch on the casing vibrated uncomfortably. He retired to one of the side seats and stood there for the duration of the voyage, uttering long quavering wails and gazing mistily shorewards like Mary Stewart leaving France. Our passengers looked at him curiously from time to time, but we tried to be nonchalant, as if we did not mind having the worst behaved dog in the world on board. We went ashore on Ensay for our picnic. This was more like it! Jet floundered to the beach and immediately began chasing the Ensay sheep. Normally he does not chase sheep: it is his one concession to canine obedience. But on Ensay he chased them right and left and up and down. We chased after him, bawling threats and entreaties. Our guests looked amused: we had just been telling them how our dog never chased sheep. I expect that is why he did it: he would not have bothered if there had been no audience to embarrass us. It was what we have come to recognise as a Ritual Humiliation Ceremony, which we are forced to undergo in various forms when he feels we are getting above ourselves.

We overcame the problem of the sheep by producing our picnic. Jet likes picnics. He had mine and Andrew's very quickly, rejected his own dog biscuits, and whuffled round the rest of the company seizing smoked salmon sandwiches and chocolate biscuits. That put him in the best of spirits. We arranged to meet everyone at the landing place in an hour.

"We'd better go off on our own so no one can see what that bloody dog is up to," said Andrew in an undertone.

Jet did not like being called a bloody dog. He chased a few more sheep. We pretended to ignore him. We walked to a small sandy bay at the far end of the island. It was very hot, and the water looked inviting, but we had not brought swimming gear. We decided to risk nudity, as everyone else had gone off in the opposite direction.

Everyone except Jet. We had no sooner reached swimming depth than we looked back to see him bounding along the water's edge, shaking Andrew's socks in his jaws. I yelled, and he disappeared behind a rock. A recurrent shower of sand betrayed the burial of the socks. As we waded hastily ashore, he reappeared with a sandy nose and eyes. I reached my clothes just as he snatched my bra and frolicked with it up the rocky slope.

By the time we had recovered our clothing, we were hot, sandy and late for our guests. At least Jet was tired: on the way home he lay on the seat rather than standing, and dozed between howls. When I got him ashore on his lead at the pier, he had recovered sufficiently to pull me flat on my face before a crowd of interested onlookers. He had had a good day. He did like the boat, in a way.

Next time we went boating we talked about leaving him at home. But he hates being left, even in the next room for five minutes. We say it is because of his insecure puppyhood. Anyway, we did not leave him at home: we decided we would drive him in the car to Leverburgh where the boat is moored, and if he showed signs of delinquency, he could be left in the car while we went out. He showed every sign of delinquency—chasing after the Leverburgh sheepdogs and peeing on people's doorsteps. But of course we couldn't leave him in the car: there was no shade to park it in. So he came to sea.

It was always the same story, as long as we had the use of *Plover*. If we went out, Jet went too, and behaved appallingly. The only boating experience we have had without him is a recent hour in a borrowed Hornet, and I was terrified we would drown and leave him an orphan. Grandparents might happily adopt our human offspring, but who would cater for the needs of a maladjusted black Labrador with a taste for comfortable sofas and expensive cuts of meat?

I need hardly say that we have given up the idea of holidays abroad. We holiday in remote rural areas, and study the maps well beforehand to make sure there is a plentiful acreage of open space without cliffs, bottomless bogs, or dangerous waterfalls. If we go to a town, we park the car in smart residential suburbs or in the better class multi-storey car-parks, and worry all the time we are away from it in case he is being stolen by vivisectionists. If we stay at hotels, we carry a bag full of our own sheets, to protect other people's beds against black fur and muddy feet. Sadly, Jet suffers now from arthritis, like many of his breed. Vets and dog lovers, observing his stiff legs, often ask accusingly if he sleeps in a cold draught. If so, he is not the only one: he long ago decided the back porch was not for him, and moved up to our bed. If he feels it is getting overcrowded, he kicks me out onto the floor for the rest of the night.

Well, that is Jet. I think it should by now be obvious how he has earned his nickname of Monster.

13

Guests and Pests

Monster likes guests. He likes the news of distant parts that they bring on the wheels of their cars, and adds his messages. He likes ogling their bitches and snarling at their dogs through safely closed car windows. He likes showing newcomers round the house and tripping them up by lying blackly on the dark stair carpet, and rolling on his back in the hall after breakfast so that departing guests can tickle his tummy. Most of all he likes the guests' diet: great haunches of roast venison and mutton, ice cream, butterscotch pie, smoked salmon and halibut baked in cream. He is disgusted by our winter eating habits: curried vegetables and stewed beans.

Guests like Monster, too. We had a certain aged earl come to visit a year or so back. Andrew went out to greet him in the car park.

"Hullo, darling! Aren't you lovely?" exclaimed the white-haired aristocrat, rather surprisingly. But before Andrew had a chance to feel flattered, a black figure padded past him to present a nose to the old gentleman, who had fallen on his knees in the presence of such canine glory. Indeed, on the few occasions I saw the earl during his stay, he was on all fours communing with Jet. His conversation to us consisted almost entirely of such remarks as "Grand dog you've got there! Are you looking after him properly?"

We thought he was a thoroughly commendable earl, and we were consternated to realise that we had almost not taken a booking from this discerning person on the sole ground of his title. Why we had arrived at such a conclusion concerning the upper classes will become clear in the course of this chapter: but in

166

any case the obvious excellence of Jet's noble admirer made us re-examine our prejudices.

In my tale of the misdeeds of the titled and landed, I had better start at the top. We had the Prince of Wales to lunch during our second season. The Prince, I must say, behaved impeccably, but the extraordinary circumstances in which Royalty lives and moves caused more than a little upheaval. The Prince's visit was part of a short tour hosted by the Highlands and Islands Development Board. He would arrive at Scarista by helicopter, would stay for approximately three quarters of an hour, and the occasion would be very informal, we were told some time in April. That was fine. We had plenty to do between April and the end of July. We would see what was good and in season when the time came, and give him a nice buffet lunch. But this is not how things are done at all. Successive parties of Highland Board officials, at first low-ranking and then high-ranking, arrived to case the joint. They scoured the neighbouring fields in their city suits, looking for likely helipads. They reviewed all our WCs to find the one most congenial to the royal bladder. They flourished a list of princely dislikes obligingly sent from Buckingham Palace, and anxiously planned the menu. The Highland Board parties were very friendly to us and very excited about their important guest, but it was obvious they were incapable of planning so much as a Sunday School picnic. We felt very anxious for them. They, for their part, were very anxious about us. Were we sure we felt confident? Would we want any professional caterers in? What about experienced waiters? Andrew said he thought he could manage as long as he wasn't expected to wear white gloves. A deputation was sent to teach us how to set tables properly. Another HIDB man was to arrive on the eve of the visit, to hearten us if we should be fainting. In fact we were fainting: we were totally worn out with weeks of anxious officials visiting and advising. They were all charming and we enjoyed their company, but they stayed up talking very late at night, and we had our normal business to run. And every lunch break, it seemed, we would just have slumped at table when the telephone would ring: about the Royal Visit—had we remembered to buy a brush and comb for the Prince's pate? Did we know he couldn't eat garlic? Could we fix up lunch for the helicopter crew somewhere?

The Day arrived at last, and it has to be conceded that it was fun—except, presumably for the poor Prince who has to do this sort of thing all the time. Three helicopters whirred down perilously near our septic tank, delighting the Harris children who had gathered in force outside. The Prince took plenty of time to chat to the onlookers, in spite of his tight schedule. He did, indeed, act quite informally, being doubtless used to harassed officials and packs of security men. These latter clumped heavily round the house, two by two, trying all the doors. My mother's dog, who was visiting, fiercely resented this, and barked furious royalist sentiments through the keyholes: she is, after all, a King Charles Spaniel.

We had bribed and bullied our regular guests that day into clearing off with a packed lunch. It was just as well the residents had agreed to a picnic of royal breaded lamb cutlets, because they would not have enhanced the occasion. We had staying at that time a party of three Majors, here to fish on a nearby estate, who had been practising rowdyism together for close on 70 years. This is a little unfair: in fact Major number one was a gentleman, and I leave him out of any further account. Major number two looked very like a chimpanzee and Major number three was brother to a baboon. If they had not so resembled their evolutionary relatives, we would have disliked them a great deal more than we did: as it was, there was a certain animal naturalness about them which was almost disarming.

Major Chimp and Major Baboon had a great deal of money and I believe they kept racehorses. Since they had left the Guards 50 years back, they had lived lives of ease and played many pranks. They smoked, drank and swore more than was good for them, and certainly more than was good for their fellow guests. They kept several cardboard boxes full of gin in the library, and more in their bedrooms. They smoked at board, bath and bed. Their language was very loud as well as very bad.

The Majors' day started early. Major Baboon would be heard at 6 a.m., rapping at Major Chimp's door.

"Are you coming out?"

No answer. Major Chimp was deaf as well as hungover.

"Hi! Bloody well wake up can't you? Are you coming out?"

"No!"

Whereat Major Baboon would clatter downstairs, rev his car noisily, and roar off for an early morning fishing session. He would of course be late for breakfast. Majors did not wait for Andrew to go through and serve them: the hatch would be thrown open, and a voice would bellow into the kitchen, "a poached egg and bacon, and I like my bacon crisp, but not as hard as yesterday." After breakfast there was peace for three hours, but Majors always wanted lunch in. After three days they didn't want that bloody salami again. After lunch and attendant libations they staggered upstairs for a nap. Their naps were deafening: they snored dreadfully. But Major Baboon was sensitive to noise, and complained if we vacuumed in the afternoon. We had just about had time to empty the ashtrays, wash the glasses, and throw out the empty bottles when they rolled downstairs again, and after a quick one or two, set off for another session on the loch. On returning, they would race each other for first bath, the excluded Major standing outside the bathroom door growling and swearing, while the winner guffawed within. Once there was a crash and a blood-curdling roar from the bathroom and a flood through the kitchen ceiling: Major Baboon had fallen into the bath, from a considerable height, I should guess. Dinner time was a fearful ordeal. The Majors took most of their calories in liquid form, and were not really interested in eating. Either they would sit down late, or leap up early if the evening invited further fishing, or both. Major Baboon did not like stew.

"It's ragout," said Andrew.

"Stew," said Major Baboon firmly. "I get it all the time from my wife."

The venison was overdone, the omelette too big, the pudding lukewarm, the meals too expensive. Major Chimp was no easier to please. He wanted two helpings of the second course and no main course. He kept bringing me fish to clean, cook and serve especially for him, with instructions not to let any other guests have so much as a mouthful. Major Gentleman ate everything politely and paid pleasant compliments, but as for his friends, we expected daily to see them turn their glasses upside down on their heads and pick up bananas in their toes.

The Majors had come in our first season. To our dismay, they booked up almost at once for the next one. We dreaded their return. I had to write to two ladies who wanted to come to Scarista for "peace and quiet" in late July to explain, in some embarrassment, that they would not find these commodities in the company they would have to keep. But we could not think of an excuse to get rid of the Majors: we were appalled to think that we might have them on our hands for ever. But in fact the second visit was the last, owing to the disgraceful behaviour of Major Chimp. On arrival that year, he got out of his car, embraced me warmly, and presented me with a tray of home-grown fruit and vegetables. I thanked him profusely: I was very touched, and thought the old man had seen the error of his ways. For I should explain that Major Chimp was one of the richest but not one of the most generous people we have ever dealt with. Though heir to millions, he wore a pre-war shirt, and got me to sew the buttons on when they parted company with the rotten cloth. He appeared one day wringing his hands in anguish, because the coin-operated telephone had eaten his 2p piece and given him no call, and Andrew had to unlock the box and retrieve his twopence. So for our Major to hand over a box of fruit and vegetables was a delightful surprise. As a compliment to his unexpected generosity, I used as much as possible of the boxful that night. After the melons had gone in, Andrew came through looking worried, but said nothing. After the raspberries, he bounded in white with rage, straight to the telephone. He seemed to be booking two single rooms at a hotel in Tarbert. Explanations followed. Major Chimp, it appeared, had intended his present for the delectation of Majors only. He was objecting in the strongest possible terms to the sight of the other diners munching his melons and raspberries. He demanded restitution—if not in kind, then a proportion off his bill. Andrew went back to tell him he had been rehoused, whereupon his companion grew very angry and told Major Chimp to shut up. Major Chimp relapsed into a sulky silence, and Major Baboon, to our great horror, rushed through to the kitchen and insisted on doing the washing up, with many unflattering and indeed unprintable asides on his friend's conduct and character. Andrew relented sufficiently to cancel the booking in Tarbert, but when Major Chimp wrote to book again (as he did, for though he sulked frequently it was never for long) we replied that we did not have suitable accommodation.

"And neither we do," said Andrew grimly. "After all, this isn't a zoo."

So that was the last of the Majors. In a way we were sorry, but we couldn't risk further outrages on the susceptibilities of less robust guests.

I have described the Majors in detail because they are the type of The Fishing Party. We had other fishing parties and found they had many things in common. Most obvious is the litter of fishing paraphernalia all over the house and garden—waders in the porch, oilskins in the baths, landing nets in the hall. A Fishing Party thinks nothing of "bagging" all the sofas in absentia by leaving trays of half-made flies spread out on them. In fact, such behaviour is the norm. They have other ways of dealing with persons of no consequence: they smoke harder, talk louder, and only about fish, swear more often, and draw up their chairs in an impenetrable phalanx round the fire. It is presumably something they teach them at school: certainly among other sections of humanity one seldom witnesses such ill manners except in children.

Indeed, our fishing parties kept up harassment of outsiders almost round the clock. Half of them would crash up to bed, whooping and shrieking like so many gibbons, at two in the morning; the other half would be rollicking out with a pack of dogs four hours later, whistling and stamping. I don't suppose they realised they were causing an abnormal disturbance: I believe noise-making at morning and evening is characteristic of many primate groups, especially among élite members. Nevertheless, by the end of a week or so we would be numb with lack of sleep: perhaps this is part of the subjection of non-élite members.

It is obligatory in fishing parties for at least one member to sport a title, either an aristocratic one, or better still a military one that has been of no military relevance since its bearer left the Guards in his early twenties. By some strange quirk of human reasoning, his continued idleness since that date invests him automatically with superior status. A regular army man is a poor fellow in comparison.

171

There are other ways in which the fishing party displays its upper-classness to the world. One of the most obvious is a pack of dogs of various sporting breeds. Members of fishing parties are no greater dog-lovers than anyone else: but sporting dogs imply sport, and sport implies wealth and privilege. So every member of the party has more dogs than he feels able to support. While the masters sit down to lobster and smoked salmon, the dogs receive a meagre dole of "complete food", an economical kind of dry biscuit. The well-bred dog further enhances his master's status by lying patiently for long periods in an unventilated car, coming to a whistle, and ignoring rabbits. A dog who behaves otherwise casts doubt on his master's pedigree as well as his own. Considerable ill-feeling was generated within one of our fishing parties by a man with two much-loved Labradors. One was golden and fat (upper class Labradors are black and thin) and they both begged publicly at the kitchen door. Their master took choice bits of his dinner out to them, and worst of all, he was once discovered kissing a wet black nose and whispering "Who's Daddy's darling then?" There was obviously a strong suspicion that he was Not a Gentleman.

Dog domination is often a major part of upper class self-expression. Presumably the dog is a useful substitute for the serfs and slaves who have vanished from our world. Certainly it is hard to see any other reason why superiority should be implicit in the oppression of a creature too good-natured to use its teeth. But then why should it be reckoned clever to outwit a poor pea-brained salmon? The Fishing Party is difficult to comprehend.

After one season we had learnt enough about fishing parties to know that we did not want to encourage any more of them. We felt obliged to let those we had collected already return, but we would not take on any new ones. I discovered an unsuspected talent for lying, and when friend after friend of Major This and Captain That rang up confidently to book accommodation for fishing parties, we were always regrettably full. In fact, as a result, we were half empty all the second summer, but it was worth every penny we didn't earn.

If I add to the foregoing that a Hellfire Club of sportsmen's dogs set upon Jet and bit his tail severely, it will be obvious why a year or so in business had made us acutely suspicious of that class of person which pronounces "off" as "oarff". The dog-loving earl was a pleasant antidote. The next earl we had to stay was a political earl, therefore not so congenial. I cannot remember why the political earl was to visit Harris: there are so many of these official progresses up and down the land. To the young civil servant who arranged the visit, however, it seemed to be a matter of intense and particular importance. With archangelic enthusiasm he told of the honour that was shortly to come our way. I thanked him, and asked for a letter of confirmation and a deposit of 16 pounds. This un-Marian response perplexed him, but no deposit, no booking: next to travel agents, government employees are the worst in the world for coolly cancelling bookings at short notice. A week or so before his visit, Gabriel rang me up again. His master would need a car to bring him from Stornoway airport to Scarista, and then from Scarista to the Berneray ferry. It must be a large car—a prestigious car—a clean and decent car—with a driver who was —he did not quite have words to describe the driver, but conveyed the impression that the average Hebridean would be considered too low-minded and evil-smelling to transport the earl. I assured him that Harris did not contain either cars or drivers of the required standard, but that I would choose the best on offer. The choice was in fact limited to one, as only one person locally had a car big enough to take the earl and his retinue, and new enough to be guaranteed clean and pure: our Harris vehicles quickly become littered with wisps of straw, crumbs of peat and other residues of rustic life. Fortunately George could do the run on the required day, and duly arrived, with the earl sitting beside him, looking bland. In the back seat were packed three young civil servants, pale, bespectacled, and overcoated, completely indistinguishable to an unpractised eye. As soon as the car stopped, they spilled out, tripping over each other and their long overcoats in an unseemly rush to get to the great man's door and open it. By the time they had disentangled themselves, he had let himself out. Disconsolately, they lined up to let him pass, and followed him into the house, bearing the luggage, which included a couple of two-foot-long black puddings the earl had bought in Stornoway, a town famed for its puddings. That evening and next morning, we witnessed, I am sure, three ambitious careers in the making. The earl appeared affable and composed: but wherever he went and whatever he said, his triple retinue bobbed and bowed, spectacles gleaming and pale brows sweating. After breakfast, the earl came to the kitchen door to say goodbye to us. Sarah, then aged three, was with us. In the manner of politicians, he spoke to her kindly, and I think considered kissing her in the approved fashion. Her exceptionally cold and piercing blue stare must have warned him off, though, and he limited himself to patting her head cautiously as he turned to go.

"Whosat?" asked the child, loudly and rudely. I hastily closed the door, but not before I had glimpsed two of the three careers in the making standing to attention as the earl passed between them, each presenting arms in the shape of a black pudding.

I have mentioned that the bookings of travel agents and bureaucrats are subject to change at short notice. There is another group who think they are doing an establishment a great favour by visiting it, and consequently think nothing of cancelling at the last minute. That is mediamen. Mediamen come in numbers from two upwards, both sexes, and nationalities. They have secretaries who are nonplussed when they can't book 20 single rooms at a week's notice in August. They make and receive endless telephone calls, especially during dinner. They smoke evil-smelling foreign cigarettes, and have poor appetites as a result. They wield cameras, notebooks and tape recorders, and promise faithfully to feature you prominently in the mediawork of the moment. These promises are not necessarily to be taken seriously—they are earnests of goodwill which may result in the mediaman getting extra friendly attention, because mediamen like to be admired, or even a reduction in his bill, because mediamen are chronically hard up.

One mediastory will exemplify the genre. On a July afternoon, a brightly painted dormobile drove into our yard. Out jumped two Danish mediamen, bright and breezy as such people always are. They were making a tourist film, they said. They had heard of the excellence of our establishment and its cuisine. They would like very much to feature us. Could they film dinner that night? We were wary. It was to be a very busy evening, and it would not make things easier to have two lanky Danes hopping round the crowded dining room. But they would not get in the way, they promised. They would come an hour before dinner time to set up their lights and equipment, and then fade into the background. It would be very good publicity for us, they assured us. Their film would be widely distributed to Scandinavian travel firms. They would send us stills and information about its progress.

Andrew went off to set tables early, to be ready to help the film-makers with their lighting arrangements. I devised the most colourful and attractive-looking meal that the available ingredients could furnish. I remember hors d'oeuvre platters containing coral-pink langoustines, a coleslaw with red cabbage, green-speckled stuffed eggs, and scarlet pepper salad among other brightly coloured things. The Danes returned, greeting us cheerfully like old friends, and began to set up their lights. About half an hour before dinner, Andrew came to warn me that they really felt they would have to eat dinner, as well as film it, as one could then be photographed at table by the other. This was problematical. I could just about stretch the food, but we had run out of chairs and tables. We got the sofa table from the drawing room and the chairs from the kitchen. There was barely room to move in our two small dining rooms, but the Danes beamed: it was wonderful, wonderful! Please not to trouble about the lack of space.

The evening went well. The diners out were entertained by the antics of the film-makers, the sunset was superb, the meal looked spectacular, and the Danes ate heartily. At the end they gathered up their lights and cameras and packed them into their van. They shook our hands warmly, and with a cheery "Goodbye" they jumped in and drove off.

Andrew and I turned to look at each other slowly.

"Well, they don't seem to have paid for their dinner," said Andrew.

"No."

For all I know they are still at it. We have certainly never heard any news from Denmark.

At least it can be said of mediamen that they keep the other guests amused. They know how to get people talking. Communications between guests are of the utmost importance to our happiness as well as to theirs. There is no worse blight than the feeling that someone has gone to bed at nine o'clock simply to avoid the other guests. Of course in a small hotel, it happens. We dread incompatibles. Scanning letters of booking just before new arrivals turn up, we are beset by anxiety. How on earth is the homely lady from Greenock, writing in a big round hand on lined paper, to be combined with the titled person from Norfolk, arrogantly scrawling across a thick cream sheet, heavily headed and crested in scarlet? How will the newlyweds from rural Lewis survive the company of the two gay gents from London? Will the Californian millionaire and his fourth wife get on with either couple?

We make some attempt to steer new guests into the right sitting room, of course, but it does not always work. In the early days, for example, we had what we thought was a compatible quartet of minor gentry staying. One couple was distantly related to a perfectly respectable earl, and the other pair was Honourable.

"They'll get on," said Andrew. "They're all snots together, after all."

But they did not get on. After a few polite preliminaries, they got down to really important issues. Did Lady X know such-and-such a lord? She replied that she did not, and enquired if the Hon. Mrs Y was related to this or that baronet. The answer was no, and uttered in a freezing tone. Neither couple, it appeared, knew anyone in the least worth knowing: and both pairs were of the opinion that the other's relatives were beneath contempt. For the rest of their respective stays, they frequented different sitting rooms and took care not to pass each other on the stairs.

The reverse can happen too. Once we dreaded for months a combination who were bound to be stuck with only each other, because they were coming so early in the season. Both couples were Londoners, and there the resemblance ended. One pair were extremely proper St John's Wood residents. She wore silk scarves and the most elegant brogues and tweeds, and his manners were of pre-war formality. The other duo were strikingly cockney. She had a liking for slinky satin boiler-suits and dramatic make-up; he wore skin-tight black gloves and black glasses, and looked very much as if he had underworld interests. We liked both couples, and were sadly convinced they were going to ruin each other's holidays. We could scarcely believe it on their first evening together when all four were still in the library at midnight. We applied an ear to the door before creeping off to bed: yes, all four voices, laughter, animation. We discovered next morning that our cockney friend had an outstanding talent for giving single handed impressions of historical battles: he had been the Battle of Jutland until two in the morning, to the great delight of his fellow-guests. It was one of the most successful quartets of the season.

But sometimes the situation is just as bad as can be expected. On one occasion our guests included a North of England couple, down to earth and uncompromisingly lugubrious as people from that area frequently are. At the same time we had an extrovert composer from London and his son. Until very recently, the public telephone was in an alcove in the library. On the opposite wall stands the piano. Most people do not use either of these amenities when there are others in the room: but the lady from the North had an infirm, deaf, octogenarian mother, who had to be telephoned every night at a set time. Meanwhile, having an artistic nature unshackled by mundane inhibitions, our composer was composing, loudly and cacophonously.

"Allo, Mum. Allo—ALLO. Yes it's me."

Clang, crash, rumble, clatter.

"It's ME, MUM. Yes, fine. I said FINE."

Hum, hum, tra-la, jangle jangle.

"What? Sorry, I can't hear you. Can you hear me? CAN YOU HEAR ME? I SAID CAN YOU HEAR ME?"

A string of arpeggios, a dozen dissonances.

"Sorry Mum. There's a bit of a noise here."

Short of ringing the fire alarm, there was nothing we could do: and I doubt if the fire alarm would have been audible over the extremely loud and modern noises issuing from the library. Certainly no one in there seemed to hear Jet, who was sitting in the hall howling dismally.

Jet greatly dislikes music: or perhaps it would be more accurate to say that he is so sensitive to music he cannot hear it without the stirring of ineffable longings, which prompt him to utter his own songs. Once we had a guest who was sociable, appreciative, no trouble in any way—except that he played the bagpipes. The inhabitants of the house other than Jet all regarded it as a pleasant diversion, when after dinner every day he played on the front lawn. Jet was appalled—inspired—frenzied. In the kitchen he howled as

177

if his heart would break. If he escaped, he would stand by the piper's side, ears down and nose up, wailing and groaning. One evening the piper slow-marched along the road to the letter box, posted his postcards, and slow-marched back again. The kilted figure was followed by a black padding shadow, and in the pauses of the music a canine dirge rose and fell.

Of course most of the time guests come and go in an orderly manner, are polite to other guests, and do not ruffle Jet's equanimity. Contrary to the experiences of many hoteliers, we find foreigners exceptionally well-behaved in general. There are the Germans—they believe everything not compulsory is Verboten; they will hardly walk to the beach without a permit. They are punctual for meals and speak more grammatical English than we do, and with more long words. The French—they live to eat. They blow kisses at the langoustines, and weep over the scallops. Whereas a respectable British guest asks me doubtfully if I am Mrs Johnson, or passes me in the yard without acknowledgement, taking me for the scullion, a Frenchman after dinner gazes at me with the worshipping eyes of a dog who sees a juicy bone coming his way. Americans—Americans, most of them, are so polite, so enthusiastic, so friendly that it is very hard to tell one from another. As successive couples come and go, we become so confused that in the back regions the current pair will be spoke of as "Mr and Mrs American".

Other races do not seem to find their way to the Outer Hebrides. I once took a difficult telephone booking from a Sheikh with very little English, but when he booked in his camel as well, I realised he was probably not genuine.

We do not suffer much from hoaxes, unless we count the myriad inspectors for this and that guidebook, who have to pretend not to be what they are. We have to pretend not to know, of course, or their feelings would be hurt. Most reveal themselves after breakfast, and we feign surprise. Occasionally, though, someone plays a worthwhile practical joke. The best was a friend who booked himself in with a few others for a meal, and proceeded to enact an Exit Club Farewell Dinner. At the pudding stage, he had convulsions and fell off his chair groaning "the soufflé!" to the surprise of the other parties in the room. Andrew was not very amused at the time: it was a mischievous allusion to the fact that I had poisoned the Tarbert WRI the previous week by using a suspect bought egg in the chocolate soufflé. It had poisoned us too, and we still felt very shaky, which accounts, perhaps, for Andrew's lack of humour on this occasion. With the nightmare memory of that salmonella-filled egg, it is time to move on to another subject —food.

14

Farm Fresh and Finger-lickin' Good

The egg in question was one from a purple box labelled "Farm Fresh Eggs". I did not at the time know as much as I now do about the intricacies of labelling, but even so I suspected that eggs so designated had probably come from a windowless prison that no normal person would call a farm, and were fresh only in the sense that they had not been pickled, frozen or canned. I bought them against my better judgement, knowing I had exhausted local supplies of genuine eggs for the next few days.

Never again. Animal feedstuffs are often highly infected with salmonella and doubtless other things besides, which can be passed into the eggs or remain in the creature's body. Hens kept in batteries eat only proprietary feeds—4 to 5 oz of it per day. If it is inedibly stale or contaminated, no matter: there is nothing else for the hens to eat, so eat they must. Our own hens get a certain amount of layer's mash, and if it tastes peculiar in any way, they complain and leave it. Of course infected feed may have no off taste, according to experts, but I suspect it usually has, because the conditions appropriate to rapid increase of organisms include warmth, damp and old age, all of which will taint the feed with the stale taste and smell of decay. Certainly the egg which sent a dozen Tarbert ladies to bed for a week looked, tasted and smelt indefinably odd: not addled like an honest egg, not smelling of fish or onions like the egg of a hen with a taste for these things, but not right. But as it was the last in the house and required to make up the cold soufflé, in it went.

My abiding objection to "fresh farm eggs" of course, is not that they are inferior in taste and texture and more likely to poison you, but that their production is fiendishly cruel, with five hens confined lifelong in a space 20″ × 18″. The farm fresh, country fresh, sun fresh, dew fresh image, with a few wholesome brown eggs pictured lying in a bed of clean straw, is one of the ugliest lies of marketing. And marketing is a business composed of lies. The stretching of language to empty it of all usually accepted sense whilst retaining a certain literality is not truth. Take the legend on the white sugar packet: "a pure natural food". Pure in the sense that any laboratory chemical is pure, and natural in the sense that the substance from which this chemical was extracted occurs in nature. If this is what pure and natural means, uranium oxide has at least as good a claim to these emotive adjectives as white sugar.

It is never wise to believe what you read on the packet. If the description is glowing, it is because the contents need promoting: if they need promoting, they would not sell on their intrinsic merits; if they would not sell, they probably taste unpleasant and have no value as nourishment. Nor can one depend on the truthfulness of the seller. Contrary to the advice given by so many ingenuous cookery writers, it is no use, for example, asking your butcher if his meat contains growth-promoters. He is not going to say yes, if he knows you will not then buy it. Would he say yes if you asked if the meat was tough, or fatty, or tasteless? Most likely he will take care not to know the answers to such questions. I do not mean to vilify butchers particularly: every salesman is in the same position, he has a living to make, and the more fool you if you come back for another hormone-plump gigot or another dozen salmonella eggs next week. You can trust no-one's judgements on food but your own, and most people's sense of taste is quite adequate, with practice, to separate wholesome from unwholesome.

Unfortunately, many people develop a liking for the unwholesome. It is easy to get used to the preservatives, anti-oxidants, emulsifiers and flavour-enhancers of modern processed foods, and to suffer withdrawal symptoms to the extent of finding unadulterated foodstuffs tasteless. But the taste for bad food (by which I mean food that does not fulfil its primary function of nourishing the body) is not a purely modern phenomenon. Even in past centuries, the wealthier, at least, ruined their teeth with sugary titbits, so that they became incapable of biting and chewing the foods worth eating—hence the prevalence of refined flour, long-boiled vegetables, and peeled fruit amongst those who could afford to choose. Elizabeth I had black teeth with eating sugared comfits. Nor is the liking for a smack of disease or decay peculiar to modern times: the Romans force-fed geese in order to eat their damaged livers just as the Burgundians do today: the "100 year old eggs" of China and the long-buried shark meat of Iceland satisfy the same sort of taste as well-hung meat, and all are traditional delicacies. Of course there are certain foods that have to undergo some sort of ripening before they become what they are—cheese and game for example. Everyone draws a different line between mature and putrid, though: when the Stilton smells of vomit and the venison of corpses they are past it, in my opinion, though that is just how many people relish them.

In such matters one cannot dictate other people's taste, but as a cook it is important to follow one's own. Otherwise, one cannot be confident that things are right. Over the years we have come more and more to a liking for fresh, clean, simple food—the sort of food that doesn't convert your own liver to foie gras.

But Scarista is not the easiest place to procure excellent fresh ingredients. The daily trip to market beloved of picturesque Francophile restaurateurs is manifestly impossible here. One simply cannot select the best produce of the day and then make use of it, except in the case of home-grown vegetables. What if the cauliflowers are freshly picked and a nice halibut arrives at six o'clock? Halibut and cauliflower is not an exciting combination. Either the cauliflowers wait till tomorrow or the halibut goes in the freezer.

In fact, one is continually forced to compromise, in order to offer any sort of variety in the menu. A lot of people tell me confidently that I never use a freezer, because of something I was once quoted as saying in the *Good Hotel Guide*, expressing mis-givings about that machine. I do indeed have very deep misgivings about it, and use it with caution and loathing. But use it I must: not to store any sort of cooked food, desserts, sauces or veg-etables, but to store certain ingredients for use when the fresh version is unavailable. Local mutton and venison are only obtainable from July to January, and have to be bought a whole beast at a time, so they are frozen more often than not. The alternative is to use bulky hormone-improved "lamb" of doubtful provenance. Fish is not a daily occurrence, either: you will get nowhere going down to the pier to meet the boats coming in, because they will be at sea except on Tuesday and Thursday evenings, when they land their catch in Stornoway. So fish appears only about twice a week, in a van or on the bus, and there is no point at all in spurning the freezer and eating refrigerated stale fish, which is what some restaurants mean by "fresh". I ate the nastiest piece of fish I have ever swallowed in a very famous Lake District restaurant. It was described as "Fresh Aberdeen Sole". In Aberdeen these particularly dull flatfish are reckoned fit only for the cat, and an Aberdonian cat wouldn't touch fish as high as that, anyway. The same applies to shellfish. If a 30lb box of langoustines or a sack of 100 scallops arrives at 10 p m., as it usually does, it is not worth keeping them in the fridge even till next day's dinner. They will not be worth eating after breakfast time, as they will lose moisture and muscle tone. Provided they are really fresh, i.e. snapping, it is best to put them straight into the freezer. They die without signs of attempted escape, and taste indistinguishable from fresh for the first three or four days. After that, for about a month, they are still much better than the travelled, stressed, dehydrated "fresh" specimens you might buy at Billingsgate or eat in an expensive London restaurant. Larger shellfish—lobster or crabs—are only edible to my mind if they are actually fresh, and can't be frozen once cooked unless for soup. They will live for twenty four hours under a damp salted towel in the fridge, but the specimens that have been packed and transported south are stale before they are even dead.

When it comes to dairy products, we have to freeze cream on occasion, and it is often so nasty when it goes in that it is no worse when it comes out. Unsalted butter is not always obtainable locally between June and August so that has to be frozen too. But the freezer is death to cheese. Never believe anyone who tells you that "Stilton freezes perfectly". If it tastes and feels the same when it comes out as when it went in, it was a Stilton not worthy of the name, probably a Milk Marketing Board fake. The same applies to any other noble cheese. As for things in foil and plastic packets, they are incapable of suffering, so freeze them if you like.

There are certain things which we have gradually stopped buying locally at all, either because the quality was poor or because the supply was erratic. We have built up a formidable list of suppliers by now. Each of the four or five types of cheese we use comes whole, direct from a dairy which uses unpasteurised milk in its manufacture: it is only raw milk that allows the subtle and complex flavours of traditional cheese to make themselves felt, but few cheesemakers use it, for it requires better hygiene, greater skill, and a strong-minded opposition to state-approved standards.* Coffees and teas come by post as well, rather than rely on whatever is going in Stornoway. Hams, bacon and sausages arrive by Datapost from a free-range farm in Devon, where Tamworths, Berkshires and Gloucester Old Spots root happily in the open air. A local haulier brings our fruit and exotic vegetables once a week from Glasgow market—not very fresh, but better than they are when they have gone first via the Inverness wholesalers and thence to their depot in Stornoway, which is the next best alternative. The same haulier brings dry goods from a workers' wholefood cooperative in Glasgow—wooden boxes of figs from Turkey, Afghan raisins and hunzas, Moroccan dates, organically grown flours and oatmeal. Because of the quick throughput in Glasgow, these are all much fresher than they would be bought from a shop, though not in fact much less expensive, as carriage costs are high. Wine arrives like this too, from half a dozen merchants each with their different specialisations. On one occasion a huge articulated lorry drew up at our gate, apparently empty. Its cumbersome tarpaulins and ropes were folded slowly back to reveal a single case of wine. Not much wonder carriage is costly.

I can claim truthfully that we have never spared either effort or expense to obtain the best possible ingredients. I wish I could claim as confidently that everything is always as fresh as we would like. But obviously it never can be: aubergines that have taken a fortnight

---

* For anyone who is interested, I strongly recommend *The Great British Cheese Book* by Patrick Rance (Macmillan, London, 1982) which gives useful lists of suppliers, with the author's comments.

between harvest and consumption and venison that has been in the freezer for six months are undoubtedly inferior to the more recently culled article. Yet often when we go and eat in hotels and restaurants in better favoured regions, where gardens are stuffed with fresh vegetables and the high streets sprout delicatessens, I am disappointed by a lack of freshness in what actually arrives on the plate in the dining room. The mangetouts may have been picked that afternoon, the coffee may have been newly roasted, but somehow the aromas have faded and the textures have blurred. Perhaps the menu is too elaborate or the dinner hour too extended for the kitchen to cope, so that some dishes, usually vegetables and sweets, are prepared ahead and kept warm or chilled, causing inevitable deterioration. Perhaps the chef is too familiar with fresh ingredients to treat them with proper respect: so many meals are ruined by indiscriminate use of the food processor, which reduces good food to mush in seconds, incorporating air and causing immediate oxidation. Purées, mousses, and smooth pâtés are very useful ways of reviving slightly tired ingredients, but they do nothing but blunt really fresh flavours. If a mousse or a quenelle is left waiting more than a few minutes, it might as well have been made with last night's leftovers. The action of air on the tiny particles of food will be causing it to decompose. The food processor has exactly the same effect as one of those cunning machines that turn lawn mowings into compost in a week.

We have fallen into all these traps at various times. Losing confidence in a no-choice dinner menu, we have offered a choice at various stages. We have had guests starting to eat at half-hour intervals, we have crammed in as many diners as the rooms could hold. I am not saying that the result is inevitably disaster, but with a small kitchen and only myself cooking, it is impossible to keep up standards when stretched in these ways. It is the same when I have attempted a run of over-elaborate desserts and finnicky starters. Recently we have, if anything, tended to simplify dinner. We like to have no more than sixteen diners. There are five courses and no choice at all, except that if forewarned, people with dietary fads and fancies may be humoured, as long as they behave themselves in other respects. Normally there is a light vegetable starter, such as individual cauliflower soufflés or a salad of melon and other things dressed with yoghurt and mint, or perhaps smoked fish or a shellfish dish. This may be succeeded or preceded by a soup: I favour those with colourful garnishes, such as gazpacho or borscht. The main course is a fish or shellfish one on at least three nights out of seven—salmon baked in flaky pastry accompanied by a casserole of courgettes and peppers, or scallops fried in oatmeal with a highly-spiced tamarind and tomato sauce, braised fennel and a mixed salad. Meat main courses are usually a roast or a pot-roast: rump of venison with rosemary and apple jelly and various vegetables, or a gigot of mutton cooked with tart apricots and cinnamon, and served on saffron rice dotted with pine kernels. I do not enjoy cooking sweet things, and am at a loss when it comes to choosing puddings, but they are usually based on whatever fresh fruit is available—griestorte with peaches or hazelnut galette with pineapple. We used to offer two every night, but we were left with so much of the revolting sugary muck on our hands that I rebelled. Our helpers can be relied on to finish up the leftovers of one type, but two often floored them. Even Jet turns up his nose at chocolate mousse and the like after the first three weeks of the season. We offer cheeses before or after the sweet course, according to guest's preference—usually four cheeses, typically a whole one each of Stilton, Wensleydale and Swaledale, and a wedge from the 60lb Cheddar which dwells in the pantry. The meal is rounded off with fresh fruit and nuts.

I cook, Andrew attends to wine, carves and runs the dining room. Two or three helpers divide their time between chopping vegetables, washing dishes, and waiting at table. Any guests who are late for dinner earn a black mark, and repeated offences may lead to a mysterious lack of accommodation next time they try to book in. To some, the dining room probably seems over-organised for this reason, but too much laxity on that side of the hatch leads to catastrophe in the kitchen. For while Andrew is decanting the claret for diners who arrived twenty minutes late, the rare beef he should be carving will be turning grey, and the vegetables spoiling while they wait for the meat to catch up. In the kitchen, there appears to be no order at all. A guest coming through five minutes before the meal to deliver wet raincoats or an empty picnic basket leaves looking shocked and pale, unable to believe that dinner could ever emerge from such chaos. Two people may be standing at a sink frantically shelling prawns. Someone else will be filling bread baskets balanced on top of the cheeses, which may themselves be set on a pile of plates. Jet will be under everyone's feet at once. Faces will be set and voices lowered, except for mine, and I will be swearing continuously. This incomprehensible and overcrowded chaos persists till the main course is over, after which everything goes suddenly slack.

At breakfast we can take all the risks that could ruin dinner, and consequently our breakfasts are among the most elaborate in the country. Breakfast foods divide themselves very conveniently into three categories: things that really can survive in the fridge for two or three days, such as stewed fruits and home-made yoghurt; things we or the hens will eat ourselves, like porridge and fancy breads; and things that can be cooked to order. The scene in the kitchen is every bit as panic-stricken and the language every bit as impure as at dinner time. I may well be juggling with three or four frying pans, boiling milk, brewing a second pot of porridge and boiling, poaching and scrambling eggs all at the same time, meanwhile trying to keep an eye on the sleepy schoolgirl who is grinding the coffee too coarse or making the tea with lukewarm water.

At breakfast, a table is laid out in the dining room containing all the cold items, to which people help themselves as many times as they want. Typically this contains fresh orange and grapefruit juice, a bowl of fresh fruit, grapefruit, melon or stewed apple or rhubarb, one or two compotes of dried fruits, yoghurt, cereals including a wholefood muesli, dates, and one of these mixtures of sliced coconut, nuts, raisins and candied fruit, which go well with cereals. Every table gets wholemeal toast and a basket of mixed breads—perhaps oatcakes and scones, or butteries and brown bread—with two kinds of honey and home-made marmalade. The rest of the meal is produced to order—oatmeal porridge with a small jug of cream, the excellent smoked Devon bacon and meaty sausages I have already mentioned, fried bread, tomatoes, mushrooms, eggs, three kinds of sliced puddings from Stornoway (black, white oatmeal, and a sweet one dotted with raisins) and local smoked fish, usually kippers. We offer two kinds of coffee and three or four types of tea. We instituted the lavish cold table supposing it would prevent people asking for large fry-ups, but it has done nothing of the sort: they simply eat twice as much breakfast as before.

Perhaps they need it. I think we probably give them rather less dinner than we used to. For the first few years, we regularly offered a fish or shellfish course followed by meat, and had far less recourse to raw fruit and vegetables. In a short time, though, our own digestions were ruined, and besides we came to dislike the unnecessary reliance on vast quantities of animal protein. Hence we evolved less gross combinations. I doubt rather if our clients actually prefer the present style. Of course fashionable eaters in the '80s have to claim to love fibre and abhor cholesterol, but in practice old habits die hard. One has only to look at a few pages of the *Good Food Guide*, that influential Consumer Association publication, to see this. The GFG is studied by every right-thinking *Guardian*-reading Foodie. Among other more useful and solid information, it has much instruction on the latest and most absurd fashions in food, which it both discovers and promotes. We have been learning for years from its asides that freshness, lightness and naturalness are the style of the age: elaborate set-pieces which cement the guts of the consumer went out with Carême, one would think. Vegetables, fish and cheeses are much in favour, heavy meats and sweet things are distinctly passé. But what does one find when one studies the ecstatic delights open to the fashion-conscious consumer? "The little golden mousse of foie gras topped with diced foie gras and served with a suprême of quail", "salad of warm duck breast, slices of duck pâté and shreds of truffle on a bed of winter chicories with hard-boiled quail's eggs . . . spinach soufflé comes filled with snails", and so on. The overt sins of cream and sugar have been banished from these august pages, but there is the same old over-elaboration of visual impact, the same old concatenation of incompatible and esoteric ingredients, the same old assumption that good eating means flesh eating. Nouvelle Cuisine, in other words, has become very like Cuisine Ancienne, and will have no better effect on your liver, your heart, or your morals.

Fortunately for us, although we have been in the *Good Food Guide* for seven years and are grateful for the business it has brought us, we are sheltered at Scarista from the worst excesses of

Foodpseudery. The keen-eyed (and often dull-palated) amateur inspector does not usually venture across the Minch, and the great names of cheffery would not consider us worth impressing by personal visits. I hate talking about the technicalities of cooking, except to someone who actually wants to learn how to do it. Conversation during which the cook is examined, marked and found wanting is totally pointless: if sense of taste won't tell you whether the mushrooms were wild or the bread had been frozen, why bother asking?

To my mind, the ability of a cook relies entirely on a keen sense of taste and smell. If the sense is acute, everything else can be added. Next to that and abetted by it comes the technique of retrieving disasters—in other words, if something tastes wrong, one has to know what to do, and do it at once. Sometimes it is simply a matter of reseasoning: for instance, say a vegetable soup ends up tasting overmuch of turnip, one may do wonders by hastily frying some freshly ground spices and splashing that in at the last moment with some lemon juice, à l'indienne. But sometimes disasters are more dramatic. A few of these more dire events averted without one's customers ever becoming aware of it are excellent boosts to self-respect. I found I felt quite cocky on the occasion when a concoction of fish in flaky pastry fell face down on the floor. I got it up intact with the aid of four fish slices, slid it on to a platter upside down, put another platter on top, reversed it, and hey presto! with a bit of dusting it was perfect. After this unscrupulous triumph I felt capable of anything for a whole week. Andrew suffered the reverse process when the same accident happened to the plum pie he was serving. As it was in the dining room he could not scoop it up as I had done. Anyway, it was shortcrust pastry and had collapsed into crumbs. He returned to the kitchen faint and sick with horror. The Dutch party who hadn't had any pie were very sympathetic and jolly, and anyway I hastily made another which they had with coffee later, but it made no difference. Andrew felt utterly disgraced, and for the next few days he looked as if he might pine away and die. It is the level of public humiliation that counts, and this is strange, because in fact guests don't on the whole mind these catastrophes. It instils fellow feeling to see us in disarray. Two stories of dreadful events in the kitchen will illustrate the point. On one occasion, I had baked a whole salmon in foil. It had seemed rather flabby raw, but I hoped for the best. When I opened the foil it smelt unpleasant, and when I tasted a fragment, it was disgustingly overripe. The second course had just gone through: that gave me perhaps fifteen minutes. Everyone fled from the kitchen as I rushed into action, chopping onions, peppers and pork and slicing and squeezing oranges. By the time the fifteen minutes were up, I had produced a very presentable substitute. We had a pleasant German couple staying at the time, and, being rather proud of my efforts, I told them all about it later. But they were not impressed. No, they had not noticed a delay, but they would much, much rather have had salmon, however bad. It could not possibly be as bad as salmon at home in Herdecke. I was considerably crestfallen. On a more recent occasion we had the corollary. I was boiling artichokes for a second course. They looked tough, and they were. Andrew and the girls were sent through to amuse the guests with light conversation while the artichokes got ready. They returned looking strained after ten minutes or so. I sent them back to sing a song or otherwise divert attention, but they retorted that everyone was sitting there looking puzzled and hungry. I tested an artichoke leaf: not only tough but bitter.

"No good," I said, "they can't eat these." I had had a sherry at seven o'clock and didn't care a bit.

Andrew looked horrified. "What shall I tell them?"

"Tell them the truth! No artichokes."

"I can't do that!"

"You'll have to. I'll have a look at the avocadoes. They begin with the same letter."

The avocadoes were underripe, but they had to have them: and furthermore they were sitting waiting for a good half hour. But no one was angry. In fact practically everyone in the dining room made a point of congratulating me personally on the wonderful way I had coped with the situation. But in spite of their kindness, once the sherry had worn off I felt like hiding under the table.

This episode points not only to the dangers of drink but also to the folly of high principles. Is the sympathy of one's guests not a more profitable asset than a fanatical devotion to their welfare? It is indeed. I must add a further illustration. In the course of a Harris summer we normally have several all-day scheduled power cuts in the interests of maintenance. What maintenance means, mostly, is clearing crows' nests off the poles. I dislike these power cuts anyway, because it seems a shame for the crows, but they are made worse by the fact that they start during breakfast—usually at 8.45. As I have already mentioned, our breakfast is elaborate and cooked to order. On a normal day it requires all rings and the oven of the electric cooker, a coffee grinder, two toasters and two electric kettles, as well as everything the aged Aga has to offer, and there is not a spare minute in the hour between 8.30 and 9.30. It was difficult enough in the days when we had only eight guests, but by 1984 we had built extra rooms. In the first power cut last year, we mentioned it to guests only insofar as shaver points and room kettles would cease to work at 8.45. Down they came to breakfast, fourteen of them, some disgruntled already at lack of morning tea, some unshaven. They did not take the hint. They ordered their usual platefuls, with some extras to make up for losing the morning brew. Couples who had always shared one or the other wanted tea and coffee, or two sorts of tea or two sorts of coffee. Others wanted fried egg, black pudding and kippers, or smoked mackerel, poached eggs and very crisp bacon. When toast was impossible, they sulked. When the coffee was ready ground out of a tin they sniffed it disapprovingly. They felt the cold plates in a meaningful way. And hot milk—suddenly coffee was quite undrinkable without it. Andrew, having suffered my wrath over demands for hot water and extra porridge, stood firm: absolutely no hot milk today. Sulks and tantrums! One gentleman refused to drink anything. A lady pleaded—surely it was not too much to ask, just a little hot milk? Andrew weakened. He very nearly got a pot of lukewarm reconstituted porridge over his head as a result.

After that I was adamant: in the next power cut, the guests could suffer, not me. So on the eve of the crow-clearing, Andrew, under threat, unwillingly passed on my message (doubtless in more graceful terms) that after 8.40 breakfast would consist of what was on the cold table, porridge, tea and stewed coffee—absolutely nothing else, not a sniff of hot milk, not a whiff of kipper. At once, people were concerned: how did we ever manage? How dreadful for us!

Of course they would be down early, or take whatever was going —or would we like them to miss breakfast altogether? And they lived up to their promises; no aggro, no sulking. There is a lot to ponder there.

Actually, we found all the sympathy rather embarrassing. We are too proud and prickly to like it. The grandiose notion we have of great personal integrity in our hotel keeping is in fact traceable to an absurd degree of arrogance. Andrew and I often argue over which of us is more arrogant than the other, and the answer is usually a dead heat. We do not like things to be out of control— guests or food or staff. Of course it happens, as much to us as to anyone else. The sense of inferiority so induced is most unwelcome, and may result any day now in a retreat to a hermitage on some remote offshore island.

In fact, our greatest bugbear was removed a couple of years ago. That was the impediment of being unable to serve drinks to our guests. It was impossible to feel or be anything but second rate when every intending customer had to be told we were unlicensed. Then there was the repeated humiliating business of seeing them wash down good dinners with cut-price German sewage from Sainsbury's, because they hadn't believed the food in the Outer Hebrides would be worth anything better. Worse still, some of the most unassuming would not bring anything to drink, in case we were really temperance fanatics who would be offended. Then there were the breezy characters who had meant to buy some when they got off the plane, but the shops were shut—lunch hour or something, do they do that here? Really!—and couldn't we just slip them the odd bottle? Most dismal of all were the serious-minded food addicts, who asked on arrival where in Harris they could buy a really *good* claret: a question which put the whole island as well as ourselves under a cloud of shame, for the best Harris can do in that line is a bottle labelled "Christopher's Claret". This is that same Christopher of whom an indignant French visitor once claimed that "'e puts ze water in ze Beaujolais"—but no matter: even Christopher's Claret is often out of stock, and the unwary gourmet could well come in to dinner disconsolately bearing a bottle of Bull's Blood or a suspect Italian something or other.

As our reputation for good food grew, the restriction imposed by the Church on the sale of alcohol on the premises became more and more irksome. To an extent, we could understand why they were unwilling to let it go: the house had been built by the labour and with the money of men who would have been scandalised to see it turned into a hostelry. Then, too, it is true that there is much drunkenness in the islands, and that some of the public bars in the region do not bear close scrutiny. We did not want a public bar and no one who comes in on two legs leaves our premises on all fours: obviously, though, the local elders of the kirk were bound to think we might be lying when we made these claims, and besides they would be anxious in case we sold up to some more riotous proprietors. To allay their fears, we made various proposals: we would serve wines only—no spirits at all; we would have Sunday completely dry; we would accept a waiver personal to ourselves, so that on being sold the property would resume its original title conditions. We tried everyone—the Minister, the eldest elder, the clerk to the Kirk Session, the General Trustees in Edinburgh. The local contingent referred us to the General Trustees and the General Trustees claimed it was all up to the local Kirk Session: but the answer was always "no". There seemed to be a certain feeling amongst the pious that they didn't mind our guests drinking as long as it was in secret—what they really could not bear was "the other churches" (the even stricter Free Presbyterian and United Free) pointing a finger at them for not standing firm: in these terms it was not an illogicality for our guests to drink themselves silly on bought-in liquor, whilst being unable to get hold of so much as a half pint of lager on the premises. Sometimes we regarded this attitude as totally Pharisaical: at other times it just seemed totally Hebridean, and we had to laugh. But we never got a laugh out of the General Trustees: we grew heartily sick of the dour conclusion that "the General Trustees have now fully considered this matter and I write to advise you that they are not prepared to vary the conditions of title."

For five years, letters and telephone calls passed to and fro, producing a half-inch thick file of correspondence. In early 1983, utterly exasperated, we eventually made application to the Lands Tribunal to have the irksome condition in our feu modified to allow a licence other than for a public bar. We were fairly sure of

winning, but the General Trustees, with characteristic unpleasantness, bluffed it out till we were well involved in expensive legal
proceedings, before bargaining with us. By mid-April, however,
they had agreed to capitulate on payment of a "grassum". I do not
know what the technical meaning of "grassum" is, but it sounds
as if someone's palm is being greased, and so it is. The Church of
Scotland, it appeared, was prepared, under threat, to relax its
principles for the sake of £1000, like Shylock. Unlike Shylock, they
got their ducats. I wish I knew that our local Kirk Session had
received the cash, but it would be indiscreet to ask, and I doubt it:
the little church across the field still only has its front painted, the
remaining three walls dirty grey. But I expect the General Trustees
have invested our money wisely and well on the advice of Mam-
mon.

This episode did nothing to enhance our respect for the Church,
but it gave us a lot of pleasure the following winter. We got a
skeleton wine list together by June, but after the season finished
we had to build it up, and to do that required much judicious
sampling. In the event, the only drunkenness resulting from our
licence was our own. Unfortunately, by the bottom of a bottle I
can never remember what the top of it tasted like, but Andrew
seemed to have sufficient grip to write quite convincing notes beside
each subject for the wine list. He began to spend many hours
crouched in the cupboard under the stairs, now referred to as
the wine cellar, arranging his bottles and leafing through lists.
Sometimes he got locked in there by mistake.

The licence gave an immediate boost to our self-respect and a
postponed but no less marked one to our occupancy. As the 1983
season was well under way by the time we sold our first liquor,
most of the guests for that season had booked supposing us to be
unlicensed. But in 1984 we had a population explosion. We had
four new bedrooms to fill, but overall we had a higher rate of
occupancy than ever before. I suspect this occurred because people
had been studying our form for years in the relevant guide-books,
but had shied off coming to a temperance establishment. Next
summer they all arrived in force. To our amazement the large
stocks of modest wines we had laid in on the previous year's
performance hardly sold at all: this lot went straight for the

Savennières, the Hermitage '71, the Château Pichon-Lalande '76, for their everyday drinking. We were left with gallons of Soave turning brown and beery, and a pyramid of what Andrew calls Halves of Piss—Piesporter Michelsberg, which he insincerely describes in the wine list as "crisp and refreshing". We were rather sorry to be lumbered with this selection for our next winter's personal drinking, whilst watching our second bottle of Lafite follow the first on to a Texan couple's table: even sorrier that having enjoyed the first bottle with venison one night, they drank the second with lobster on another. If we had had a third in stock I expect they would have taken it away to drink in mid-Minch with Caledonian MacBrayne's pie and chips. There is a lot of money in Texas.

15

Marking Time

Over the years we have seen the hotel's reputation soar, level off —and what next? Almost certainly, it will deflate like a balloon left over from Christmas. We do not have many illusions about it. In the guide books, lobsters and Johnsons and langoustines and black pudding float in baroque clouds of posturing epithets, occasionally inclining to the golden sands and flowery meads of the island paradise. But the bed-and-breakfast ladies along the road suspect us, not without reason, of being a vastly overpriced guest-house. The urban rich of Stornoway regard us as a rustic imitation of their smartest hotel. The local hauliers think us very small fish because we have no weekly load of beer kegs, like the real pub down the road.

Even our friends the Macaulays treated us with pitying concern for the first few years: they simply could not believe we were a success. With hindsight, this is not surprising. After all, John Angus knows that half our furniture came out of his byre and that our early guests were fed largely from clandestine Macaulay gifts, delivered at midnight with a warning, "Don't say anything to anybody about this." I think he worried in case our customers would refuse to pay their bills if they knew we hadn't paid for their dinners.

John Angus and Calum, concerned as always, imagined us set for bankruptcy. Sometimes they asked us cautiously if we wouldn't have done better to carry on teaching. The disaster they foresaw but were too kind to mention outright has not happened; but though the likelihood of its occurrence has withdrawn as our business expanded, a more insidious rot has set in. The hotel has brought us self-confidence and flourishing reputation—even some money.

By the end of the second season, we could see it coming. We could expand, we could put up our prices, we could pontificate. We could buy smart clothes or a new car, or go to the hairdresser's instead of hacking at each other with kitchen scissors. Someday we would be able to holiday in expensive hotels and spend the winters abroad, if we kept our noses to the grindstone. But we were bored with all that before it ever happened. We had proved to ourselves that we could do what we set out to do, and after that we felt aimless, marking time until some new goal surfaced.

We have tried some of the above diversions, of course. We had one holiday in Italy, but when we got back Jet had a nervous rash on his ear, and forbade any further ventures of that kind. We went to some expensive hotels and restaurants, but usually I couldn't sleep for indigestion, and hotels are very embarrassing when you have a self-willed dog and a ratty infant in tow, so now we usually camp. We once bought a new car, but what we considered great wealth was only enough for a basic Polo. We have not even begun to attempt clothes or coiffures.

From a personal viewpoint, the hotel business had really outlived its usefulness after a couple of seasons. There was no question of selling up: we loved Harris and particularly Scarista, and still do, and besides, we were in considerable debt to the Highland Board. Indeed, we had to expand the business to keep it going at all, and in fact the building works involved offered a welcome change from the routine organisation and sweated indoor labours of the summer. In the second season, there were increasing numbers of non-residents clamouring for dinners and lunches. We had never advertised locally, but word of mouth is powerful in a community like this. People were quite prepared to drive the round trip from Stornoway, over 100 miles, for a pleasant evening out. Some came from the outlying parts of Lewis, making their drive nearer 200 miles. Increasingly, we had to turn down many dinner bookings for lack of space. I did not really want to cook for more than 14 or so people, which was all our dining room would hold, with our bulky old furniture. At the same time, we could obviously do with the extra money, and even more pressingly, it was miserable disappointing people, often locals whom we knew, trying to book weeks in advance for a special family occasion. At first we tried feeding people in two or three sittings, but the food suffered, and so did we.

The dining room contained a cupboard in the thickness of the wall, behind which was a single storey wing, really just a shed, with no floor or ceiling and bare stone walls. One end had been knocked out to make a rough and ready garage. We had had thoughts of turning this into a sun lounge, but decided to make it an extra dining room, with access through the old cupboard. It was an interesting room to design, as we had decided to make it more cottagey than the rest of the house. There were various bits of bric-a-brac that we wanted to find a place for—a ship's wheel, a fine hanging paraffin lamp, an assortment of brass candlesticks, a collection of Scottish working-horse harness. Planning backwards from these, we fitted the room round them. We put windows across the end, where the wall had been knocked out, and unblocked an aperture at the front, giving us two windows in that wall. This allowed splendid sunset views at any time of year, from south-west to north-west. Andrew made the two little 12-paned sash windows for the front, and they looked pleasantly rustic in their slightly squint openings. We exposed their heavy wooden lintels and blackened them to match the beams. We left the bare stone walls, painted white. The broken old wood floor, once removed, showed a pit full of ancient sheep droppings most nourishing to the garden, where they accordingly went. We filled the area with concrete, and covered it with glazed ceramic tiles in a pleasing Italianate design of buff, sepia and pale green. The effect was delightful, except that as usual I did the grouting with my fingers, only to find that that particular type of grout was a potent skin remover. I had none on any of my finger tips for a fortnight. Andrew had his nasty moment too—an Acrojack that was propping a loose beam crashed down on his hip joint as he was bending, a very painful accident.

We had not been used to having accidents. They happen when you are distracted, and the causes of distraction were not difficult to find: a whining dog and a squalling baby. When we looked back on that winter's work and realised we had completed one room in the time it had previously taken to do six, we were appalled. It was even worse when the guests came along and said: "Ah, I see you just left the bare walls—much simpler!" or "Oh, you just left the beams—how nice!"

JUST! The mouldering walls, with their stained mortar of dubious composition, had taken weeks to scrape, brush, point, stabilise with sticky fluid, and then paint. Immediately they turned brown. We tried four different kinds of paint. They stained through all of them, and still do. As for the beams, there is an intricate jigsaw of plasterboard between them, much more time-consuming than sticking up whole sheets. Well, that is guests. These same guests thought it was absolutely wonderful having a baby in the house, and the ladies at least came down to breakfast with moonstruck smiles because they had been wakened at 5 a.m. by "the little one cooing"—that is to say, screeching with rage. I couldn't believe it. There we were trying to carry on as normal, while feeling rather like survivors of Hiroshima, and our efforts were entirely wasted. All the female guests required for perfect happiness was to see, hear, touch and smell the baby. If their husbands protested they were ruthlessly stamped on. Jet was as disgusted as I was. Perfectly normal people who had petted him and taken him to the beach the previous season now walked straight past him, bearing gifts in pretty paper to the undeserving and undiscerning infant. Jet does not like other people getting presents to unwrap unless he gets one too. He does not under any circumstances allow the members of his family to be admired in case they become spoiled. He turned to innumerable delinquencies to prove these points. His victory was inevitable, of course. He required concessionary treatment: by the time Sarah was three months old he had achieved his long-held ambition to sleep in our bed. He would swagger up there when we were too busy to stop him, about nine at night, and simply refuse to budge at bedtime. He could make himself three times his normal weight at will. He had decided, I suppose, that if he was vigilant and slept between us, he could prevent any other baby making an appearance. Once he had settled this to his satisfaction, he became quite benign towards Sarah, in a rather distant and leonine way. He has remained the most respected figure in her world. Any day now she will realise that God is simply Dog spelt backwards.

Jet quite liked the new dining room once it was finished: the tiled floor was cool on hot days. He was personally responsible for the first stage in its making, too, which was to evict the feral tomcat who was living there at the time, with only a little help from Andrew and a hosepipe. But the work in between he did not enjoy. He sat behind us and howled. He sat in front of us and squeaked. He stood on our toes and yelped. Why weren't we rabbiting? Why waste energy knocking down walls only to put them up again? When we jumped clear of a shower of falling masonry we had to jump back to pull out Jet, at the expense of our own feet and fingers. When we painted the walls, there he was, spotted white like an inside out Dalmatian. When we screeded the concrete, he danced upon it Shiva-like, with rolling eyes and many paws. Not much wonder we met with industrial accidents, not surprising we never traced the leak which to this day pours through the south east corner of the room from the gable above.

As far as the guests were concerned, the room was a great success —such a great success that it was as difficult as ever to get a booking. In the third season people still had to telephone up to five weeks ahead. We now seated up to 22, and in the kitchen that caused chaos. The cooking facilities and work-space had been planned with 10 in mind, and only ourselves working there. We might now have an extra three bodies in the kitchen, which is no bigger than the equivalent room in a superior modern bungalow. There were other problems, too. As it was always someone's special night out, the no-choice menu had to be very conservative, so as not to disappoint the very old, the very young, the toothless, the faddy, the hard up: the red-faced husbands dragged in against their will in church-going suits, the timid little girls whose boyfriends were treating them as a preliminary to proposing. In a big restaurant, you don't notice your clients in this way, but we were in a position to know something about practically everyone who came to eat. The menus settled into a most uncomfortable rut: prawn cocktail or some variation of it, roast duck, roast beef, steak, Beef Wellington, sweets with gallons of cream and acres of meringue. Of course this sort of food is eminently suitable for the special night out, and it was always someone's special night out: but it is deathly boredom to cook such stuff night after night. It is also, of course, extraordinarily expensive for a fixed-price menu, though we would not have minded that if the preparation had been challenging and enjoyable. The only challenge lay in trying to organise 20 steaks for simultaneous consumption on a grill designed to take six. We began to feel desperate. We knew, though, that the dining-out trade would slacken off as our novelty value decreased, and that in a year or so we would be left only with customers who really wanted to come, and were prepared to put up with our style of food: we looked forward to the day. To hasten it along, we stopped asking people when they booked if there was anything they specially fancied, and instead merely asked if they had any special dislikes. When intending diners informed us that six of the party wanted duck, duck and nothing but duck, and that the other two would "just have steak", we demurred. If we were feeling particularly overworked, we would even suggest that if the party coming on July 20th didn't eat game, shellfish, fish or pork, they might be better going elsewhere. At first we felt very hard hearted, and inevitably people were disappointed, but at least we were certain that the prawns-and-steak brigade could get that sort of dinner in Stornoway. If they wanted to come for the surround-ings or for a different sort of meal, they would come happily enough to us. This has continued to be our policy and works reasonably well. Of course, we still know who is coming, so if it is a party of elderly ladies from the Bays of Harris, we do not present them with, say, stewed octopus, which only young teeth can tackle and which most islanders hold in distinct dis-esteem.

Almost as soon as the new dining room was finished, we started planning another project. Our rear boundary fell just inside the old steadings, a long, low group of buildings with hideously decayed corrugated iron roof, all too visible from the car park and the drawing room window. "Are you going to do something with these sheds soon?" people would ask, brightly. It was a sore point. We had asked the Church to sell, but they would not. We had tried planting a hedge, but that disappeared in a matter of months. We began to consider building something to obscure the collapsing steading roof. We consulted the Building Regulations to see what we could squeeze in between the electricity pole and our boundary. After a lot of sums, we arrived at a structure 100 feet long, 18 feet wide, and 18 feet high. This would comply with regulations and would blot out the hated corrugated roof from the drive, the car park and the drawing room. There were only two drawbacks: we did not have the money to erect such a structure, and had no use for it once it was up. The HIDB would give financial assistance to any tourism project, but we did not really want more tourists. The dining room was full to overflowing with steak-eaters, but we could not even fill our four guest bedrooms. We did not want to operate a steak-house, and had no hope, it seemed, of filling a hotel annexe. Eventually we decided on self-catering units—long thin ones. It was quite enjoyable dovetailing three two-bedroom cottages into our extraordinary ribbon development, at least on paper. The building was to look superficially like a conversion of the old range of outbuildings it obscured, with white walls and a similar pitch to the roof. With three front doors, it should not at a glance look too different from the rows of labourers' cottages seen all over the Scottish countryside. It was fun drawing and redrawing plans to make ingenious use of the cramped space whilst retaining a set pattern of doors and windows on the outside.

But when we actually thought of the effort and expense involved in putting up such a unit, we had no heart for it. To afford it at all, we would do all the work ourselves, over two or three winters. To build what amounted to three small houses by ourselves in the vicious, wet, windy Harris winters, we needed a sense of personal commitment, and it was not there. All we would be building would be holiday cottages, which would be standing empty for six months of the year, while elsewhere in the island families could not find or afford homes. And then we hit on a lovely Plot. If we changed the designation of one of these cottages to "Housekeeper's Apartment" on the plans, someone would get a house out of the scheme. Of course, at the time we did not need a housekeeper: but we could probably need one if we tried hard enough. We had a candidate in mind, who certainly needed a house. Lena Maclennan had worked for us in our second season, and had just joined us for the third. She had worked before her marriage in the same establishment as Jet's first master, and had many tales to tell of his exceedingly naughty puppyhood. Jet had received her graciously in his new home and would obviously be prepared to let her live at the end of his garden. Her daughter had been born on the same day as Sarah, and the two babies were already companionable. For weeks we considered whether to reveal the Plot to Lena. It might look like interfering, she might be too embarrassed to back out of it, the HIDB might wonder why on earth we needed a housekeeper's cottage and turn the scheme down. There was a lot of argument on the type "Go on, you ask her", "No, *you* ask her." Eventually, one of us plucked up courage. We need not have worried: both Lena and her husband were immediately enthusiastic.

For the next few months we waited anxiously while the papers shuffled round various council departments. "Housekeeper's Cottage" looked very official and important on the plans. We were astonished and jubilant when the HIDB accepted the project for grant assistance, but looking back, it is hardly surprising. Though we were a very small concern and by now had three or four part-time staff, we worked grindingly hard. There was, in fact, plenty of work for a housekeeper, and we had no need of the preposterous excuses we were hatching in case anyone asked why we wanted one.

On Boxing Day in the snow, a digger came along and cleared the turf from the new site. After that it was down to spades. Lena came in to baby-sit and do the housework in the mornings while I escaped to the building site. Uisdean came along to give a hand when he could. He and Andrew worked many dark evenings with a couple of inspection lamps brought out on a long lead from the house. I was confined inside in the evenings, not by Sarah, who was asleep, but by Jet. He hated this new form of time-wasting, and did his best to bring it to a halt. He would sit by the cement mixer uttering long piercing squeaks, shivering pathetically, making it quite impossible to throw sand and gravel into the moving drum. He would jump on the edges of the newly dug trenches till they crumbled, and then lollop off rolling his eyes and flashing his teeth. He would jostle the blocks for the footings till he pushed them askew, tie himself up in the measuring lines, lie down in front of approaching wheelbarrows, and pee very deliberately on the clean sand kept for concrete. He sulked dreadfully if he were left indoors with Lena, and as soon as the door was opened, he would escape and make his way back to the building site to express his displeasure. In daylight he was dangerous enough, but at night he was lethal, being completely black. It is impossible to swing a pick or guide a loaded barrow up a ramp with confidence, if one expects every moment to hear a howl of pain from the darkness or to trip over a black obstacle. Eventually, we discovered a way of reducing his interference to a tolerable level. Though Monster protested vehemently at being left in the house, he was usually quite happy to spend the mornings and evenings in the car, which accordingly became known as the Site Hut. Once the gaffer was ensconced there, he could be sure we could not do anything interesting without him: he was already in position if there was a trip to the dump in view, or a journey to Tarbert to buy more cement. In the summer, he became more friendly towards the new building, as by that time the cavity wall was about three feet high, and its purpose had become clear: it was a superior sort of rabbit trap. Young bunnies would hop in through the ventilators and hide in the narrow space between the two leaves of blocks. Jet was ecstatic. He spent many happy summer evenings optimistically scrabbling and snorting at the ventilators. The rabbits, of course, simply waited till he had wedged his nose into a hole, and then hopped off about their usual business of eating the carnations. Sometimes they investigated the many lengths of drain pipe lying around the site. Jet would seize one end of the pipe in his teeth and rush around trying to shake the rabbit out, occasionally appealing to us for help: but when Andrew did dislodge one about two feet from his jaws, he was too astonished to chase it.

In the event, three winters passed before Lena's house was completed. We had to get the whole of the basic structure up and roofed and the windows in before we could concentrate on finishing her section. It was all most enjoyable. The work was quite different from the conversion of the old house, where there had been so much patching and repair. Block walls are not of themselves inspiring or beautiful, but it was interesting to put them up for the first time. Andrew thoroughly relished the roof carpentry, particularly the interesting details round the off-centre chimney in Lena's house. Our local building inspector was highly amused by his meticulous craftsmanship, and he declared it could have come straight out of one of these old textbooks where the carpenter wears a bowler hat. I was more harassed than amused. I was always being found out with a block a degree off vertical, or a crumb of cement on a wall-tie.

Andrew wouldn't notice if the kitchen weren't swept for a month, but he would spot a nail out of place on his building site at a hundred yards. Dropping a hammer down the wall cavity was apparently quite a different sort of crime from using the washing up bowl for sump oil.

Gradually, the Nordic hall 40 feet long by 16 feet wide, with a blackbird's nest in one corner and sparrows flying in and out, became a house, with two bedrooms, a kitchen, a living room, and a bathroom tucked ingeniously round the back of the chimney. I kept eyeing up the space and telling everyone the bath would never fit in there, and neither it did, without gouging a trench in the plaster of the chimney column. The finishing touches were very exciting, the pretty tiles in the bathroom, the oak-fronted kitchen cupboards, the glassed-in shelf units in the living room. Uisdean's parents' loft yielded up boxes of ornaments and teasets and pictures that Lena had hardly seen since they arrived as wedding presents, and the shelves and cupboards were occupied. Furniture was hauled out from the back of our attic where it had been stored, and the tiny rooms filled up alarmingly quickly. But somehow everything got in, followed by Lena, Uisdean, Tina and Calum Alex, Shep the collie and Topsy the cat, and the place had become a home. It was a great moment. I think Andrew and I enjoyed it far more than we had enjoyed setting up our own house: there was more time to stand back and admire. Sarah and Tina were delighted with the new arrangement. The only shadow, and it was a big black one, was cast by Jet, who had regarded the new house, and particularly the sofa and fireplace, as his property. He conceived an undying hatred of Shep, who cordially returned the sentiment. There were noisy and terrifying territorial disputes. After a few uneasy days, however, we noticed that each was too scared of the other to bite, and so it has continued, with a great deal of bluff and swagger. If one dog is away for the day, the other will slink into hostile territory, and leave an insulting pile of turds as near the enemy doorstep as he dares. It adds spice to both their lives.

By the time Lena had actually moved in, it had become clear that we did, in fact, need the housekeeper we had invented. Each summer had brought an increasingly higher room-occupancy, and our season had extended to take in most of April and October, which is long by Highland standards. In addition, there was a fair amount of winter trade for dinners and at weekends, this being one reason why the new building was behind schedule. It was becoming difficult to get away for a day's shopping or a holiday even in winter, because of the organisation required to man the telephone and see to deliveries. In fact, Lena has never become a housekeeper, strictly speaking. She is much more useful, because she can do bits of everything. An extension telephone and an intercom to her house provide a very elastic situation. Look after the 'phone for three weeks—run over to Leverburgh to collect prawns—put Sarah up for the night—lend a pound of sugar—tell these people coming up the drive we're out—get that hen out of the back garden. Best of all, Lena's house provides Sarah with playmates, outings, and often board and bed. A network of grand-parents, great-aunts and great-great-aunts is open to her. She has acquired a second family, a second language, a second culture. The two girls go to school together, bicker interminably, and collaborate in making endless stomach-turning dinners up in the filthy old outbuildings.

These vexatious outbuildings have continued to be an embarrassment, except to the children and the hens, who relish them greatly. No sooner had we got the foundations for the new building down, than the Church decided they would sell the old steadings after all. We were in a quandary. We no longer wanted them, and could ill afford them at that stage, having put all our money into concrete blocks and timber. On the other hand, we could not risk their being bought by anyone else. So we now have them, but have never had the time or inclination so far to do anything to them. The only slated section of roof collapsed in a bad gale soon after we bought them, but the crazy, rusty corrugated iron remains. Occasionally we make plans for them. They could make delightful cottages, or equally delightful hen houses. It depends on whether we decide to keep more people or more hens. At the moment the hens are winning.

In fact, the prospect of having more people around the place became more inevitable and less attractive as the new block approached completion. At a very early stage in the building work, we had changed our minds about their purpose. Suddenly, we had discovered that we could not only fill the bedrooms we had, but could do with several more. We were now at the same stage with would-be residents as we had been for some time with would-be diners. It was flattering to be so much in demand, and tantalising to turn away such an increase in profits. Besides, we reasoned, if we could almost fill our new dining room with extra residents, we could get out of the prawns-and-steak rut. Residents usually stay for several nights at a stretch: they can put up with braised conger and blackcurrant-leaf water ice one night, if they get good old roast beef and creamy meringues the next. This was all self interest: but also, it was wretched disappointing so many people—a day's 'phone calls typically represented more disappointments than successes. The obvious conclusion was that we didn't need self-catering units, we needed more bedrooms. We revised the plans for the internal layout of the new building, leaving the outside as before, to give us four more bedrooms with bathrooms en suite.

We planned fairly extravagant decor for these rooms, to compensate for the fact that they were separated from the public rooms by a windy back garden and car park. We had done nothing so lavish in the house itself, and it was fun choosing the coloured bathroom suites, the Italian tiles, the curtainings and bed linen and all the little accessories like door-handles and light fittings. All this was laid in stock by the time Lena and Uisdean moved in. We had thought we would be anxious to see it all in place, but the impetus had gone.

"More rooms means more guests, and there's too many of them already," Andrew kept repeating, ominously.

For of course, we had changed our minds again. We had got callously used to turning disappointed customers away: we had hard-heartedly eased out of the prawns-and-steak dinners: and we did not need any more money, because if our four bedrooms were reasonably well occupied, we had more than enough to live on, it turned out. The trouble was that the new block had started as an interesting building exercise, and once Lena's house was finished, that was its only point.

"I'll carry on building it, as long as you don't take any bookings for it," Andrew said. He then spent many happy weeks installing ingenious and contorted plumbing and executing decorative joinery for all four rooms in turn. Of course, I did take bookings for the year after Lena's house was completed. Even so, the first occupants of one room caught us out by arriving off an early ferry, to find their curtains unhemmed. They were very sporting about it—in fact one of the ladies hemmed them. I was very grateful, for I was by then in the same state of boggled exhaustion as on our original opening day. There is such a long haul between "nearly finished" and "finished".

The completion (or at least near-completion) of the work had been very exciting, and we had even begun to feel kindly towards our guests again, imagining how they would view the attractive rooms as they first saw them. Because of the original plan of the building, there are two front doors, with two rooms off each lobby. Each pair of rooms is identical to the other pair, except for a slight difference in length. To get away from the monotonous box-like look of modern interiors, we worked out very different decorative schemes. Hardly any of what we would require was obtainable on the island, and most of the time we were shopping blind, through mail-order catalogues and in mainland shops and warehouses. Holding up tiny snippets of material and sanitaryware colour cards, we skulked round the Aberdeen stores and John Lewis's in Edinburgh. Everything came back to Harris wrapped and boxed, and it was only at the last moment that we could see whether or not things would hang together. Mostly we got off with it, except in one room, which is pink—every shade of pink—and could upset the over-sensitive.

We used the curtain fabrics, bought on the basis of samples or spotted in a sale in Aberdeen, as the starting point of the decoration. There is the Sultan's Hunt—a black fabric with a design of prancing Persian horsemen and graceful animals in tones of persimmon, olive green and ochre. The bed sits in an ogee topped recess, with a corded and tasselled banner at the head. Ogees on either side are filled with mirror. Opposite the bed, a complementary trio of ogees surround the recessed wardrobe and the doors to the lobby and bathroom. The colours are all shadowy neutrals, except for the surround of the arches, which pick up the persimmon of the curtains. All the light fittings and door and drawer handles are in heavy brass, and a few tasselled cushions and black and white goatskin rugs complete the opulent effect. We have to watch who we put in this one: it does not suit the meek and elderly. On the opposite side of the tan and white lobby is the slightly unsatisfactory pink room, with a charming fabric called Palace Birds, showing an exotic aviary of crested and long-tailed birds that never were among water lilies and flowering branches. This one has all light cane furniture, delicate petalled glass lamps and porcelain door knobs. The bathroom tiling is particularly pretty, with a flowing design of softly-coloured wisteria hanging in irregular swags as if from the ceiling. For these non-symmetrical designs, I arranged each "wall" on the bedroom floor, transferring it to its place tile by tile. This one, starting from the top, is somehow more attractive than the other three, which start low and "grow" up the wall. Off the other lobby, which is blue, is a completely traditional mahogany room, in dark blue and very pale pink, with an apple blossom design on the curtains. The skirtings and door-surrounds are done with one of Andrew's old moulding planes. Opposite this is a room in pale aquamarine—very hard to keep clean: I do not recommend it for carpets. We refer to it as "Chinese", but purists would of course object. The curtaining has, let us say, a Chinese-style design of chrysanthemums in clear pastel colours on a light blue-green background, the border being stripes of pinks and blues. We repeated this border on the paintwork of the door surrounds, and there is an appliqué of a pale pink knot design taken from the curtains on the doors themselves. Andrew concocted a further piece of Chinese knottery in the bedhead, to my mind very convincing. We put honeymoon couples in this one. Unfortunately, Sarah, Tina and Calum Alex tend to play outside its back window, though often reproved, and we are always nervous in case some pair of romantics should be startled by three grinning little faces at windowsill level.

In spite of our misgivings, we finished the new rooms in a flush of pride and enthusiasm. Every room had a lovely view, and every room was sunlit and pristine. The guests were bound to be delighted, we thought. But they were not, or at least a few of them were not. It was unpleasantly clear what was running in their minds: if the annexe rooms were this good, the rooms in the house must be much better. Why should they be fobbed off with an annexe? What might the *real* rooms contain—four posters, colour television, free champagne, florist's bouquets? There seems to be a natural human impulse to assume that one is being cheated. Or perhaps an animal impulse: our hens will always desert their breakfast in a body to steal what I am putting out for the seagulls, and Shep will leave his own dog-meal untouched, then sneak into our porch to eat Jet's—or vice versa. In animals it looks what it is—natural. In creatures who drive Mercedes cars and bedeck themselves with gold bracelets, it is grotesque. Such little foibles make one exclaim, with Othello, "apes and monkeys!". We generally find, however, that once such rich and spoilt anthropoids have sneaked upstairs, to pry into the bedrooms in the house, they make less chatter about being cramped or cold or otherwise ill-used "out at the back", for the new rooms are larger, warmer and better furnished than the old, on purpose to compensate for that walk across the garden. Many people, of course, are quite happy with

210

whatever they get, and there has been plenty of admiration for the new rooms, as well as moans.

Most of our guests, in fact, are very nice people; the same goes for our staff. As individuals we like all of them, and yet we have fallen into the ridiculous trap of dreading the summer all winter, and wishing it were winter all summer. This is manifestly a waste of life, and something has to change. The damage has been cumulative, and is mainly, I think, a result of lack of privacy. We have no private quarters, except for our bedroom, which can't be reached without encountering guests: and anyway, while it would doubtless be in order to retreat to an office,* one can't retire to a bedroom without causing staff morale to slump. This is hardly surprising: everyone is working hard, and naturally suspects everyone else of working less hard. So we stay around, eating our much-interrupted meals in the kitchen, and doing the accounts in the dining room with the cleaning going on around. As we are always about, it has never seemed worth delegating anything: if the 'phone rings, I rush in from the garden or down from the attic to answer it: if deliveries arrive, Andrew leaves his window cleaning or fuel fetching to see them in. It is a disjointed, hectic existence, and the maddening thing is that it need not be so. Other people could do all these things, but we have never got anyone into the habit, far less trained anyone to cook a meal or make up a greengrocer's order. It is entirely our own fault. We are inveterate do-it-yourselfers, and bad managers. Of course, as the numbers of guests have increased, so have the numbers of people required to look after them, and it is always a pleasant surprise to realise that Lena or Morag or one of the others has quietly gone and done something we had arrogantly supposed only we could do. So each year, we have a little more leisure, but unfortunately a lot less privacy, and lack of privacy leads to a peculiar sort of disintegration, which by September can amount almost to shell-shock—a dreadful feeling that everything is completely out of control, and the recurring question, what on earth are we doing here?

It is a grave question. When it crops up, it is high time to stop

---

* After this was written we took over a guest bedroom as an office. It is very nice but still insufficiently inviolate. Next season we may install an electrified door knob and a portcullis.

and take stock of one's life. Andrew favours a spell in prison to facilitate reflection, but I assure him it would do no good: what with cell-mates telling you their life-history, warders inspecting you, and a constant procession of talkative chaplains, social workers, psychiatrists and doctors all intent on improving your lot, there is probably just as much hubbub at Barlinnie as at Scarista.

16

Dropping Out Again?

The question "what on earth are we doing here?" is not really one that people in our position could be expected to ask. It is obvious what we are doing: running a fairly flourishing business in the summer, and enjoying a long holiday in the winter. Such an existence must appear enviable: we are our own bosses, we are financially secure, and if we work hard for half the year, we can live in as much luxury as we like for the other half. As far as most of our guests are concerned, the hotel is delightful; as far as our staff are concerned, they are pleased to have work in a jobless area; as far as Harris is concerned, the fact that Scarista House has credit in national and international guidebooks is a matter of local pride. In fact we are doing very well and our enterprise is not even anti-social. But we have more doubts than a sensitive curate.

The rot really set in with Jet's arrival. As soon as we had a dog, one or both of us was absolutely obliged to spend an hour a day tramping along the dunes with the relentless Monster. Commonly, it is whichever of us is in a more enfeebled state and therefore less useful at home who accompanies him. The combination of physical or mental weakness with hearty exercise in filthy weather is of extraordinary spiritual benefit, or at least it is less unpleasant than putting up with Jet if he hasn't had his walk. In such circumstances the Walk is both challenge and therapy. When a piece of scaffolding fractured my skull, I went for a walk instead of taking it to the doctor. Likewise, when Andrew sliced a finger in two, he tied it up in a lot of scarves and staggered off along the beach, plainly unfit for unloading the lorry that had just arrived. For sprained ankle, toothache, bronchitis, concussion, acute exhaustion and suicidal inclination, there is one imperative—"you take Jet today".

213

It is the best possible treatment: having survived it, you feel you are not so feeble after all.

The Walk shows that the meaning of life is not to be found in a fat bank balance and respectability. How can such mundane achievements weigh against the bliss of whuffling after rabbits through the marram grass? But there are other more solemn reflections, too. The preoccupations of the West Loch days have surfaced again. Is it possible to live harmlessly, without oppressing the lives of other creatures? And if not, is it worth living at all?

The sea and sky do not care at all who lives or dies. In the low light of winter, crumbs of ice whipped by the wind tinkle an eerie tune on the frozen pools. A family of whooper swans sings a wistful echo, white wings flashing like ice against a turquoise and orange sky. If they are crying for soft mud and open water, they will not get it. The saltings below Chaipaval are indifferent. In the heat haze of midsummer, the sand shimmers and dissolves out of focus. The sky vibrates and sparkles with white terns and their frenzied remonstrances. But no deus ex machina will rend the blue sky to eject the deaf and heartless picnickers who are sunbathing on their nests.

Swans, terns and picnickers are alike insignificant. The white mountains of winter and the blue mountains of summer, the level sand of low tide and the uphill slope of high tide, keep their times and seasons before and after all of them.

You cannot walk on this beach without feeling cut down to size. So inhuman is this area of wind-sculpted dunes, bare sand and moving water that its very indifference eventually makes welcome a sense of kinship with the other short-lived things of flesh and blood that blow and scuttle across it. Our footmarks criss-cross with the round-toed prints of an otter, the long lope of a rabbit, a black-back's clumsy webs, the scurry of a rat. The impassivity of the mountains and the sands leads to speculation: what were they doing, what do they feel? And the tracks will often tell. The big dog otter lives up the stream: he went fishing when the moon rose, and home before dawn. The female came down later with two cubs running sedately in her footsteps, but there they broke rank, and played King of the Castle on a hump of dried seaweed. The rabbits were playing as well, round and round in the sand in a crazy bouncing dance. The black-backs had a lovely find, a fragrant dogfish corpse: they dragged it up and down the sand, beating off envious crows and herring gulls. But the rat went home hungry. The shells he turned over were empty and the sheep's jaw bone dry. The marks of man on this vast landscape of sand, sea and sky are ugly and impotent, mere malicious scratching; a litter of post and wire fences, crazy collapsing corrugated iron sheds, broken whisky bottles, tangled, wind-blown plastic flotsam. Harris is not like England: no old-world cottages veiled in honeysuckle, no time-hallowed churches sleeping among yew trees. The wind here scours away all the vegetation that softens the impact of human habitation. The less aggressive outlines of ancient man-made things, won with difficulty from a harsh environment, the black houses of stone and thatch and the winding lazy beds, are soon flattened by weather. What remain are the all too easy products of an age of steel and concrete, jagged, alien and futile: shabby houses with no one living in them, broken fences that keep nothing in or out, abandoned wrecked cars. No branches will ever grow over them and wind and wet are powerless to crumble them. And man-made cruelties as unconsidered and ugly as these structures blot the face of nature. An unshepherded ewe has caught her fleece in barbed wire, and torn the skin of her throat and shoulders raw in her struggles to escape. The rabbits once prized for food are not wanted now, and have been given myxomatosis: they stagger blindly with pus and blood dripping from the tumours above their eyes. The disease has not killed enough of them, and now they have started gassing them. The corncrakes get less every year, preyed on by the unwanted feral descendants of domestic cats. Mink also prey on ground-nesting birds, and are themselves harried and trapped mercilessly: they escaped from a fur farm 30 years back and now infest the island. The otter, for all its legally protected status, is shot for enquiring too closely into a fish-farmer's close-packed cage of wretched captive salmon. A dead seal lolls on the tide-line, still warm, with a red hole in the back of her head: she was sun-bathing too near someone's front door.

Such depredations are not peculiar to Harris: indeed, it is because the encroachment of human towns and human agriculture is less thorough-going than elsewhere that one has the chance to notice what is happening. In more advanced parts of Britain, the vermin have long since been exterminated, the farm animals shut up in windowless sheds where no one need see their misery, and the only wildlife left is a pretty flock of little birds in the suburban garden. Thank God the Western Isles have not yet reached that stage of civilisation.

Harris has taught us two salutary lessons. One concerns the duty of neighbourliness, the obligation of mutual tolerance under normal circumstances, and unconditional help in times of crisis. We have been generously treated in our community, not out of kinship or friendship, but because we are neighbours: fellow-men. And the other lesson is that, not only in Harris but outside any human community, half-routed, struggling, but not quite dispossessed, is the rest of the world that is not human, which has no rights, towards which there is no obligation. On the one hand, courtesy and charity: on the other, exploitation and oppression.

And yet it would seem so obvious that neighbourliness should not stop where hands become paws or wings or hooves. We would like to spread that message. As hoteliers, however, our chances of evangelisation are limited. We do what we can. We point our guests towards otters and seals, and say our bit about free range hens, who are always available free of charge for photographic sessions. We ban television and daily papers, with their scab-picking anxieties and human-centred drivelling. We feed a diet free of factory-farmed meat or other barbarous products. We leave animal welfare propaganda in a discreet corner of the porch and improving ecological studies on the library table. But it is still a compromise. You can't spread a gospel till you have tried to live it. We would like to put our money where our mouths are, and buy some piece of land, not in order to own it, but to secure ownership for the creatures who live there already, because there is nowhere that wildlife is safe from human interference without such sanctuaries.

It would be nice to end this book by declaring that we had bought such and such an island and were about to set sail for it to live in harmony with the seals and puffins. Well, it hasn't happened yet. The boat is sitting on her trailer in the yard: I hope she will sail there some day. Andrew's advice is to tell a literary lie: a much better ending.

"But what if someone comes to interview us for 'Woman's Hour', and asks 'which island?'" I objected.

"Point at the misty horizon, and say, 'Out there!'"

Perhaps he is right. A journalist once described us in an article as "amateur drop-outs". Where better to drop, than out there?

Scarista Style

*A free-range and humane approach to cooking
and eating*

Contents

CONTENTS

CONTENTS

CONTENTS

CONTENTS

About the Athene Trust and
Compassion in World Farming

The copyright and author's income from this book have been given to the Athene Trust, which has been set up to further the educational work of Compassion in World Farming.

CIWF is an organisation formed to oppose the exploitation of animals and land in modern agricultural practice. In the past thirty years, factory farming has become very big business. Vast numbers of meat animals are mass-produced in cruelly confined conditions. To feed them, the most fertile farmlands are constantly overcropped to produce cereals and oilseeds. It is the belief of CIWF that the only sane policy is to reduce reliance on animal protein, use our best croplands to produce food for direct human consumption, and realign the research and expertise now devoted to intensive animal husbandry towards less wasteful production.

The Athene Trust is designed with young people in mind, to provide information through schools and educational establishments, by means of project packs, films and so on. But young or old, we all need educating. It is easy for us, as consumers, to hide from the ugly facts of factory farming. The animals are shut away in windowless sheds, where we cannot see, hear, or smell their suffering. There is plenty food for us to buy in the shops, so we need never find out that the other face of our wasteful Western plenty is Third World famine. CIWF aims to make plain to consumers the twin immoralities of large scale animal abuse and wastage of global resources inherent in modern agriculture, and to publicise alternatives. Their message is "Don't buy your food in ignorance", and so is mine.

If you would like further information about the work of the Athene Trust and CIWF you can contact them at 20 Lavant Street, Petersfield, Hampshire, GU32 3EW.

Introduction

When I telephone suppliers for the first time, and say I am speaking from Harris, they nearly always repeat "Paris", knowledgeably.

"No, H-arris!"

"Harris? where's that?"

If you look at the top left-hand corner of a map of Britain, you may see Harris. On some maps, it is put in a box, or missed out altogether. Scarista is on its western side, looking out across the empty Atlantic.

We bought Scarista House as a dismal semi-ruin ten years ago. After an enjoyable do-it-yourself conversion period, I retreated to the kitchen and Andrew sallied out front, and we opened our doors as an hotel. We were "noticed" immediately by some of the major hotel guides, which was just as well, since we had no money and few customers. Inflated with righteous pride, we set high standards. We bought ingredients with regard to quality, not price, and I cooked (and still cook) in a last minute frenzy, to ensure freshness.

For the first few years that was the challenge, to produce food of excellent quality in an unlikely location: and unlikely it is, for we are fifty-five miles from the nearest supermarket, and home-grown vegetables blow away as often as they take root in our breezy garden. We availed ourselves of the fine local venison and seafood, built up a network of suppliers, and eschewed all processed imitations of real food. Gradually, tins and packets were edged out of the larder. Last to go were chicken stock cubes. We noticed our dog would snort in disgust at gravy containing even a crumb of them. We respected his judgment: really, they did taste a bit odd. But then chicken tasted a bit odd. And having got this particular oddness up our noses, there was a certain something about duck . . . and pork . . . and bacon. Not to put too fine a point on it, "*Ça sent la merde*"; each animal's flesh was faintly permeated with the odour of its own dung. Why? Had they been rolling in it? Penned up in the fumes of it?

We had heard of factory farming, but it is pleasanter to forget about it. When we actually began to enquire, we found that the life and death of our poultry and pigs was even more gruesome than our suspicions had suggested. When we knew enough to be unable to forget it any longer, we excluded totally all intensively farmed meat and eggs from our kitchen, together with the worst productions of cruel rearing methods or inhumane slaughter. We have never regretted it or found the new regime hard to manage. We use less animal protein and a greater variety of fruit and vegetables than before, and the proportion of shellfish and game has risen. No animal remains are wasted now: I pressure cook all fish trimmings with vegetable peelings into a delectable goo for the hens, our dog dines off the toughest portions of meat, and the seagulls have all the fat and kipper skins. Our reputation for fine food has not suffered. We can feed people well and imaginatively at dinner with only one dish containing meat or fish, and the rest of the courses built upon fresh fruit and vegetables, free range eggs and farmhouse cheeses. More and more people want to come, and our profits have not decreased: in other words, it is perfectly possible to run a hotel and restaurant business on these lines, and it should certainly not be more difficult to do so with an ordinary household.

But why bother, if food is convenient and a good bargain, and you haven't yet smelt the dung in it? Why look for trouble? Certainly, the giants of the processing, packaging and marketing world will do everything possible to keep you blindfolded. Their wares are appetisingly clean and neat: their wrappings are bucolically cheerful with dancing pigs and flowery milkmaids, chirpy chickens and thatched cottages. But these are elaborate lies designed to conceal squalid realities.

Let's start at the luxury end of the market. Take, for example, the hygienic package of frog's legs you can buy in a delicatessen: "cuisses de grenouilles" in a smart restaurant. The cuisses, delicately sauced upon your plate, were probably sliced from a living frog in Bangladesh. The head, body and pathetically groping forelegs were left to die slowly: one death for every two legs on the plate. To compound the evil, these frogs used to keep down insect pests for human farmers in the famine-stricken areas where they are caught. No frogs now—so the farmers turn to the chemical insecticides, many such as DDT and dieldrin long since banned in the rich West, and cynically exported to more desperate markets. They poison people and wildlife as well as insects: that is why we have got rid of them here. So what is the answer? Don't eat frog's legs, say compassion and common sense. Farm frogs for gourmets, cries ingenious greed.

My claim is that we should only eat what we could bear to see killed before dinner. If you could not eat frog's legs while frog's bodies dragged themselves painfully round your table—don't eat frog's legs. Remember, too, that nicely breaded scampi were the tails pulled from living langoustines, and that the crab claws all folksy and tartan in a west highland dining room were wrenched off a living body.

Don't be misled by the red-herring of cold-bloodedness. We have no proof at all that cold-blooded creatures don't feel pain. A creature that did not have sensation would not flee from danger. There is every evidence that frogs, fish and crustaceans are sensitive to touch: and such sensitivity cannot be disassociated from pain. Don't listen to pseudo-scientific nonsense about "flight reactions" and "negative stimuli". Human beings have a flight reaction too, if threatened with the negative stimulus of a red-hot poker.

In any case, the warm-blooded fare no better at human hands. You may forgo the cuisses de grenouilles and plump for the pâté de foie gras. Plump is right: the stuff is 55% fat—deliberately diseased by the disgusting practice of *gavage*, force-feeding geese up to 6½ lb (3 kg) of salty, fatty maize in a day. The goose is restrained—it may have its feet nailed to the floor, or be sat on by a fat grandmother, traditionally: in more modern and even more fiendish circumstances, it is held fast in a brace and attached to a hellish engine worked by a foot-pedal, which simultaneously stretches its neck, forces its gullet open, and pumps the maize down its throat. An elastic band round its neck prevents it vomiting the food up again. This isn't a scene from a nasty video: it happens every day to millions of birds like those you may have watched with pleasure waddling round an old-fashioned farm, or flying overhead with haunting cries in autumn and early spring. Think about it before ordering any Strasbourg pâté next Christmas. And while in that restaurant, don't have the escalope of veal, it is tender and pale because the animal was deliberately deprived of exercise and iron. To produce white veal, the calves are kept from a few days old to slaughter in individual crates 24 in (60 cm) wide. In other words, they can't turn round even to groom themselves. They can't touch or see their fellows, far less play or run about. The floors of their pens are slatted wood, without straw, because if they had straw they would eat it in a desperate search for roughage, which ruminants require. Instead they are kept on an all-liquid diet, to produce the flabby pale flesh said to be desired by the consumer. There is in fact a humane British system of veal-raising, where calves are kept in small groups in straw covered yards. But their flesh is not pallid enough for the gourmet market: hence about ninety per cent of the veal sold in restaurants—any veal that is pale—comes from the inhumane crate system. True, a lot of it is imported from France and Holland, but no room for congratulation here: great numbers of British calves are sent, often at a few days old, by road to the continent, as far south as Italy, destined for crate-rearing. Their wretched journey can take 48 hours, without rest or food. Anyone who has seen a new-born calf can imagine their miseries.

Well, not many of us have frequent access to such doubtful luxuries as foie gras and white veal. But what about those cheap and convenient forms of protein, the chicken and the egg? Chickens—and turkeys and ducks—are reared crammed together in huge, dim, warm sheds, where they will not waste valuable feed by exercising. Feeding and watering is automatic. Almost the only human touch is to remove corpses and cull runtish birds. When the flock is full grown, they are stuffed into crates, with considerably less care than a market gardener stows his cabbages, often sustaining broken wings and legs. The crates are piled into a lorry, and moved to the slaughterhouse. If you are driving in a city or on a motorway very early in the morning, you may end up behind one of these ghastly loads—feathers and the odd wing or leg sticking out between the slats of the crates. Don't try to forget the sight—try to remember it. These weren't feather dusters, but live birds: and their next torment is to be hung upside down on a conveyor belt, stunned, bled and dipped in boiling water. Most are dead by the boiling water stage, but not all. Slightly larger or smaller birds can miss the automatic stunner and knife and be scalded alive. So your chicken may be half-boiled before it ever gets in the bag. That is the life and death of your country-fresh, down-home style, happy valley chicken—or turkey, or duck, or nowadays even quail or partridge.

And eggs? Worse and worse. Ninety per cent of British eggs come from battery units, where laying pullets are crammed sometimes five or even six to a wire cage 18 in × 20 in (45 × 50 cm) for their whole miserable lives, day and night. They cannot perch, scratch, dustbathe or even stretch their wings. They often lose their feathers—they don't need them, the producers explain, in the warm battery house. If they are released from the cages, they can't stand or walk: they don't need legs either, to be egg-laying machines. Lay they must: they are specially bred for that ability, and contrary to popular myth, ovulation does not cease because of mental or physical deprivation. If it did there would be no human famine in Ethiopia and elsewhere, for when life became too wretched, people would be unable to breed; convenient if true—but not true, either for people or hens. So don't assume with Mother Katherine of the Convent of the Order of the Passion of Jesus, which keeps a very intensive battery egg unit near Daventry that "if they weren't happy they wouldn't lay so many eggs". Eggs may be obscenely mislabelled—fresh farm eggs, country eggs. Supermarkets may feature photographs of straw nests harbouring a homely clutch. But unless the box is clearly marked "free range", don't be fooled. I would also say, unless it is labelled "free range", don't buy it. Free range will cost pennies more—probably no more than 20p per dozen. For an average family, the money you might save on buying hell's eggs will get you, in a year, the cost of a new hair-do or a couple of bottles of gin. And if you are visiting that French restaurant again, forget the quail's eggs. These days they, too, are produced in battery conditions.

Once you have your free-range eggs, what about the bacon to go with them? The outlook is poor. Don't buy Danish, that's for sure: and if you buy British, you won't do much better. About sixty per cent of the nation's pigs are intensively housed. This means that the pregnant sows are permanently penned on concrete, usually without straw, and without room to turn. These are the infamous "dry sow stalls". In the farrowing crate, piglets have a separate compartment from which they can reach the confined sow's teats—indeed, she cannot escape from them for an instant. The sow's only relief from imprisonment is when she is put to the boar to be served: then the whole life-in-death cycle begins again. For millions of pigs there is never a chance to root or wallow, or to interact with others of their kind. Pigs are intelligent animals, particularly prone to boredom and stress. To alleviate boredom, they gnaw the bars of their cages. As for stress, they sometimes die of it on their way to the slaughterhouse, or if they don't die of it the signs of suffering are evident in unusually pallid, rather wet meat. The worst is discarded, presumably made into pork pies, but some of it finds its way into the shops: I know I have handled pork like that before I realised what caused it. If you can buy local pork and bacon in an area where you actually see numerous pigs rooting in the fields, you are in luck; but if you haven't seen a pig for years fear the worst: it is probably the truth.

And the rot keeps spreading. In the south, you are seeing more and more "Scotch salmon". It is farmed from the stripped eggs of that magnificent wild Atlantic fish, with its intense migratory instinct. The fish are reared entirely in net cages, so close crammed that when ready for "harvest" there are 10 per cubic metre. To prevent the flesh becoming too flabby the cages may be placed in a current so that the fish have to swim constantly to avoid being crushed against the cage wall.

Nothing is getting better for the animals we eat. If you see rabbit meat, it will probably be hutch-reared: and modern "hutches" are bare mesh cages without litter. Pheasants may have been reared in pens, fitted with metal bits or painfully debeaked to prevent their boredom finding an outlet in feather-pecking. Red deer are being farmed now —as yet fairly humanely, but for how long? Much beef in America and more and more in this country is being reared in feed-lots and barns, cramped together and fed on concentrates. Experiments are afoot to see if there is profit in cage-bred lamb.

There is big money in all this: big money and little employment. It takes few workers to monitor the automatically fed, watered, warmed and ventilated stock in the windowless factory farms. True, the intended automation may fail, so that beasts starve, freeze or suffocate: if fire breaks out, they may often burn to death. But what does it matter? The law has not been broken, and insurance covers losses. There are government codes of practice which appear to offer minimal protection to intensively farmed livestock, but these codes are constantly flouted, and never enforced.

The only way the consumer can beat the system is not to buy the products of it, however it is dressed up in pretty packaging, with smiling cows, contented hens, and flowers and trees. It is not only the oven-ready chickens and veal cutlets that come under suspicion, but all the processed foods and ready meals containing battery-farmed products. Stock cubes—canned soups—pet food—made-up pies and pâtés: all these make the profit margins worthwhile for the big producers. Read the list of ingredients carefully: if you are not put off by the first five or six, which are probably chemicals, look hard at the next, which may be "chicken".

Consider dairy produce carefully, too. The dairy cow, comparatively speaking, does not have a bad life. She is a sensitive creature, and lactation can be considerably reduced by stress, so it doesn't pay to torment her. Most cross-bred calves are reared for beef, and if they are grass-reared that is not as bad a fate as some animals suffer. Other dairy calves of pure breed are slaughtered at a few days old. But the less lucky are sold to the crated veal industry. Veal is simply a by-product of dairying.

Any reader who has not given up by now on this catalogue of abuses is probably feeling depressed. What is there left to eat? Is it worth bothering, when so much is wrong? Certainly, it is worth it. There are degrees of evil in the system: I would put battery egg production lowest of the low, of the common abuses, and regard dairy produce with ambivalence, but these are personal judgements. *The important thing is to make judgements at all*. Even in the crazed world of EEC quotas, ultimately demand must decide supply. It may take a long time, but if consumers simply do not buy the products of intensive farming, the monolithic indifference of governments will be shaken. Either the product will fade from the scene, or more humane methods of production will be found: in many cases, such methods are already known. Eventually, laws are changed in line with public opinion. Switzerland is phasing out the battery cage by 1991; in West Germany, the state of Hessen has taken up and enforced a Federal ruling that such cages are illegal; in Holland, 13 per cent of eggs come from "scratching hens". In this country, legislation is on its way to phase out the veal crate by 1990. Small victories, but significant.

As consumers, we all have the power to change things, by thinking before buying. Of course the choice of animal protein is then narrowed —you eat less of it—maybe none of it—but this is no bad thing. Quite apart from the misery of the animals concerned, there are other arguments. The health factor is well known, in spite of the meat trade's attempts to suppress it. Everyone is aware by now that the too carnivorous suffer more of every ailment from cancer to acne. Not quite so well known is the terrible waste of grain, pulse and fish protein—up to nine tenths wastage—in producing meat, especially beef, poultry and pork. In a world where many people are starving, everyone in the rich west must take responsibility for that. In 1984 we imported about £1½ million worth of oilseed for animal feed from the farmland of Ethiopia. Even less publicised is the export of the techniques and apparatus of intensive animal husbandry to third world countries, fostering not only animal abuse but the very waste of vegetable proteins and human health these methods have produced in the west. Least considered of all, perhaps, is the massive destruction of wildlife habitat caused by our flesh eating propensities. Tropical forests are axed to make way for the Great American Steak; nearer home, sophisticated fishing gear nets not only the fish, but the egg and larval stages of many species, thousands of sea birds, seals, and "non-commercial species"—and all this often for fish meal, to feed the intensively-kept meat animals.

Knowing what you are eating, I think, is enough to achieve a reduction in animal abuse. The mere facts, pondered on, remove the desire for excessive animal protein. But habit is not so easy to break. We are used to bacon and eggs, meat and two veg, pâté sandwiches, sausage rolls. How on earth do you plan a special dinner party? What can you offer weekend guests for breakfast? There are, of course, plenty of vegetarian cookery books, but not everyone wants to be a vegetarian. In fact, a sudden switch can be traumatic and discouraging: once, in days when I was more carnivorous and more orthodox, I gave up meat for Lent, and thought about nothing but steaks for forty days and forty nights. In recent years, I have given up Lent, and steaks. But I still cook for non-vegetarians. The recipes which follow can, I hope, be used by people of both persuasions. Outside the main course sections, hardly anything contains meat or fish, and many of the second section can be used as vegetarian main dishes. At the end you will find some dinner menus. If you try them, I hope you will be impressed by their lightness and balance, rather than depressed by the lack of truffled pâté and quails' eggs.

And for those who have borne patiently with me this far, and are still thinking longingly of roast dinners, here is the heart-cry of a fellow sufferer:

A priest once tried to teach a wolf his letters . . .
"A", said the priest, starting the rule.
"A", said the wolf, who was no fool.
"B", said the priest, "Say that with me!"
"B", said the wolf, "I do agree."
"C", said the priest, "Do carry on!"
"C", said the wolf. "When will this be done?"
The priest replied: "You say it through!"
The wolf said: "That I cannot do."
"Then spell out the sounds from any name!"
"LAMB!" said the wolf. "LAMB! LAMB! LAMB! LAMB!"
The priest observed the sense of this.
Wolf's mouth spelled out Wolf's thoughts.*

* From *Medieval Fables of Marie de France*, translated by Jeanette Beer (Dragon's World, 1981).

236

A Note on Serving Quantities

The recipes in this book are designed to serve 6 amply as part of a full meal, unless otherwise stated. The exceptions are to be found among the Appetisers and Cereal and Vegetable Side Dishes, which will serve 6 in those capacities, or 2–4 as a vegetarian main course, where suitable.

A Note on Oven Temperatures

I am exceptionally vague about cooking temperatures. I have a very old Aga which alternately sulks and rages. Also an electric cooker: our electricity supply travels a long way over the mountains from Stornaway and comes in three varieties—too much, too little and none at all. So I am seldom in a position to cook things for 7½ minutes at 185°C. Where accuracy is desirable for a particular recipe, I have put a Centigrade temperature in the text (with its Fahrenheit equivalent). Likewise if preheating is essential to the success of a dish, I have mentioned it. For those lucky cooks with well-behaved ovens, I append a scale of equivalent temperatures.

	°C	°F	Regulo
Very slow	115–135	240–280	¼–½
Slow	135–160	280–320	1
Very moderate	160–170	320–340	3
Moderate	170–185	340–370	4
Moderately hot	185–205	370–400	5–6
Hot	205–225	400–440	7
Very hot	225–250	440–480	8–9

Soups

Don't you like our turtle soup? No!
Throw it out the old front door.

Thus sang Ivor Cutler soulfully, and since I hold firmly to the conservationist party line on turtle abuse, I cannot but agree with the forceful negative. The implied waste in the follow-up, however, shocks me to the core. Soup is by its very nature the most rewardingly frugal and nourishing of foods, as you cook all the ingredients together, losing none of the flavour or nutrients. Soup in one form or another is the mainstay of delicate convalescents and hearty peasants, tender infants and toothless elders. Queen Henrietta Maria started each day with "a good porringer full" of hen broth. Alexis Soyer revitalised the Parisian poor with wholesome brews of unpeeled vegetables.

At Scarista I serve soup about five days out of seven as a first or second course. This is not actually for any of the reasons expressed in the above eulogy, but because we possess twenty-three soup-cups and only fifty-two small flat plates. If we use most of these for the first two courses, there's an awful lot of washing-up to be done before anyone can have cheese or pudding. Inevitably, someone (not *me*) has put them in the dishwasher, so that they are unappetisingly hot and soapy when required for the chocolate mousse. That may be a poor reason for serving soup often, but it's what is known as a secret of the trade.

Carrots provide thickening without the addition of flour, forming a light, aromatic base, which supports fruit and herbs well. These combinations are a good start to a rich meal, offering the cleanness of a salad even in climatic conditions that would make salad eaters turn blue.

Apricot and Carrot Soup

Use only the sourest type of apricot. The more wizened and shabby they look, the better, for savoury dishes. They will resemble biltong to start with, but in quarter of an hour they will be plump and perfumed.

    2 oz (50 g) dried apricots
    1½ oz (40 g) butter
    3 medium carrots, coarsely grated
    1 medium onion, finely chopped
    ½-inch (1.25 cm) piece of
        cinnamon stick
    a pinch of dried basil
    salt and sugar to taste
    1 pt (570 ml) water

Stew the apricots in the water till tender, and liquidise. Melt the butter, put in the cinnamon, and add the carrots and onion as you get them ready. Do not brown this mixture. Add the basil and the apricot purée. Simmer till the vegetables are tender.

Add salt and sugar to taste—get the balance right or it will taste dreadful, but properly seasoned it is teasingly aromatic.

Carrot and Orange Soup

    1 lb (450 g) carrots
    ½ lb (225 g) onions
    2 oz (50 g) butter
    3-inch (7.5 cm) strip of orange peel
    1 pt (570 ml) water
    salt
    juice of 1 large orange

Cut up the onion and carrots roughly. Remove the orange peel very thinly, without pith: a carrot peeler is ideal for this job.

Put everything except the orange juice in a pan and simmer, covered, for about half an hour. Liquidise or sieve. Add the orange juice, test for salt and reheat, but don't reboil or the delicate scent of orange will disappear.

Kail and Oatmeal Soup

Curly Kail is one of the few vegetables I can grow easily. It is daunting to caterpillars, unappetising to rabbits, impervious to rain. It thrives on frost and snow. Eventually winter gales finish it off, but it puts up a fight first. Not much wonder it is a traditional vegetable in the North of Scotland. Scottish vegetable gardens used to be called "kailyards": kail being any of the cabbage family, but typically Curly Kail, defiantly tough and green in all weathers. Kail and oatmeal is a time-honoured combination. "Kail Brose" was made by stirring raw oatmeal into the boiling liquor strained from cooked kail: a dour and economical dish to keep farm labourers labouring diligently at little expense. This soup is a slightly more sophisticated version.

about 1 lb (450 g) curly kail
2 large onions
3 oz (75 g) butter
3 oz (75 g) medium oatmeal
salt
about 1½ pt (825 ml) water

If the kail leaves are large, cut out the ribs. If the leaves are small use the ribs too; you will then only need ¾ lb (350 g). Shred the kail across in ¼-inch (6 mm) strips.

Chop the onion, not too fine, and fry in 2 oz (50 g) of the butter till just beginning to brown. Stir in 2 oz (50 g) of the oatmeal, the kail, the water and salt. Simmer for 15 minutes, stirring occasionally, as oatmeal tends to collect in the bottom of the pan and stick.

Meanwhile, fry the remaining meal in the rest of the butter till it turns pale and slightly crisp. Add a little salt and a lot of freshly ground pepper. Dish the soup with the fried meal sprinkled on top. You can add cream before dishing if you want a richer soup.

Cauliflowers are another useful soup vegetable. A classic cream of cauliflower will only be as good as the cauliflower was fresh, but if you have to deal with execrable objects looking fit only for the compost heap, you can still produce interesting flavours by adding some strong-tasting complement. The first example is unashamedly à l'Indienne. The other combination was suggested by Rhoda, our butcher's office lady, when fennel first appeared in Hebridean shops. To persuade her family that the exotic new arrival was edible, she had cooked it along with the more familiar cauliflower, and it was delicious, she told me. She was quite right.

Spicy Cauliflower Soup

Ready-ground spices are all right for the discreet touches required in baking or in Middle Eastern cookery, but they are no good at all for a dish which relies on spicing for its main impact. However, grinding in a pestle and mortar is very laborious. I recommend using an old coffee grinder. Don't bother trying to get the mix too fine unless you are the sort of person who screams at a tomato seed. If you only have one coffee grinder, you can still risk using it occasionally for spices: but wipe it out AT ONCE with a lightly oiled piece of kitchen paper, then a dry piece: then put a tablespoon of kitchen salt into the grinder and switch it on for its maximum time. Do this two or three times, empty it, and wipe it out again. Dried pomegranate seeds can sometimes be had from Pakistani or Indian grocers, but if you can't get them, omit them, and grate a small tart apple in with the ginger.

For the soup
2 teaspoons coriander seeds
1 teaspoon cumin seeds
½ teaspoon black peppercorns
½ teaspoon turmeric
2 teaspoons dried pomegranate
   seeds
2 oz (50 g) butter
1 large onion fairly finely chopped
1-inch (2.5 cm) piece of fresh
   ginger, grated
2 cloves of garlic, crushed
1 cauliflower pulled into small sprigs
1 pt (570 ml) water
salt to taste
juice of ½ to 1 lemon

For the garnish:
½ oz (15 g) butter
1 oz (25 g) coarsely chopped
   blanched almonds
1 teaspoon paprika
(1 teaspoon sesame seeds
   —optional)
(1 teaspoon poppy seeds
   —optional)

Grind the first five ingredients and fry them in the butter for about one minute. Add the onion, ginger and garlic, and fry for another few minutes. Put in the cauliflower, add water, and about 1 level teaspoon of salt. Stir well and simmer till very tender—about 20 minutes. Liquidise about half the mixture, and return it to the pan, leaving the rest rough. Add lemon juice and extra water if necessary, but leave it fairly thick. Reheat without boiling. Fry the almonds and paprika in the ½ oz (15 g) of butter. You can add a spoonful of poppy seeds or sesame seeds if you like. Scatter this mixture on each serving of soup.

Cauliflower and Fennel Soup

Don't overcook this: any of the cabbage family tastes much too cabbagey if boiled for long.

1 small cauliflower
an equal weight of fennel
1 medium onion
2 oz (50 g) butter
¾ pt (425 ml) water
up to ½ pt (275 ml) cream
juice of 1 lemon
salt to taste

Save some of the best feathery leaves of the fennel. Chop finely and set aside.

Slice the remaining vegetables roughly and put in a pan with the butter and stew gently till the onion loses its crispness. Cover with water. Simmer for 10 minutes. Liquidise, adding more water if necessary to make a thick purée.

Add the lemon juice, cream and salt to taste, then reheat without boiling. Garnish with the chopped fennel leaves.

Kailkenny Soup

"Kailkenny" is an uncompromisingly grim Scottish dish of mashed potatoes and long-boiled cabbage. But since it is a pretty name, I appropriated it for this soup, as sounding more enticing than sprout-and-potato. You can use nasty old sprouts for this, as long as you take care to cut away all the dingy ochre and slimy black bits on the outside, and wash away the taint of these unpleasantnesses before proceeding further.

1 lb (450 g) potatoes	1 pt (570 ml) water
1 lb (450 g) brussels sprouts	½ pt (275 ml) creamy milk or
2 medium onions	cream
2 oz (50 g) butter	salt, pepper and nutmeg

Prepare the sprouts, peel the potatoes and cut them into slices, chop the onions. Turn the vegetables in the melting butter, add water and simmer till just tender—not more than 15 minutes, or the sprouts will taste sulphurous. Liquidise, add milk or cream, and season to taste. Serve with croûtons and a sprinkling of chopped chives or parsley.

Lovage and Celery Soup

You will be glad of this recipe if you grow lovage, as it will have taken over your garden and you won't know what to do with it. "The root grows thick, great and deep, spreading much and enduring long . . . It is planted in gardens, where it grows large," says Culpeper blandly, adding that "a decoction of the root is a remedy for ague." If you don't live in a malarial marsh, you will find you have a large surplus of this particular herb.

This is one of my favourite soups, and worth suffering the rampages of the plant for.

2 medium onions	3 large handfuls lovage leaves
1 head celery	¾ pt (425 ml) water
2 large potatoes	½ pt (275 ml) milk
2 oz (50 g) butter	¼ pt (150 ml) cream

Chop the onion, celery and potatoes coarsely and sweat them in the butter for a few minutes. Add the water and lovage and bring to the boil. Cover and simmer till the vegetables are very soft. Stir it occasionally, as the mixture will be thick and inclined to stick.

The soup now has to be sieved, as celery is hairy stuff. It is easier to do this if you liquidise it first, adding the milk as you do so.

Return the soup to the pan, add salt to taste and the cream. Reheat without boiling. Serve with a blob of cream or some freshly chopped lovage on top.

Tomato and Sweet Pepper Soup

It seems to have become an old cookery wives' tale that tinned tomatoes are preferable in flavour to all but the best in true Brit. type tomatoes. Certainly the sickly-hued November "fresh" item in the shops tastes of very little. Here it differs from the bright red tinned version, which tastes of very little but tin. Tinned tomatoes, in my opinion, are fine in a dish with other flavours stronger than tin—strong spices, red wine, or half a sack of onions will usually overcome. But for a fresh-tasting vegetable soup, you should use raw tomatoes. I concede, however, that a teaspoon or so of tomato purée and a good pinch of sugar will give body to the more aqueously underripe, without tasting suspect. In the recipe below, red peppers seem to ripen the flavour of tomatoes without recourse to canning. To get rid of tomato skins and seeds, I prefer to cook everything together in large chunks, then liquidise and sieve. That way no flavour is lost. You could get the same result by chopping finely before cooking and sieving. I don't advise blanching and seeding for this tomato recipe.

For the soup:	For the garnish:
2 medium onions	1 tablespoon yoghurt
2 medium red peppers	1 tablespoon cream
1½ lb (675 g) tomatoes	a little salt
1½ oz (40 g) butter	paprika or freshly chopped green
1½ oz (40 g) flour	herbs (parsley, mint or
1 pt (570 ml) water	marjoram)
salt and pepper	

Cut up the vegetables coarsely. Make a light roux with the flour and butter and add the vegetables. Stir in the water, and cook till just tender—the onion and pepper should not have gone soggy, though. Liquidise the mixture and then press it through a sieve, season to taste and reheat. For the garnish, mix the yoghurt and cream with a pinch of salt. Put a blob of this in each serving, and a scattering of red or green over that.

Nettle Soup

It is such a fiddle picking nettles that I hardly ever make this soup, which is a pity as it is distinctive and delicious. You can wear rubber gloves to pick and wash nettles, but being too impatient for that I usually just grab them and curse. Grasp a nettle by its stem and it will flick back up your sleeve and sting your wrist. Jump back swearing and its sister will get you in the back of the knees.

young nettle shoots to fill a 2-pint (1.2-litre) jug, loosely packed
1 medium onion
2 oz (50 g) butter
2 oz (50 g) wholemeal flour
a 2-inch (5 cm) strip of lemon rind
1¼ pt (700 ml) water
salt, black pepper, nutmeg and lemon juice to taste

Wash the nettles—they collect earth and bits of grass. Chop the onion finely and sauté in the butter. Stir in the flour and then the nettles and water. Simmer, but not for too long or the nettles will lose their fresh colour. The onion can afford to be slightly crisp in this soup.

You can either liquidise everything, if you want a smooth soup, or leave it as it is, providing your nettles were in small pieces to start with. I prefer to liquidise half and mix it back in—this gives the most intense flavour without losing the interesting texture. Season to taste. You can add cream if you like it.

Orkney Soup

I don't know if this soup originates in the Orkneys at all. I think it is probably rather like Steak Bonnie Prince Charlie or Robert the Bruce's Spider Cookies, but leaving the Romance of Scotland aside, it is an unusually flavoured yet immediately appealing dish. I have found it very popular.

2 carrots
a chunk of swede or turnip—about 4 oz (100 g)
3 stalks celery
3 medium onions
2 or 3 leeks *and/or* a few green cabbage leaves
1 oz (25 g) butter
2 tablespoons oatmeal (pinhead is best)
1½ pt (825 ml) stock
½ pt (275 ml) milk
chopped parsley

Chop all the vegetables fairly fine. The leeks will need to be well washed to get any earth out. Turn the vegetables in the melting butter and add the oatmeal—the coarsest you can find. Add stock and salt and pepper. Simmer for 30–40 minutes. Dilute with water if too thick. Add the milk, adjust the seasoning, and reheat. Stir in the parsley or sprinkle it on top.

If you don't have all the suggested vegetables, carrot, onion and one other will still make a tasty soup.

Mushroom Soup

This is best made with big coarse Horse Mushrooms; we find those that grow in the heather have the most aromatic flavour. Failing these, cultivated mushrooms will do, but they should be the dark open kind, not buttons. If they are looking a bit past it, all the better for this soup, as it should be slightly pungent. There is no need to chop the mushrooms if you are going to liquidise it, but if not, break up the caps and chop the stalks. The soup should have chunks of mushroom and onion: it is not a purée.

½–¾ lb (225–350 g) mushrooms
1½ oz (40 g) butter
1 medium onion
1½ oz (40 g) flour (plain or
    wholemeal)
1-inch (2.5 cm) strip lemon rind
1 blade mace
1 small bay leaf
1 large pinch of thyme
1 pt (570 ml) light stock or water
salt and pepper
(cream or creamy milk or dry
    sherry—optional)

Chop the onion and turn in the butter with the mushrooms. Stir in the flour. Add everything else except the optional ingredients and stir to prevent sticking. Simmer, covered, for 20 minutes, but watch it at first as it tends to boil over.

Remove the bay leaf (if you can find it) and give the soup a short burst in the liquidiser. Reheat, add cream or sherry to taste, and adjust the seasoning.

Split Pea Soup with Cumin

This is an ordinary dull pea soup with a sprightly garnish. The result is lively and interesting, but you must serve it at once after adding the onion mixture, or the aroma will disappear.

For the soup:
¾ lb (350 g) onions, chopped
3 cloves of garlic, crushed
6 oz (175 g) yellow split peas
2 pt (1.2 l) water
salt

For the garnish:
1 oz (25 g) butter
1 medium onion finely sliced or chopped
½ a green pepper, chopped
1 tablespoon of chopped fresh mint
2 teaspoons of cumin seed
To finish:
yoghurt or cream

Put all the soup ingredients in a pan and cook till the peas are soft. If you soak them overnight first, this will only take about an hour —otherwise at least two hours. When the soup is ready, add more water if necessary and adjust the seasoning. Just before serving, fry all the garnish ingredients till the onion and pepper are softened but still slightly crisp. Splash this mixture into the hot soup and finish with a swirl of yoghurt or cream.

Potato Soup with Yoghurt

It is amazing how many spices curry haters will eat as long as you don't use the word "curry". This soup is, in fact, a very liquid curry, and if you want to make it hotter, a couple of chillies will do the trick.

¾ lb (350 g) onions, sliced fairly fine
2 oz (50 g) butter
2 teaspoons of fennel seeds
½ teaspoon of fenugreek seeds
½ teaspoon of mustard seeds
a large pinch of asafoetida
1 large bay leaf

2 cloves of garlic, crushed
1 teaspoon brown sugar
3 tomatoes, finely sliced
1 lb (450 g) potatoes, scrubbed and cubed
salt
1 pt (570 ml) water
¼ pt (150 ml) yoghurt

Grind the fennel, fenugreek and mustard. Fry the onions in the butter and when very hot add the ground spices, asafoetida and bay leaf. Stir for half a minute, then add the garlic and stir again. Add everything else except the yoghurt. Do not peel the potatoes or you will lose a lot of flavour, but if you can't stand tomato skin blanch the tomatoes first. Simmer the soup for about half an hour. If the potatoes are still intact, mash them a bit, but not too smooth. Adjust the salt, remove from the heat and stir in the yoghurt. Garnish with a pinch of paprika or chopped parsley.

Spinach Soup with Orange

This is my favourite soup and you will love it if you like spinach. If you don't like spinach much, you will find the orange disguises the taste quite pleasantly. If you detest spinach utterly, you will loathe a bowl of this stuff.

    2 medium potatoes
    2 medium onions
    2 oz (50 g) butter
    about 4 pints (2.4 l) of spinach
        leaves, pressed down firmly
    2–3 inch (5–7.5 cm) strip orange
        rind
    ¼ pt (150 ml) water
    juice of 1–2 oranges

Peel the onions and potatoes and cut them up roughly. Stew them in the butter while you wash the spinach. There is no need to remove the stems, but pick out seeding heads. Don't dry the spinach. Put it in on top of the other vegetables dripping wet and add the water and orange peel. Cook fairly fast till the spinach has shrunk and turned bright green, then simmer till the potato and onion are just cooked. Liquidise everything, adding more water if necessary. Add the orange juice and some salt, little by little, till the balance is right. Reheat without boiling. Garnish with a few shreds of freshly-pared orange rind. People won't eat them, but the colour contrast is pretty.

Two Chilled Soups

We don't usually have much need for cold soups in Harris. A hot afternoon may suggest pre-prandial drinks on the lawn, open windows, and a light cold supper, but by eight o'clock there is usually a forceful breeze and guests are donning woolly cardigans and looking hopefully at the unlit fire. However, there is occasionally a place for these two favourites. Borshcht is particularly useful, because if the weather deteriorates it can become a hot starter without altering the balance of the menu too much.

Borshcht

This recipe is a completely bogus adaptation of an assemblage of scholarly variants all claiming authenticity.

For the soup:
3 beetroots (about 1 lb (450 g) weight)
3 tomatoes
2 medium onions
1 medium carrot
3 stalks celery
1 oz (25 g) butter *or* 1 tablespoon oil*
1 teaspoon dill seeds or caraway seeds
1 pt (570 ml) water
salt and vinegar *or* lemon juice to taste*

For the garnish:
2 tablespoons sour cream (*or* 1 tablespoon cream & yoghurt)
a little salt
1 hard boiled egg
chopped parsley, dill or chives

*butter and lemon juice are better for a hot soup: oil and vinegar if to be served cold.

Twist off the leaves of the beetroots and put them in a pan of water *without skinning*. If you peel them all the juice and taste will bleed out. Boil till getting tender—about 15 minutes.

Skin the tomatoes and chop the flesh. Strain the seeds to save the juice. Chop all the other vegetables fairly finely and sauté in the butter for a couple of minutes. Add the tomato and its juice, dill or caraway, and salt.

Put the half-cooked beetroot into cold water and slip off the skins. Chop a third of the beetroot finely and add it and the whole beetroot to the soup. Simmer everything for about 15 minutes. Now fish out the whole beetroot, cut in chunks if large, and place in the liquidiser with a couple of ladles of the soup. Blend till smooth and return to the pan. Add the vinegar or lemon juice. (If you are serving the soup cold, cool and then chill it before seasoning to taste with vinegar and more salt if necessary). For the garnish, chop the hard-boiled egg and herbs separately. Salt the cream.

Hot or cold, this is a most colourful dish—bright crimson, marbled with the white of the cream and dusted with bright yellow and green from the egg and herbs.

Gazpacho

My Gazpacho is just as bogus as my Borshcht. The nearest I've been to España is at the bottom of a bottle of Xérès.

For the soup:
1 large cucumber *or* 2 small ones
1 red pepper
1 green pepper
4 tomatoes (about ¾ lb (350 g))
1 small onion
2 cloves garlic
1 tablespoon pine kernels *or* hazelnuts

1 tablespoon good olive oil
1 tablespoon wine vinegar
salt
2 sprigs of mint (about 10 leaves)
water
For the garnish:
cucumber, pepper, tomato and hard boiled egg, all chopped separately

Skin and seed the tomatoes. Strain and keep the juice from the seeds. Reserve the garnishes. You will need 1½ inches (3.75 cm) of the cucumber, a third of each pepper, a third of the tomato flesh, and one hard boiled egg.

Peel the rest of the cucumber, the onion and garlic. Cut these up enough to go in the liquidiser, with the oil, vinegar, tomatoes and juice. Add about ¼ pt (150 ml) water. As it liquefies, add all the other ingredients. If everything won't go in at once, it doesn't matter—you can stir it all together afterwards. You should end up with about two pints (1.2 l). Taste for seasoning—you may want more olive oil and vinegar than this.

Chill the soup while you chop the garnish finely. Arrange the chopped vegetables and egg in a delightful pattern on a pretty dish. Put a cube of ice in each bowl of soup and hand the garnishes separately.

The next two recipes are for shellfish. Velvet crabs, recognisable from their cobalt blue markings and pugnacious habits, often come up in lobster pots, so if you have ever put down your own pots, you have probably seen them. At the moment they are intensively fished for the European market, so they may not be with us long. Don't try to keep lobsters alive in a plastic bag or under a heap of seaweed: unless conditions are very cold, they will suffocate. You can keep them instead for up to 48 hours in a not too cold fridge (about 7°C/45°F). Wring out a towel in fairly salty cold water. Spread it out on the fridge shelf, lay the lobsters on it, and fold the towel over. When the door is closed, it will be dark, cool and quiet and the lobsters will lie doggo: they are used to spending a lot of time hiding in dark crevices. Do not leave lobsters out in the air or in a bright light, both of which are distressing for a secretive creature of the seabed.

Crabs are more difficult to keep, especially small ones: they should really be killed and used at once. For instructions on humane killing of shellfish, see the preamble to the "Shellfish" section on pp. 284–6. Don't buy dead crustaceans. They have almost certainly been boiled alive. Even for a single lobster in a large pot of fast boiling water death can take up to four minutes, but the method in common use is much more fiendish. Dozens of crustaceans are crammed together in wire baskets and placed in boiling vats, so that the heat takes God knows how long to kill off those in the middle. (The method is highly reminiscent of the twenty-foot high wickerwork giants stuffed with men and cats which the Druids annually sacrificed in a bonfire.)

I wouldn't recommend buying live crustaceans either, except on the quayside. They are often slow and moribund, having travelled for many hours, even days, packed in boxes, stressed, dehydrated and subjected to unfamiliar light, noise and movement. A proportion always die in transport. A healthy creature is snappy and lively when handled and doesn't blow bubbles.

You will notice I haven't mentioned the usual bogey of food poisoning. If you eat maltreated lobsters and crabs, I sincerely hope you get it, and badly.

Lobster Bisque

    1 lobster of about 1 lb (450 g)
      weight
    2 oz (50 g) butter
    1 medium onion, finely chopped
    2 teaspoons chopped tarragon
    some parsley stalks
    a 2-inch (5 cm) piece of lemon peel
    1 oz (25 g) plain flour
    1 pt (570 ml) water
    1 glass white wine
    salt, cayenne pepper, nutmeg
    1 glass dry sherry
    ¼ pt (150 ml) cream

Kill the lobster by any of the recommended methods given on p. 285 and split it lengthwise. Keep the tail meat aside. Crack each joint of the large claws with a hammer and scrape the meat out with the handle of a teaspoon. Put this in a bowl, and add to it the greenish-yellow liver and the coral (if any). Pull out the stomach and digestive tract and discard. Pull out the body contents, scraping out any bits of meat you can get at, and (if the lobster was cooked) the curdy substance adhering to the inside of the shell. You are now left with a lot of small claws and bits of shell and a pool of juice. Crush all this somewhat with a hammer and put it in a sieve over a bowl to drain if it was very juicy.

Melt the butter and sauté the onion in 1 oz (25 g) butter till golden. Add the drained lobster shells, turn the heat high, and fry the shell till some of its orange colour transfers to the butter. Add the tarragon, parsley stalks, lemon peel, water and wine. Boil this quite fiercely together for five minutes, and strain off and keep the resulting shellfish stock.

Put the stock in the liquidiser and add the contents of your bowl and the lobster juice if any. Blend well.

Melt the remaining butter, make a roux with the flour, and stir in the contents of the liquidiser. Simmer, stirring, for about three minutes—a bit longer if you started with a raw lobster. Season to taste.

Cut up the tail meat finely and add. If raw, simmer a further two minutes. If cooked, add the sherry and cream at once; after these go in, do not reboil. Adjust the seasoning—you may need a little lemon juice. Serve very hot, with a swirl of cream and a dusting of parsley or chervil on top.

Velvet Crab Soup

8 to 12 velvet crabs
water to cover the crabs
1 medium onion
2 cloves garlic, crushed
1 stick celery
2 oz (50 g) butter
1½ oz (40 g) flour
juice of half a lemon or a teaspoon
    of tomato purée

1 teaspoon French mustard
1 small bayleaf
1 blade mace
thyme and parsley
1 small glass very dry sherry or
    tannic red wine
cream or creamy milk to taste
salt

Stab the crabs and cook them for 10 minutes with just enough water to cover. Reserve the cooking liquid. If you have plenty of crabs, keep a few whole for people to crunch with their soup. For the rest, dismember them and make three heaps. (1) Twist off the large claws. (2) Press the line around the small claws on the underside till the body part comes free with these claws attached. (3) Remove the stomach sac and keep the body shells hollow side up to retain the juices and curd.

Now hammer the large claws to get out what meat you can. Put it in a bowl. Add any scraps you can pick from the underside portions, but don't bother to be too thorough. Scrape out the juices from the body shells but not the rest of the shells, which will still be meaty.

Melt the butter and chop the celery and onion finely. Sauté these gently with the garlic while you continue.

Put the shells you have left into the liquidiser, a few at a time, with a couple of ladles of the crab cooking liquid. Blend very thoroughly (this will sound dreadful). Strain the resulting mud through first one sieve and then another, adding more crab stock if necessary. When you have done this with all the shells, make up your strained liquid to 1¼ pints (700 ml) with crab stock.

Now stir the flour into the vegetable mixture and add the 1¼ pints (700 ml) of strained crab juices. Stir till it thickens. Add the crab meat in the bowl and all the other ingredients except the cream. Simmer for five minutes. Remove the bay leaf and mace, adjust the seasoning, and add as much cream or milk as you fancy. You may prefer more sherry. A good manzanilla is best.

I dish this soup in shallow plates with a crab swimming in each. Some people like to munch and suck the crabs. Others do not rejoice at the sight of their prey, but I don't see why they shouldn't be reminded of what they are eating.

Appetisers and Vegetarian Main Course Dishes

Except for the first few, most of the recipes in this section can also be used as vegetarian main dishes. The quantities given will serve six as a starter, or four as a main course in a full dinner menu. None of these recipes uses fish or meat. The sort of restaurant menu that sprouts game soups, pig terrines and shellfish mousses over the first two courses, followed by veal and poultry accompanied by lardon-bespattered salads and vegetables, gives me indigestion, physical and moral. I sometimes feel that the carnivorous would gladly complete the meal with sweetbreads in caramel or Stilton and pork crackling—are there ideas there for some ambitious young chef?

Light starters

First of all, a note on the terms "water ice", "granita", and "sorbet". Sorbet is a French concept. Fruit pulp is sweetened with sugar syrup and whipped egg white is added part way through freezing. To my mind, the result is too sweet, too bland, and too smooth for anything but a pudding. A granita has no egg white, the degree of sweetening is optional, and the texture is a sort of grainy slush. "Water ice" is a rather loose term. It used to be an English equivalent for both sorbet and granita. I would define it as a granita mixture which has been allowed to set rather firm. To their credit, and unlike sorbets, water ices and granitas can't be successfully kept. You must use them when they reach the correct texture, or they will become tasteless and lumpy.

Melon with Blackcurrant or Plum Water Ice

1 large ripe melon
For the ice:
1 lb (450 g) blackcurrants or santa
   rosa plums
light muscovado sugar to taste
water as required

Sieve the blackcurrants or plums. I liquidise them first, stones, stalks and all, and then press the pulp through a strainer using the back of a metal ladle. You should get about 1 pint (570 ml) of purée. Make it up with water if it is short. Sweeten to taste with muscovado sugar, a little at a time as it can easily get too sweet. The flavour should be fresh and intense. The ice will take about 1 to 1½ hours to freeze, during which you should mash it several times with a fork.

Cut off the very end pieces of the melon and divide it horizontally into six slices. Remove the seeds, and lay each slice on a flat plate. Put a scoop of the ice in the centre and decorate with attractive leaves or little sprigs of currants.

Redcurrants and Victoria plums also make good ices for serving with melon, but the colour contrast is not so attractive.

Grapefruit Water Ice

3 large or 5 small grapefruits
1 large orange
caster sugar to taste
¼ pt (150 ml) water

Using a very sharp knife, halve the grapefruits, cutting them zig-zag round their middles. Squeeze the grapefruit halves carefully, taking care not to damage the skins. Put the skins into a bowl of lukewarm water. Squeeze the orange, and strain and mix the two juices. You should have about 1¼ pints (700 ml)—if less, squeeze another grapefruit. Add the water, and sweeten to taste with caster sugar. Stir it vigorously to dissolve it before you decide to add more. Pour this mixture into a flat metal dish and freeze for about 1½–2 hours, mashing it well several times.

With a teaspoon, scrape the membrane and untidy bits out of the grapefruit skins. The soaking in water makes this easier. Dry the skins and freeze till the ice is ready. Serve the ice in the grapefruit cups.

For a party, these grapefruit ices look spectacular piled up on a silver or crystal dish full of cracked ice, bedecked with sprays of mint or other fresh greenery. The ice will keep them firm till people come to the table.

Avocado with Tomato Granita

3 avocadoes
a little lemon juice *or* French
   dressing
For the granita:
½ clove garlic
1 lb (450 g) tomatoes
1-inch (2.5 cm) strip orange rind
a sprig of marjoram or basil
a pinch of sugar
salt to taste
¼ pt (150 ml) water
To garnish:
6 nice sprigs of a compatible fresh
   herb—mint, basil or marjoram

Start the granita about two hours before you want to serve it. Put all the ingredients in the liquidiser, or chop finely. Sieve the mush, and test for seasoning. It should not be too salty, but not tasteless either. Pour into a flat-bottomed dish, preferably metal, and set on the floor of your freezing compartment. After ¾ hour, mash it with a fork, and repeat this as necessary to keep the mixture slushy and stop it sticking in a block to the bottom of the dish. If it does this at any stage, leave it at room temperature till it can be mashed again.

Slice the avocadoes lengthwise, just before serving, and taste a sliver. If they are dire, sprinkle liberally with French dressing: if they are so-so, brush with lemon juice: if they are superb, don't do anything to them. Serve a spoonful of tomato ice in the cavity, and garnish with the fresh herbs. (You can also use whole prawns as a garnish.)

Avocado and Walnut Salad

For the salad:
3 ripe avocadoes
2 large oranges
2 oz (50 g) shelled walnuts
For the dressing:
1 teaspoon chopped sweet cicely or
    mint
1 teaspoon honey
2 tablespoons yoghurt *or*
    1 tablespoon lemon juice and
    1 tablespoon sunflower oil
a pinch of salt
For the garnish:
lettuce leaves

Cut the avocado flesh into chunks and place in a deep bowl. Scatter on the walnut pieces. Obviously fresh newly shelled nuts are best, but others will do up to the very rim of rancidity.

Now place a strainer over the bowl. Using a very sharp knife, peel the oranges, round and round as you would apples, removing all the pith. Do this over the strainer so as not to lose any of the juice. With a fine saw-edged knife, cut out the orange segments, leaving all the membrane behind. Squeeze the remains of the orange hard in your fist over the strainer to get out the last of the juice. Mix the orange segments carefully with the avocado.

For the dressing:

Mix all the ingredients together. Sweet cicely is a common country wild flower, with a delicate aniseed flavour, but if you don't have it, mint will do. If your walnuts were grotty, use the oil dressing rather than yoghurt, but don't be tempted to use walnut oil for this salad—it is much too heavy.

Pour the dressing over the salad and mix, but gently. Chill, but not for more than half an hour. Dish surrounded by the lettuce and garnished with sprigs of the herb you used.

Melon with Mint and Yoghurt Dressing

3 ogen melons *or* 1 large honeydew
    melon
For the dressing:
¼ pt (150 ml) yoghurt
1 dessertspoon of honey, preferably
    heather
2 teaspoons lemon or orange juice
1 tablespoon finely chopped mint
For the garnish:
sprigs of mint

Chill the melons. Mix all the ingredients for the dressing: don't use an insipid honey. Lemon juice is best for ogens and orange for honeydew.

If using ogens, cut through the middle, remove the seeds and pour the dressing into the cavities. If using honeydew, get the flesh out with a melon-baller or cut into chunks. Divide between six glass dishes and pour the dressing over. Garnish with the sprigs of mint.

Vegetable Soufflés

The basic method for all hot soufflés is the same: you add egg yolks and the flavouring agent, puréed or chopped, and then fold in the stiffly whisked egg whites. A 3½-egg mixture will give you at least 8 individual soufflés. There are a few slight variations on the method, so I shall give separate hints for my favourite versions, after the basic instructions.

Soufflés are not entirely predictable. You may follow all the directions carefully and still end up with total collapse or failure to rise. However, the soufflés will still taste good—don't be too sensitive about such events. There are a few general hints here which will help to eliminate mistakes.

(1) Don't incorporate hidden water—it will affect the rising power of the egg whites, so:

Make sure all utensils are dry and at room temperature, to avoid condensation.

Don't work in a steamy kitchen or leave the separated egg whites in a damp atmosphere.

Drain your vegetables well, and if the purée is rather thin make the white sauce correspondingly thicker.

(2) Use only very fresh eggs. Don't leave the whisked egg whites standing—incorporate them immediately.

(3) Don't have too much top heat, which will form a hard crust and prevent the bottom from rising properly. Place your soufflés mid-way down the oven or a little lower. If you are really pernickity, place the filled soufflé dishes on a pre-heated baking sheet to get the rising started from the bottom first.

(4) Don't admit draughts or jolts. Open and close the oven very carefully, and when you are carrying the finished soufflés to the table, shut the windows. A sudden gust will shrivel them up. I have had several sad experiences when the dog has been deciding whether to go in or out or half-way through the back door at this unpropitious moment.

Basic Method

> 1½ oz (40 g) butter
> 1 oz (25 g) flour
> ¼ pt (150 ml) milk
> 4 eggs separated, *or* 3 yolks and
>   4 whites
> ½–¾ pt (275–425 ml) cooked
>   vegetables chopped very finely or
>   puréed
> seasoning

Pre-heat the oven to 200°C/400°F.

Butter 8 to 10 small ramekins or soufflé dishes lightly—not too much buttering or the rising mixture will slip back down the dish. Melt the butter, stir in the flour, and cook till it turns pale. Stir in the milk and boil, beating till you have a smooth thick sauce. Turn this into a wide bowl. Put a piece of wet greaseproof paper over it if the vegetable purée isn't ready, or a skin will form.

Beat in the vegetable purée and when it has cooled slightly, the egg yolks. Season to taste, quite highly—the egg whites will blunt the flavour somewhat.

Whisk the egg whites very stiff, and fold a third into the vegetable mixture, followed by the other two thirds. Use a rubber spatula or a metal spoon, with a light semi-circular slicing movement. Turn the mixture gently into the prepared dishes (filling within ¼ inch (6 mm) of the top is safe but not completely full or your soufflé will escape).

Bake the soufflés immediately for 35 minutes. Don't open the oven door till at least 30 have elapsed. If they look cooked then, experiment by pushing one dish slightly with your finger. If the contents quake, they're not quite ready.

For Cauliflower soufflés

Use one small head of cauliflower. Cut into small sprigs and cook in minimal water till tender. Purée with a little of the cooking water or milk and use less than ¼ pt (150 ml) of milk, for the white sauce. Beat in the purée while the sauce is hot. Sprinkling the tops of these soufflés with grated cheese is a wise precaution, as the cauliflower mixture tends to lack stamina and may collapse.

For Fennel soufflés

Use 1 lb (450 g) of fennel. Keep the nice bits of green and chop them finely. Trim and slice the heads and simmer in a little water with a knob of butter and a squeeze of lemon juice. Mash very well or purée, with its liquid, of which there should be very little. Fold this into the sauce with the chopped green leaves and 1 tablespoon of Pernod.

For Sweet Pepper soufflés

Slice 2 large red peppers and ½ a medium onion. Cook gently in 2 teaspoons oil till very soft. Rub through a sieve with the back of a ladle. Don't add extra liquid to this purée: this type of soufflé tends to sink anyway, but it is worth making for its brilliant colour and fresh summery taste.

For Spinach soufflés

Wash 1½ lb (675 g) of spinach. Put in a pan without added water. Cook till the leaves have wilted and the juices have run. Drain very well, chop finely, and add to the sauce. If you prefer, liquidise the spinach with some of the cooking liquid, and use less than ¼ pt (150 ml) milk for the sauce, but be sure to beat the purée into the sauce while it is hot or it will be very stiff to work. Season with nutmeg and freshly ground pepper.

While on the subject of soufflés, here is a related recipe.

Spinach Soufflé Flan

You could of course use any soufflé mixture to fill a pastry case, but this filling is less rich, though more collapsible.

For the pastry:
6 oz (175 g) wholewheat flour
5 tablespoons sunflower oil
2 oz (50 g) strong grated cheese
water to mix

For the filling:
1 lb (450 g) fresh spinach *or*
    1 × 12 oz (340 g) tin
½ oz (15 g) butter
½ oz (15 g) flour
salt
nutmeg or coriander
2 eggs
(1 tablespoon grated
    cheese—optional)

Preheat the oven to 200°C/400°F.
For the pastry:
Mix all the ingredients, using just enough water to make a firm dough. Roll out carefully. It will break up, but press it bit by bit into an 8-inch (20 cm) flan ring placed on a baking sheet. Bake blind till just firm, about 20 minutes. Remove from the oven, cool slightly, and carefully lift off the flan ring. If the pastry starts breaking, leave the ring on—it will look inelegant, but at least the filling won't escape.
For the filling:
If using fresh spinach, wash well, shake off excess water, and cook till wilted. Drain well, reserving the liquid, and chop the leaves. For tinned spinach, drain and keep the juice.

Make a roux with the butter and flour. When it turns pale, add spinach juice cautiously to make a very thick sauce. Put this in a wide bowl with the chopped spinach and beaten egg yolks. Mix well and season.

Whisk the egg whites very stiff and fold lightly into the spinach mixture. Turn this gently into the prepared flan case (it can mound up in the middle, but if it slops over the edges, take a bit out and cook it separately in a greased dish).

Scatter the grated cheese on top, and return to the oven for about 30 minutes. Look in cautiously and touch the centre at that point—if it is liquid underneath give it another five minutes.

Stuffed Vegetables

Stuffed vegetables are delicious either as a starter or a main course but they do tend to look awful. Their original bright colours are subdued to dingy shades of khaki and brown; they exude puddles of watery juice on the plate; they break up on serving and disembowel themselves slowly on the diners' plates or in extreme cases into their laps. There isn't really all that much to be done about this: a smothering of chopped parsley is the best policy, but I often don't have any because our heavy dog sunbathes in the parsley patch.

If you are serving these dishes as a main course, a sauce made with the juices and a roux of flour and butter will improve the appearance and make more of a meal. Make your sauce, taste, and season with what you fancy—white wine, lemon juice, tomato purée, grated cheese, etc. Don't let the flavouring overpower the stuffing, though. I don't advise over-enthusiastic applications of Worcester sauce, curry powder or French mustard, for example.

Apple-stuffed Mushrooms

If possible, choose large mushrooms 2 inches (5 cm) or more in diameter for this dish. You will need about 12 of that size for this quantity of stuffing. You can use smaller ones but they are more fiddly to deal with.

15 large mushrooms or	2 large tart eating apples
¾ lb (350 g) small ones	salt and freshly ground pepper
1 medium onion	thyme, marjoram and parsley to taste
4 oz (100 g) butter	½ glass white wine

Take the stems out of the mushrooms and chop them finely with three of the large caps or 2 oz (50 g) of the smaller mushrooms. Lay the whole caps close together in one layer in an ovenproof dish.

Chop the onion fairly finely and cook it gently till it softens in 3 oz (75 g) of the butter.

Grate the apples, skin and all, and add to the onion along with the chopped mushrooms. Add seasoning and herbs to taste.

Divide this mixture between the mushroom caps, pressing it down with a finger. Melt the rest of the butter and dribble this over the mushrooms. Pour the white wine into the dish.

Bake the mushrooms, uncovered, in a moderate oven for 15 minutes. When you dish them, spoon over any juice: the mushrooms will re-absorb it.

263

Stuffed Peppers

A very similar stuffing to the last one makes an unusual and unstodgy complement to peppers. The most attractive effect is achieved by using peppers of different colours, red, green, and yellow.

    1 tablespoon olive oil
    6 smallish peppers
    1 medium onion
    3 oz (75 g) butter
    6 oz (175 g) mushrooms
    2 tart eating apples
    1 tablespoon almond kernels
    salt and ground black pepper
    thyme and parsley
    lemon juice

Put the olive oil in a casserole in which the peppers can sit upright close together. Cut off the tops of the peppers, but keep them. Discard the seeds. Trim the bases if they are too knobbly to stand, but try not to make holes. Put the peppers in the casserole.

Chop the onions and fry in the butter till golden. Chop the mushrooms, grate the apples, skin and all, and chop the almonds coarsely: blanch them or not, as you please. Add all these ingredients to the onions. Season to taste. If the mixture is too sweet, add lemon juice, but you may not need it.

Fill this stuffing into the peppers. Replace the tops and put about two tablespoons of water in the casserole. Cover with a lid or foil and bake in a moderate oven for about 40 minutes. Check once or twice to make sure there is still a little liquid in the base of the dish.

These peppers are best accompanied by a sauce. I make about half a pint (275 ml) of thick white sauce and add 2 oz (50 g) grated cheese and the pan juices. If there isn't much juice, make a thinner sauce and add a good squeeze of lemon or a tablespoon of dry vermouth.

Sesame-stuffed Aubergines

Not everyone likes aubergines. Perhaps it is their funereal colour. When dealing with them, there are three points to remember.

(1) If not salted and drained first they can be bitter, and are indefinably unpleasant in texture.

(2) They will drink as much oil as you give them at once—gallons of it—and then you will get indigestion: so add it bit by bit, as sparingly as possible.

(3) Undercooked aubergines are repulsive.

Properly treated, they are superb, particularly in spicy dishes. This one was invented to use up a large bag of sesame seeds, but the combination is so good I now use it often—see another example in the section on cereals and vegetable side dishes (p. 313).

3 medium aubergines	¼ pt (150 ml) yoghurt
1 tablespoon coriander seeds	2 medium onions, roughly chopped
1 teaspoon black peppercorns	1 clove garlic
2 teaspoons paprika	a few sprigs of mint
a large pinch of asafoetida	juice of half a lemon
2 oz (50 g) butter	
2 tablespoons unhulled sesame seeds	

Slice the aubergines in half lengthwise. Scoop out the flesh, leaving the skin intact. Chop the flesh roughly. Salt the chopped aubergine and put it in a colander. Salt the skin cases on the inside, and turn them hollow side down on top of the contents of the colander. Allow the whole lot to drain for 45 minutes, then wash it in cold water and pat it dry in a tea-towel.

Grind the coriander and pepper and set aside.

Put the yoghurt, lemon juice, onions, garlic and mint in a liquidiser and reduce to a paste. If you haven't a liquidiser, grate the onion and chop the mint finely, crush the garlic, and mix these into the yoghurt with the lemon juice.

Get the butter very hot. Fry the coriander, pepper, paprika and asafoetida for half a minute. Add the sesame seed and the chopped aubergine and stir well. Pour in the yoghurt mixture. Lower the heat and cook gently, uncovered, till the aubergine is fairly soft—about 10 minutes. Arrange the scooped-out aubergine shells in a shallow oven-proof dish, keeping them close together to support each other. Fill with the cooked mixture. Sprinkle with sesame oil or dot with butter, and bake for about 40 minutes in a moderately hot oven. If they look like drying up, reduce the heat and pour a tablespoon or so of water into the dish.

Spicy Stuffed Tomatoes

The stuffing is really just a very thick dahl. For the spices, consult any recipe for garam masala, or make up your own, but don't use ready ground spices.

Suggested combinations: coriander, cumin, cinnamon, cloves.
coriander, cumin, cardamoms, bay leaf.
coriander, kalonji, cinnamon, asafoetida.

Add a fresh chilli to the lentils if you want it to be hot.

6 large tomatoes
1-inch (2.5 cm) piece of tamarind
  pulp *or* juice of 1 lemon
2 oz (50 g) red lentils
1 small onion
2 cloves garlic
1 oz (25 g) butter
1 dessertspoon of freshly ground
  spices
1 tablespoon chopped parsley or
  mint
salt

Cut lids off the tomatoes and scoop out the seeds. Set them close together in a greased ovenproof dish or 6 ramekins. Soak the tamarind in half a cup of hot water and strain this through a sieve, or squeeze the lemon. Simmer the lentils for ¾ hour with twice their volume of water and the tamarind or lemon juice. Check now and again to forestall sticking.

Grate the onion and crush the garlic. Fry in the butter till browning. Add the spices and fry for one more minute.

When the lentils are soft and have absorbed the water, mix them with the spices and onions and the fresh herbs. Salt to taste. Stuff the tomatoes with this mixture and bake uncovered in a moderate oven for 10 to 15 minutes.

Other Vegetable Appetisers

I have chosen these because they are attractive to look at—important for a first course—and also easy to prepare. Except for the mushroom dish, they don't need last minute attention, but don't keep them standing once cooked: most cooked vegetables weep and you will find them looking distinctly depressed if they are kept warm for more than five minutes.

Aubergine Pizza

For the base:
2 large aubergines (about 1½ lb)
    (675 g)
For the topping:
3 tablespoons olive oil
1 medium onion
3 cloves garlic
2 lb (900 g) tomatoes
1 teaspoon dried oregano or basil,
    or a mixture
3 oz (75 g) grated cheddar or other
    tasty cheese
salt
10 black olives

Slice the aubergines into rings a bit less than ½-inch (1.25 cm) thick. Put the slices in a colander, salt them liberally and leave to drain for 45 minutes.

Chop the onion and garlic fairly fine. Fry gently in the hot oil till they soften slightly. Add the tomatoes cut in half and the herbs. Simmer till the onion is very soft—about 20 minutes. If the mixture looks watery, raise the heat and boil till it thickens.

Press this mixture through a sieve if you want a dressier dish. Add 2 oz (50 g) of the cheese and salt to taste. Now turn the aubergines into a basin of cold water to rinse off the salt. Dry them thoroughly in a tea-towel. Oil a pizza plate very well. (If you don't have one, any large shallow ovenproof dish will do: my favourite is a huge cast iron gratin dish.) Lay the aubergines all over the bottom, close together or overlapping. Pour the topping on and scatter the remaining cheese over and decorate with the olives. Bake in a moderately hot oven for 20–30 minutes. To test for readiness, poke a knife into the centre: if there is no resistance, the aubergine is cooked.

267

Courgettes with Cheese

It goes without saying that this is best made with very young fresh
courgettes. It can also be adapted as an accompanying vegetable
dish—in which case use 1 lb (450 g) of courgettes and ¾ pt (425 ml)
milk and omit the cream.

½ lb (225 g) courgettes	¼ pt (150 ml) cream
1 small onion	½ pt (275 ml) milk
½ oz (15 g) butter	salt, pepper and nutmeg
1 whole egg + 2 yolks	3 oz (75 g) grated cheese.

Slice the courgettes thinly—about ¼ inch (6 mm) thick. Drop the slices
into a pan of boiling water and simmer till just tender. This will take
from one to three minutes depending on the age of the courgettes.
Drain them well.

Chop the onion finely and fry till soft in the butter.

Butter 6 small ramekins or a two-pint (1.2 litre) ovenproof dish. Put
the onion in at the bottom and the courgettes on top.

Beat the remaining ingredients together and pour over the courgettes. Stir while you are doing this or the cheese will be unevenly
distributed.

Bake in a moderately hot oven till just set and brown on top—about
15 minutes for the small dishes and 25 minutes for the large.

Carrot Cake

This is bastard oriental. It looks very attractive and tastes a lot better
than the list of ingredients might lead you to expect.

    2 large carrots (about ¾ lb)
    20 cardamoms
    2 teaspoons oil—sesame oil is best
       with carrots
    salt
    1 tablespoon raisins
    1 large leek

Grate the carrot and fry in the oil. Add the black seeds scraped out of
the cardamoms—discard the husks. When the carrot is golden add a
tablespoon of water and continue cooking while this evaporates. Add
salt.

Butter a 7-inch (17.5 cm) sandwich tin, preferably non-stick. Scatter the raisins on the bottom, then the carrot mixture. Cut the leek into narrow rings, wash to remove grit, drain, and press the leek down on top of the carrot. Cover with a greased paper. Bakewell rounds are great for the purpose.

Cook for 15 minutes in a moderately hot oven. Remove from the oven, press down on the paper, and allow the tin to stand for 5 minutes. Remove the paper, run a knife round the edge of the tin, and turn out on a plate.

Curd Cheese Ramekins

Here's the humble carrot again, but you will find it difficult to detect. The curd cheese is made with drained yoghurt—for details see p. 369.

For the base:
6 oz (175 g) curd cheese
3 oz (75 g) wholemeal
 breadcrumbs
3 oz (75 g) cheddar cheese, grated
1 medium carrot
1 small onion
2 oz (50 g) mushrooms
1 tablespoon parsley
1 tablespoon double cream
1 egg
milk to mix
salt and pepper

For the sauce:
½ pt (275 ml) milk
1 small onion
1 teaspoon dried thyme
1 oz (25 g) butter
1 oz (25 g) flour
salt

For the base:
Grate the carrot and chop the onion, mushrooms and parsley. Mix all the ingredients together, but reserve 1 oz (25 g) each of the breadcrumbs and grated cheese. Use only enough milk to produce a thick paste. Butter 6 small ramekins or a two-pint (1.2 litre) ovenproof dish, and spread the curd mixture in the bottom.

For the sauce:
Heat the milk gently for 15 minutes, with the sliced onion and thyme. Strain the milk and use it to make a white sauce with the remaining ingredients. Pour this over the curd mixture and sprinkle on the rest of the crumbs and cheese. Make sure the dishes have at least ½ inch (1.25 cm) spare room at the top or they will bubble over. Bake in a moderate oven for 25–30 minutes.

Gougère of Mushrooms and Peppers

A classic gougère is made with a choux paste incorporating small chunks of gruyère cheese. As I can't get gruyère cheese and don't like it anyway, I use grated cheddar. We get majestic aged whole farmhouse cheeses weighing a portly half hundredweight, of a character and substance far exceeding any flighty continental, so I use cheddar for practically every cheesey purpose. Indeed, I would be afraid to use anything else, with one of these enthroned on its trestle eyeing me sternly from the pantry. I need hardly say that there is no point at all in using grated orange plastic from the supermarket.

Gougère is quite a dressy dish, well worth mastering. You can vary it by omitting the cheese or using different fillings, but whatever you put in the middle should be piquantly seasoned and not too watery. Certain vegetables are worth avoiding in this context. Gougère of cabbage and turnip?

For the pastry:
3¾ oz (100 g) plain flour
3 oz (80 g) butter
7½ fl oz (200 ml) water
3 well beaten eggs
1½ oz (40 g) grated cheese

For the filling:
1 tablespoon oil
1 medium onion
1 clove garlic
2 medium red peppers
2 teaspoons tomato purée
2 teaspoons fresh chopped marjoram, or ½ teaspoon dried
2 teaspoons fresh chopped parsley
½ lb (225 g) mushrooms
salt and a pinch of sugar

Preheat the oven to 190°C/375°F.
For the pastry:
Sift the flour on to a sheet of paper.

Cut the butter into chunks and place in a wide pan with the water, over a medium heat. When the butter melts, turn up the heat so that the mixture boils up. Remove from the heat immediately and tip in the flour all at once. Beat hard till the mixture leaves the sides of the pan. Beat in the eggs bit by bit—if they are large, you will probably need only about 2½. The paste should be soft, but hold its shape. Lastly beat in the grated cheese.

Grease an 8-inch (20 cm) diameter baking dish and arrange the paste in spoonfuls evenly round the edge. It puffs up enormously so don't be alarmed at how meagre it looks. Place in the middle of the oven and when the pastry has puffed up but not darkened (about 25 minutes) raise the heat to 205°C/400°F and give it a further 10 minutes. It should be light, crisp and golden brown.

For the filling:

Chop up the onion finely and sauté in the hot oil till tender. Add the pepper, finely sliced, and the crushed garlic. Turn these in the oil, cover, and cook on a very low heat for 10 minutes. Slice the mushrooms, stalks and all. Put them with all the remaining ingredients in the pan and mix well. If no juice formed round the stewing pepper and onion, you will need to add two tablespoons of water. Cover the pan again and remove from the heat: the mushrooms and herbs should not be overcooked.

When the gougère is ready to come out of the oven, heat up the filling quickly on a high heat, take out the gougère, and pour the filling into the hole in the centre. Serve at once if possible, but you can return it to the turned-off oven for 5 minutes if necessary.

Pepper Fritters with Tomato Granita

Tomato ice is a delicious surprise with hot vegetable fritters. The combination is agonising for those with sensitive teeth.

  1 quantity tomato granita *(see
  recipe for Avocado with tomato
  granita on p. 41)*
  1 red and 1 green pepper
  4 oz (100 g) plain flour
  1 egg, separated
  ¼ pt (150 ml) milk
  ½ teaspoon salt
  fat for deep frying

Sift the flour and salt, and mix in the egg yolk and milk till smooth. Beat well and set aside. Slice the peppers into long strips not more than ½ inch (1.25 cm) wide. Heat the fat to the correct temperature—about 205°C/400°F.

Whisk the egg white stiffly and fold into the fritter batter, then put the pepper strips into the bowl. Fry them in batches till golden and drain on kitchen paper. While they are cooking, dish a scoop of the granita on to cold plates. Arrange the fritters round the granita and serve at once, before they go cold or soggy.

Devilled Mushrooms

I call these "devilled mushrooms" for want of a better name, but the dish is not exceptionally spicy. The main flavouring is actually mint. I have an embarrassment of this herb. It is one of the few that grow enthusiastically here, and I feel obliged to use it frequently. It is extremely good with mushrooms. Mushroom Humbug, perhaps.

For the mushrooms:
2 oz (50 g) butter
1 small onion
¾ lb (350 g) mushrooms
2 cloves garlic
1-inch (2.5 cm) piece of fresh
    ginger (optional)
1 tablespoon chopped mint
1 teaspoon brown sugar
juice of half a lemon
salt, black pepper and nutmeg
1–2 teaspoons flour
3 tablespoons cream

For the topping:
1 oz (25 g) butter
1 clove garlic
2 tablespoons brown breadcrumbs
chilli powder or cayenne pepper

Chop the onion finely and sauté in the butter. Chop the mushroom stems and a few of the caps, crush the garlic, and grate the ginger. When the onion is tender, add all these ingredients and fry together over a medium heat for two minutes.

Add the mint, sugar, lemon juice and other seasonings, and stir till the lemon juice is absorbed. Sprinkle in the flour and cook a further minute—you may need a little more butter.

Add the cream, and let the mixture just bubble. Remove from the heat. You can do this much up to half an hour ahead.

Now prepare the topping. Crush the garlic and fry it with the breadcrumbs and butter till crisp. Add chilli cautiously to the strength you like. You can do this ahead, too.

To serve, stir the reserved mushroom caps into the mushroom sauce and reheat quickly, but without boiling. Dish into individual hot bowls or plates and sprinkle on the spiced breadcrumbs.

Fish

We are lucky in being able to obtain a reasonable variety of fresh fish locally, though usually only two or three types are available in any one week. Where possible I favour large energetic fish, as they are usually clouted on the head when hauled inboard to stop them wreaking havoc with the gear, and so suffer a less miserable end than the smaller creatures left to flap and suffocate.

Most popular with guests is salmon. Islanders, on the whole, think little of it, after the first few summer meals. They cram their freezers with it, to assuage the longings of visiting winter relatives. They feed it to dogs and hens and stuff it into sandwiches for their bed and breakfast visitors' late night snack. In the old days they used to salt it, and nowadays some people have some smoked at MacDonald's excellent smokehouse in Stornoway (no relation of the hamburgers).

While the populace at large are turning green at the sight of salmon, the Barbour-bedecked and fly-festooned rod fishermen eagerly flog loch and river for the first bite of the season. Their fish may cost them £500 a whack. They must be crazy. Also cruel: would they like to spend their last half hour being dragged along by a hook through the cheek or nostril? I prefer salmon to be netted, as they then drown quite quickly. Monofilament nets are atrocious, though, as they maim and kill not only their intended catch, but also otters, seals, and seabirds in vast numbers.

The next three recipes are for **halibut**. I think this is the best of all fish, firm-fleshed and clean-tasting. If, like me, you get your fish whole and are then faced with gutting, filleting and skinning, it is the easiest of all to deal with. It is not slimy, or oily. Its skin doesn't tear, its guts don't stink, and its bones don't jab you. There is very little wasted of the body weight, and the pressure-cooked head makes a delicious breakfast for hens. It is an inoffensive creature in life and death, a peaceful bottom-feeder relying on camouflage to induce the world to pass it by. Unlike the sad-faced whiting, it does not conceal a gulletful of its smaller fellows. In recent years my respectful affection for the halibut has come in the way of my taste for its flesh, but I can still vouch for the excellence of these three recipes.

Halibut with Mushrooms

This is delicious with new potatoes. It is good cold as the basis for a salad, too. If the cream you are going to use is fresh and unadulterated and the halibut likewise, you will not need flour in the sauce, as it will set to a delicious curd anyway. Our cream rarely lives up to our fish, so I usually add the flour, reluctantly. It tastes better without. Do not overcook this dish—halibut is not at all disgusting even a bit on the raw side.

1½–2 lb (675–900 g) piece of
   halibut on the bone
6 oz (175 g) mushrooms
1 small onion
1 oz (25 g) butter
½ teaspoon each dried thyme and
   tarragon

1 teaspoon flour (optional)
2 teaspoons tomato purée
4 tablespoons double cream
salt and pepper

Cut the fish into steaks about ¾-inch (2 cm) thick, or skin and fillet it and cut into even-sized portions.

Chop the onion finely and sauté in the butter till transparent. Chop the mushroom stalks finely, break the caps into three or four pieces, and stir into the onion mixture till the fat is absorbed.

Add the flour if you are going to use it and then all the remaining ingredients. Spread half this mixture on the bottom of an ovenproof dish of a size to take the fish in a single close-packed layer. Spread the rest of the mushroom mix on top of the fish and bake in a moderate oven for 15–20 minutes.

Halibut in Tomato Cream

1½–2 lb (675–900 g) piece of halibut
1½ lb (675 g) ripe tomatoes
1 small onion
½ teaspoon dried tarragon or basil
1-inch (2.5 cm) strip orange or lemon peel

¼ pt (150 ml) double cream
salt
chopped parsley or slices of raw tomato for garnish

Cut up the fish as for the preceding recipe. This dish looks more attractive if the dark skin at least is removed.

Chop the onion finely and cut the tomatoes in half. Put these ingredients in a wide pan with the herbs and peel. Prod this about over a high heat till the juice runs from the tomatoes, then lower to a simmer and cook for 10 minutes. If is sticks, add a little water—don't let it darken, which tomatoes do if they dry out.

Press this mixture through a sieve. Add the cream, and salt to taste. Lay the pieces of fish in a shallow dish and pour the sauce over. Bake uncovered in a very moderate oven for 20–25 minutes. Don't let the edges brown; the sauce should keep its clear colour. Decorate with chopped parsley or the tomato slices.

Halibut with Herbs and Lemon

This is a very easy and delicious way of baking any sort of white fish.

1½–2 lb (675–900 g) piece of halibut
juice of 1 lemon and grated rind of ½ lemon
¼ pt (150 ml) double cream + 2 tablespoons top of the milk

salt
1 tablespoon chopped parsley
1 tablespoon snipped chives
1 tablespoon any other mixed fresh herbs—dill, chervil, thyme, tarragon

Cut up the fish as in the preceding recipes. Mix all the ingredients for the sauce together and pour over the fish. Bake uncovered in a very moderate oven for 20–25 minutes. The sauce will probably curdle even at a low heat but it is still very good.

Turbot with Dill Sauce

Turbot is highly esteemed by most discriminating persons including our dog, but I don't like dealing with it. In its whole state it is too rhomboidal for any vessel but a turbotière, an extravagant and unstoreable piece of equipment. If you cut it up, it blunts your knives, breaks your scissors, and smears you with irritant and irremovable slime. It wears pathetic knobbly camouflage on its dark side, and its face is understandably one of failure and sadness. But for all that it is a delicacy, with its rich creamy flesh, so I give one recipe here.

2 lb (900 g) turbot fillet
For the sauce:
4 egg yolks
1 teaspoon vinegar
8 oz (225 g) unsalted butter
juice of half an orange
finely grated rind of 1 orange

6 green olives
1 teaspoon capers
2 tablespoons dill
2 teaspoons snipped chives
For the garnish:
1 orange

Fillet the turbot and cut into serving pieces. Leave the skin on, and lay skin down on a buttered trivet or baking dish. Steam, or bake in a moderate oven covered with buttered greaseproof paper. It will only take about 10 minutes. It remains very firm but turns opaque when cooked.

For the sauce:

Start as for a hollandaise sauce. Put the egg yolks in a bowl or double boiler with the vinegar and a small lump of the butter, which should be very soft. Set the bowl over (*not* in) a pan of steaming water and stir constantly while you add the rest of the butter bit by bit. If you are lazy and reckless, put the butter in by halves. Beat away at the first half till it has melted, then do the same with the other half. By then it should be thick and lukewarm, no hotter or it will curdle.

Chop the olives, capers and dill, snip the chives, grate the orange rind and squeeze the juice. Add all these to the sauce and taste for salt. Keep the sauce just warm—no more.

For the garnish:

Slice the orange into very thin slices through the middle.

Dish the turbot, pour the sauce over, decorate with the orange slices and serve at once.

Mackerel are the subject of the next two recipes.

People suspect that mackerel are cheap, if not free. It is therefore impossible to serve them to our hotel guests without causing sulks. This is a pity, because fresh mackerel is unbeatable. They are oily so should be spiked with some sharply aromatic flavour. The following method made a virtue of necessity when a friend and I were barbecuing freshly caught fish on a remote beach. Investigating the hillside for thyme or juniper, we found none, but smelt bog-myrtle. We suspected it might be poisonous, but stuffed the bellies of the fish with it anyway. It was delicious. Bog-myrtle won't grow in your garden, but it can be gathered and dried like bay.

Kill the mackerel as soon as you take them off the hook. It is in your interest as well as theirs. Comparisons in our fish-catching days showed that our fish (instantly despatched) always tasted better than friends' fish caught at the same time and left to suffocate. The latter had an indescribable off-taste, slightly metallic, not quite clean, even in a very fresh fish. Presumably the chemicals produced by stress cause the change. It is well known that the production of adrenalin in warm-blooded animals just before slaughter affects the quality of the meat. Depraved tastes prefer this tortured flesh: Rouennais ducklings are smothered and dogs in the Philippines and South Korea are slowly strangled to lend a fiendish goût to the meat.

Grilled Mackerel

To more cheerful matters. Do thus with your cleanly killed mackerel.

6 mackerel (about 12 oz (350 g)
 each)
½ oz (15 g) butter per fish
3 sprigs bog-myrtle per fish (or use
 thyme instead)

Gut the fish and remove the heads. Make 3 diagonal slashes about ½ inch (1.25 cm) deep on each side. Put a flake of butter in each cut, and the remainder into the cavity with the bog-myrtle.

Grill at medium heat for about 7 minutes each side. If you are doubtful about doneness, poke a sharp knife between flesh and spine at the thickest part. If it doesn't come away easily, grill for a few minutes longer.

Pour the pan-juices over the fish and serve with lemon and mustard separately.

Smoked Mackerel Salad

This will serve six as a starter, or two to three as a lunch dish with a green salad. A sweetish brown bread is good with this.

For the salad:
2 large fillets of smoked mackerel
2 sticks celery
1 eating apple
½ small onion
For the dressing:
2 tablespoons mayonnaise *(for a recipe, see p. 72)*
2 teaspoons French mustard, preferably Dijon
3 tablespoons yoghurt
cayenne pepper and freshly ground black pepper
For the garnish:
parsley and lemon slices

To take the mackerel off the skin, hold the tail end under your left hand, and slice from the other end, slanting each cut to the right and twisting the blade flat as you reach the skin. Cut across into ½-inch (1.25 cm) slices. Slice the celery and apple thinly and chop the onion finely. Mix all these in a bowl.

For the dressing:

Combine all the ingredients in a separate bowl. If it is too bland, add lemon juice and more cayenne pepper. It should be quite sharp and tingling. Mix salad and dressing just before serving and decorate with parsley and lemon slices.

Haddock Mousse

This cold dish—rather solid for a mousse really—is suitable for a salad lunch or supper, or for a starter. If it is set in a fish-shaped mould, you can have great fun decorating it. Use strips of pimento for a sad fishy mouth, capers for eyes, and thin half slices of cucumber for scales, with a scattering of paprika on the back. Surround your masterpiece with lettuce leaves, tomato slices and fronds of dill. This is the best fun since making tri-coloured jelly at the age of five.

The recipe also works well with salmon, smoked salmon and smoked haddock.

For the mousse:
¾ lb (350 g) haddock fillet *or* 1½
    lb (675 g) whole fish
½ pt (275 ml) milk
½ bay leaf or a blade of mace
2 teaspoons gelatine + 2
    tablespoons water
1 oz (25 g) butter
1 oz (25 g) flour
any or all of the following:
    2 teaspoons lemon juice
    a dash of tabasco
    a tablespoon of finely chopped
      parsley
about half a small carton of double
    cream

For the garnish:
any salad things or fresh herbs
tomato-flavoured mayonnaise
    (optional)

Gut the fish if whole. Poach gently in the milk with the bay leaf and mace. It will take about 10–15 minutes, either in a very moderate oven or on the stove top. Cool slightly, remove all skin and bone, and crush the flesh. You can either chop it very finely, or put it briefly in a liquidiser with the minimum necessary of the cooking liquor.

Make a white sauce with the butter, flour and the remaining liquor from the fish. You may need a bit more or less milk—it shouldn't be runny, but should still fall from the spoon easily. Turn it into a wide bowl and add the chopped fish.

Soften the gelatine in the cold water and dissolve over gentle heat. If it boils it won't work properly.

Add the gelatine to the fish mixture together with the chosen flavourings, and salt to taste. Put aside to cool, stirring occasionally or it will set round the edges. If you are in a hurry, put the bowl in the freezer or in a basin of iced water. Whip the cream till it just holds its shape. When the mixture in the bowl is cold and setting, fold in the cream. Turn it into a dampened mould to set.

To serve, dip the mould very briefly (try 3 seconds) in very hot water. Loosen the mousse by pressing a finger over the top of it till it pulls away from the edges of the mould. Turn it on to a plate and decorate attractively. You can serve tomato mayonaise separately.

To make tomato mayonnaise, add two tablespoons of thin cream, two teaspoons of tomato purée and a few drops of tabasco to ¼ pint (150 ml) of bland mayonnaise (there is a recipe for mayonnaise on p. 72). This sauce does nothing at all for the smoked fish mousse or for salmon, but is good with haddock.

Turnover of Sole

This sounds like a lot of work, but it is actually not much trouble, as long as you have something else to keep you busy while the pastry is chilling, the stock brewing, and the sauce cooling.

If you had a fine Dover sole, you would not waste it on this dish, but it is a good way of using undistinguished flatfish such as lemon sole, megrims or witch. Years ago I used to use frozen puff pastry, and everyone thought it was a triumph. Now I always make my own and great lumps of it are left. Nevertheless, I continue to believe that even the roughest of homemade pastry is more wholesome than anything out of a shop freezer. If you like the taste of anti-oxidants and are addicted to glucose syrup, by all means use the packet stuff. Or try plasticine instead.

For the pastry:
9 oz (250 g) plain flour
a pinch of salt
5 oz (150 g) butter, straight from
    the fridge
ice-cold water
beaten egg to glaze

For the filling:
3–4 lb (1.4–1.8 kg) whole flatfish
    or 1¼ lb (550 g) fillets
1 bay leaf
1 small onion
1 small glass white wine
¼ pt (150 ml) milk, or more
1 oz (25 g) butter
1½ oz (40 g) flour
2 tablespoons cream
½ teaspoon dried tarragon or
    1 tablespoon chopped parsley
salt and pepper

For the pastry:

Mix the flour and salt in a wide bowl. Cut the butter into chunks (roughly ½-inch (1.25 cm) cubes) and drop into the flour. Add enough cold water to make a pliant dough, softer than shortcrust but not as soft as scones.

Knead out lightly into an oblong on a well-floured board. *Roll out to about ¼ inch (6 mm) thick, keeping everything well floured. Mark the oblong into thirds across its long dimension. Fold the right flap over the middle section and the left flap over that. Turn it so that the right-hand edge is facing you.*

Repeat the section between asterisks twice more. If your kitchen is hot, you may need to chill the pastry between operations, but this is only a distant and slovenly relation of puff pastry, so don't get too worked up about it. However, once the rolling is all finished, you are best to chill the pastry for at least half an hour.

For the filling:

If you start with whole fish, fillet them, and if you are fussy remove at least the dark skins. If you are leaving the skins on, do scale the fish before you start. Put all the trimmings in a wide pan with the onion, bay leaf, wine and ¼ pt (150 ml) of water. Leave the lid slightly off, and boil on a high heat for 5 minutes. Cover the pan, remove from the heat, and leave to sit till you are ready for it.

If you are using fillets, chop the onion, and infuse it with the bay leaf in the milk for 10 minutes over gentle heat, then strain.

Melt the butter, stir in the flour, and when it turns pale, add the milk. Beat till smooth. Add the strained fish liquor if you have it, or the wine if you started with fillets. If the sauce is still very thick, add more milk. Add the herbs and seasonings and simmer for 2 minutes. Fold in the cream and cool.

Cut the pastry in half and roll out into 2 oblongs about ⅛ inch (3 mm) thick. (One turnover would be too difficult to lift off the tray.) Place the sheets of pastry at opposite ends of a baking sheet, with one half of each piece hanging over the end of the tray. Brush the edges of the sections on the tray with beaten egg.

Lay the fish on the pastry, leaving the eggy margins free. Make a slight dent in the fish to keep the sauce in. Pour the sauce on, and immediately flop the pastry over and press down round the edges. Do this with one turnover at a time, or the sauce will escape.

Brush the tops and edges with beaten egg: be careful if your sauce was still warm, as the pastry will then tear easily. If it does, grit your teeth and patch up with scraps from the edges glued with egg.

If you aren't the sort of person who suffers from tearing pastry and leaking sauce, display your perfections by decorating the turnovers prettily with leaves or fish. If you are really talented, you can even fold your pastry to form a fish, and give it fins and eyes. I did that once and was most impressed by my own genius, till I discovered I had forgotten to put the sauce in.

Bake in a hot oven for about 20 minutes, till a rich golden brown.

Salmon

The wild salmon has an instinctive migratory urge which takes it on a sea journey of up to four years and five thousand miles, before it returns to its native river to breed. It is this free-swimming migrating stock which produces the fish crammed lifelong into pens along the Highland coastline. For that reason, do not buy farmed salmon any more than you would cage a swallow. Don't be fooled by such optimisms as "fresh" or "Scottish": if it is not labelled "wild" it is almost certainly farmed. This applies to the smoked article as well.

In spite of the enthusiastic assurances of marketing, farmed fish tastes bland, sweetish and subtly disgusting to anyone who is used to the wild salmon; you would do well to avoid it for that reason alone.

Good salmon is best when cooked gently and minimally in its own juices. Don't handle it more than necessary, but do scrape all the blood away from the backbone inside the cavity. If you are cooking a whole fish or large piece, you don't need to scale it, but if the piece is less than 2 lb (900 g), you had better scrape off the scales, as they will wander onto the cut surface of the fish.

Either steam the fish on a trivet, or wrap it in kitchen foil (not too tightly) and cook it in simmering water or in the oven. Forget the seasonings, the butter and the court bouillon: a fresh wild fish has no need of these adornments.

Cooking times for these methods are as follows, or at least I hope so. I quite often get it wrong: you might do better to consult another book at this point.

Steaming, or simmering in foil:

    1–3 lb (450 g–1.4 kg)   15–25 minutes

    3–5 lb (1.4–2.3 kg)   25–40 minutes

    5–10 lb (2.3–4.5 kg)   40 minutes–1 hour

Baking in foil:

    1–3 lb (450 g–1.4 kg)   30–45 minutes

    3–5 lb (1.4–2.3 kg)   45 minutes–1 hour

    5–10 lb (2.3–4.5 kg)   1–2 hours

The usual sauces for salmon are hollandaise if it is hot or mayonnaise if it is cold. Nothing could be better than these, along with plenty of new potatoes. However, if the weather is close, or the rest of the meal elaborate, I strongly recommend dispensing with a sauce and accompanying the fish, hot or cold, with a separate bowl of Raita, a refreshing preparation familiar from Indian restaurants.

Raita

½ a cucumber
½ pt (275 ml) yoghurt
1 teaspoon chopped mint
salt, paprika

Chop the cucumber coarsely. I prefer to leave the skin on for colour and taste. Mix in the yoghurt, mint and salt, and sprinkle the top with paprika.

Don't combine the ingredients until just before serving, or it will go watery.

Shellfish

The world is divided into people who adore shellfish and people who are allergic to them. Often one of the first group is married to one of the second. This makes for awkwardness in the planning of set dinner menus. "1 no shellfish" is scribbled by the name of many couples in our bookings register. When other names on the same night bear such legends as "no game", "hates cheese", "avoid citrus", "no tomatoes", etc., the atmosphere in the kitchen is bad and the language foul. Allergies are something of a growth-industry at present. They are particularly popular with well-to-do women. In America even men have them: I find this somehow rather shocking, like my discovery that Marks and Spencers now stock pale pink Y-fronts.

Some people have genuine and very serious allergies, of course, like our black Labrador, Jet. He comes out in enormous lumps if he takes aspirin. If you can imagine a cross between a warthog and a black pudding, you will picture the horror of the effect. The first time it happened, he reduced a perky collie to a quaking wreck simply by staring through his car window.

But to return to shellfish. We can obtain them very fresh from local boats, though every year there are ominous rumours of further decline in stocks, and small inshore boats are pushed out by predators from East and South. But as long as there is still a catch to cook, our concern is to kill it by the most humane method for the particular species.

We freeze scallops whole. Bivalves are less likely than crustaceans to feel pain, but give them the benefit of the doubt. Heat penetration takes quite a long time to kill something as large as a scallop and if you force them open with a knife they palpate for some time afterwards. From common observation, it seems that cold-blooded creatures respond to falling temperatures by a slowing of all physical functions, so I think this is the surest method, insofar as we can be sure. We do the same with langoustines, which being crustaceans are more active. If they found the freezer uncongenial, they would try to escape, as lobsters quite certainly do from boiling water.

We use an electrical stun-tank for lobsters and crabs, but this is hardly practicable for most people. The Universities Federation for Animal Welfare now recommend freezing (in a plastic bag at −10° to −15°C). I have tried this, and it seems to work well. Freeze for at least 5 hours, but not more than 24 hours: after that the texture of the flesh softens. Thaw for only 2−3 hours at kitchen temperature. Boil 10−20 minutes depending on size.

However, I am very doubtful about UFAW's other claim, that fast boiling is a humane death. They assert optimistically that "the lobster should die within 15 seconds", but J. R. Baker's experiments at Oxford tell a different story, almost two minutes of struggling. A method heating the lobster very slowly from cold used to be considered humane, but recently doubts have been cast on it. I used to do this, and I think I would recommend it but very cautiously and only with the following provisos:

(1) Use sea water or water as salty as that.

(2) Use a very heavy pan with a folded towel in the bottom of it.

(3) Heat VERY SLOWLY on a very low heat. The water should take half an hour to become even lukewarm, and the heat should not be raised until it is as hot as a hot bath.

(4) If the lobster becomes more rather than less active at any time, reduce the heat.

A very quick way of killing a lobster is to cut it in half with a stout knife. Have the lobster back up on the table, with the tail outstretched and held in your left hand. Look for the cross-shaped mark at the bottom of the carapace, where it joins the tail. Plunge the knife into this mark and cut quickly up to the head, pushing the knife right through to the belly, and then immediately cut down the middle of the tail. The lobster's nerve ganglia are now destroyed, and it is dead, but be prepared for strong reflex jerks of the two separate halves; macabre, but at less cost of suffering to the lobster than other ways. This method means you can't boil the lobster but you can sauté it or steam it; if you are steaming, lay the halves cut side up, and cook for 10 minutes.

Crabs can be killed almost instantly by stabbing. Arm yourself with a marlin spike or a stout skewer, and pliers. Twist a towel into a ring on the table and lay the crab on that, belly up. Pull back the tail, which will be curled up under the body. You will see a small hole with a groove running back to it. Holding the skewer fractionally tilted towards the head, stick it firmly in at least half an inch (1.25 cm) at this hole. Twist it in all directions. The crab is now paralysed but not dead, so finish it off at once by destroying the other nerve centre, in the head. The easiest way is to put the pliers over the whole face (mouth parts) and close them firmly. If this sounds too horrible (but it is best for the crab) find the small depression between the mouth parts and the two movable plates. Slope the skewer far towards the head and pierce this point by quarter of an inch (6 mm). All this sounds a lot more complicated than it is: if you have a crab in front of you it becomes instantly clear.

Anything is better than buying ready-cooked shellfish to save yourself a squeamish chill. Such creatures will have been killed by boiling crammed together, which prolongs the agony, or by steaming (ever had a steam burn?).

Crab Soufflé

I dread being offered a gift of a bag of crab claws. Amongst lobster fishermen it is a common practice to twist the claws off the crabs which are caught stealing the bait in the creels, and throw the still living bodies back in the sea. So if you see crab claws offered in a restaurant, suspect them.

Don't deal with your first crab before an important dinner party, as they are the most fiddly of all shellfish to prepare. The cooked flesh freezes well for a short time, certainly well enough for made-up dishes.

Kill the crab by either of the suggested methods. Boil it for 10 minutes if it is small, 20 minutes if large. To get out the meat, start by pressing hard on the line running round the under-shell at the top and sides. The middle part of the shell will crack out. Put it to one side. Remove the digestive organs (a small sack at the mouth) and discard. Scrape out the brown meat, but keep it—it lends flavour to the rest. Crack the large claws with a hammer to get out the flesh. If it is a huge crab do the small claws too. Take the piece you lifted out of the underside and use a teaspoon handle to extract the meat from it: it is contained in a series of pockets on each side.

Now you have the crab ready and can continue with the recipe.

The meat of 1 large crab or 6 small
    ones (about 8 inches (20 cm) and
    3 inches (7.5 cm) respectively
    across the carapace)
a little dried tarragon
½ teaspoon French mustard
1 tablespoon Pernod or brandy
a scrape of nutmeg
salt and cayenne pepper
2 oz (50 g) butter
1½ oz (40 g) flour
⅓ pt (190 ml) milk
4 eggs + 1 extra white
Parmesan cheese

Preheat oven to 190°C/375°F and read the general remarks for vegetable soufflés (see pp. 259–61).

Mash the crab meat together with the flavourings. If you have no Pernod or brandy use 2 teaspoons of Worcester sauce.

Make a thick white sauce with the butter, flour and milk. Add it to the crab. Cool this slightly while you grease a 2 pt (1.2 litre) soufflé dish or casserole.

Beat the egg yolks into the crab mixture. Whisk the whites VERY stiff and fold lightly into the rest, turn at once into the dish, sprinkle with the cheese, and bake for 35–40 minutes.

Lobster

Sunday is a short-staffed day with us, so we simplify dinner by cutting out a course. To make it up, the main dish is a whole boiled lobster per person, weather permitting. A windy Saturday means a lobsterless Sunday.

Some people, I think, wish the lobster were less whole, when they see it sitting there in its habit as it lived like the ghost in *Hamlet*, proffering a pot of mayonnaise between outstretched claws.

For remarks on how to kill lobsters see p. 285.

Lobster is quite a robust meat and goes satisfactorily with baked potatoes and a salad. Don't overcook lobster: for a 1 lb (450 g) one, it is enough to bring the water back to a rolling boil for 2 minutes, then turn out the heat and leave the pan covered for a further 10. Even if you are serving them cold, don't cook them too far ahead. They deteriorate quickly and are tasteless chilled, best eaten tepid and wetly juicy.

Lobster Mayonnaise

Here is the strong-flavoured mayonnaise I prefer for lobster. Use only first-pressing unrefined oils.

    1 egg yolk
    ¼ teaspoon salt
    ½ teaspoon mustard (French or
      English)
    1 tablespoon wine vinegar
    almost ½ pt (275 ml) of mixed
      olive oil and sunflower oil

To prevent curdling, have all the ingredients at the same temperature, add some of the acid with the egg yolk, and add the oil VERY slowly at first. This applies to any mayonnaise.

Put the egg yolk in a small basin with the salt, mustard and 2 teaspoons of the vinegar. Beat or whisk till lightish in colour.

Mix the oils in a small jug that pours well. Drip in a drop at a time, a little more if you are using a rotary whisk and it can trickle slowly down the blades. Beat between each drop and after 10 such additions add splashes rather than drops. Once the mixture thickens you can add the rest of the oil quite recklessly. If it gets too stiff, add some of the vinegar. Test for sharpness: you may like more or less vinegar.

A more bland mayonnaise suitable for vegetables or fish can be made with less mustard and all sunflower oil. Lemon juice can be substituted for vinegar. I never add sugar to mayonnaise but some people like it. If you do, put it in at the beginning, as it (and salt) remain gritty if added at the end.

Langoustines

These are also known as Dublin Bay prawns or scampi. In North West Scotland they are simply prawns. They have long nippy claws like lobsters. In the larger ones of six inches (15 cm) upwards there is a fair bit of meat in these claws, and the body contains tasty yellowy green liver which is good in small quantities. So it is worth serving the big specimens whole, but the diners must be prepared to use animal methods to extract the goodies. Sometimes you can watch an otter perched on a rock, scrunching and sucking at a crab, with eyes half-closed in bliss, and this is the way to eat whole langoustines —though you needn't sit on a rock.

Langoustines with Sour Cream and Herb Dressing

Langoustines need very little cooking: it is enough to bring the water back to the boil. Allow five large ones per person for a starter, ten for a main course. Provide a finger bowl, a plate for débris, and the following dressing.

Sour cream and herb dressing
4¼ pt (150 ml) double cream
juice of ½ lemon
¼ pt (150 ml) yoghurt

2 tablespoons fresh herbs, chopped
1-inch (2.5 cm) long piece of
    cucumber
salt

Whip the cream with the lemon juice till stiff. Add the yoghurt, the finely-chopped cucumber, and the herbs. Parsley and chives should definitely be included, with smaller quantities of dill, fennel, tarragon, chervil, mint or lovage, as available. Salt cautiously.

You can use cultured sour cream instead of cream with lemon juice. If you like a very rich dressing, use extra cream instead of yoghurt.

Spiced Langoustines

This quantity is enough for a starter for six people. For a main course, double everything, and serve with rice or a flat wholewheat bread. Though bogus, this tastes Indian enough to be part of a curry meal.

30 langoustines
1 bay leaf
1 tablespoon fennel seeds
1 tablespoon coriander seeds
1 teaspoon turmeric
½ teaspoon chilli powder (more or
    less according to taste)

2 cloves garlic
½ teaspoon salt
juice of 2 lemons
2 tablespoons finely chopped mint
4 oz (100 g) butter

Grind all the spices together. Crush the garlic with salt. Melt the butter and add to it everything except the langoustines.

With a very sharp knife, slit the belly shell lengthwise. Prise it apart slightly (a prickly job) and stuff in a bit of spiced butter. Do this to all the langoustines and lay them stretched out belly down, on a baking tray. Paste the remaining spiced butter over their backs. If you have the patience, stab each shell a few times first.

It is best to leave the shellfish in a cool place for several hours at this point, though not essential. Bake them in a hot oven for 5 minutes. Don't waste the juices—pour them over when you serve.

Mussels

We used to go to endless lengths to clean mussels, even turning them in the cement mixer to knock off barnacles. Now I cook them barnacles and all: the grot comes off when the liquor boils up, and what doesn't rubs off easily. The beards often disappear too, or can be easily tweaked out by pinching the shell closed. Of course, you have to strain the juice through muslin or a teatowel before using it.

Mussels being small, they open quickly in heat, so probably this is no worse a way for them to die than by freezing. You may snort at the idea of a mussel feeling pain, but if it doesn't, why does it bother to form pearls round uncomfortable bits of grit? Mussels do this just like oysters, though the pearls are not of commercial size.

If you gather your own mussels, be very careful. They thrive on sewage, but you won't. I have only once gathered mussels within sight of human habitation. They were recommended as particularly plump and juicy by strong-stomached friends. I was spectacularly ill afterwards, though it may have been quantity rather than quality that did it.

Nowadays our shores are festooned with farmed mussels. I don't think the mussels mind it, but the product is unpleasantly sweet and flabby. They feed naturally, but more intensively than wild mussels, as they are not intertidal; so they are as pudgy and bloated as dyspeptic businessmen.

Good mussels have a distinct and strong flavour, and go well with many vegetables—onions, garlic, tomatoes, peppers, fennel. They need a wine which is tasty but not too subtle. I prefer a good Muscadet, and recommend broaching it for the sauce of the next recipe.

Mussels with Fennel

3 quarts mussels
¼ pt (150 ml) dry white wine
1 large bulb fennel
1 medium onion
1½ oz (40 g) butter
1 oz (25 g) flour
3 tablespoons double cream

Slice the onion and fennel finely, reserving some of the green fennel tops for garnish. Stew them in the butter over a gentle heat, covered, till tender. This will take up to 15 minutes.

Wash the mussels to get rid of loose grit. Discard any that stay open when tapped. Put them in a covered pan with the wine. Set this on a high heat. As soon as this boils up and over the mussels, they will open.

Strain the mussel liquor into a jug. Discard one shell from each mussel and keep the rest warm.

Stir the flour into the fennel and make a sauce by adding 1 pt (570 ml) of the mussel liquor. Simmer for 2 minutes.

Dish the mussels into shallow bowls. Add the cream and chopped fennel tops to the sauce, and ladle over the mussels. Serve with warm bread to soak up the sauce.

Mussels Provençales

This is very quick and tasty, but only Provençal for want of a better name. It makes a good sauce for pasta.

    3 quarts mussels
    ¼ pt (150 ml) water
    2 tablespoons olive oil
    1 red pepper
    3 cloves garlic, crushed
    1 large tin of tomatoes
    1 tablespoon tomato purée
    1 tablespoon chopped parsley
    1 tablespoon Pernod or ferocious
      red wine

Cook the mussels as for the preceding recipe, but using water instead of wine. For this dish shell the mussels completely. Strain ¼ pt (150 ml) of the liquid, and discard the rest.

Slice the pepper finely. Simmer it with all the other ingredients, uncovered, for about 10 minutes, or till the liquid has boiled in. Cautiously add the mussel liquor, but don't get it too salty—use some water if it is very salty. Replace the shelled mussels in the sauce and reheat.

If you omit the mussel liquor, this makes a nice pizza topping.

Scallops

The well-educated call these bivalves scollops and correct me firmly when I say scallops. In Harris they are always called clams anyway. The biggest and freshest are got by diving, and these select shellfish cost half as much again as the dredged catch. Clam-divers are invested with high earnings and an air of romance—till something goes wrong. It is a physically taxing and very risky career. We always try to buy from divers. Not only are their scallops finer, smelling of the sea rather than bilge-water, but they do no harm to the sea-bed. A dredge claws the bottom like a giant harrow, tearing out every scallop, large and tiny, whole and broken, and devastating the entire plant and animal community of the sea bed. Regeneration takes years, if indeed it ever happens.

Most classic recipes for "coquilles" are too rich and cloying to use with really fresh scallops though convenient for disguising the aforementioned bilge-water flavour if it is pronounced. The recipes given below are very simple.

Scallops in oatmeal

The Scots use oatmeal as a coating for various types of fish. Herring in oatmeal, trout in oatmeal, so why not scallops in oatmeal? Less bother than egg and breadcrumbs, and more interesting too.

For the scallops:
18–24 scallops
about 4 oz (100 g) fine oatmeal
3–4 oz (75–100 g) butter

For the garnish:
1 lemon
1 large tomato
shredded lettuce

For the scallops:
If the scallops have been frozen they will be very easy to shell. Using a stout knife, prise the two halves apart near the hinge. Discard every thing except the round white bit and the bright orange coral. In addition cut off the very opaque fibres down one side of the white, and the tough grey-brown piece at the thicker end of the coral. Save 6 of the deep shells. Cut the white part into two or three rounds, ½ inch (1.25 cm) thick. Leave the corals whole. (Sometimes there are none.) Using one hand only (it's a sticky job) dip the pieces in the dry oatmeal. Start frying with just 1 oz (25 g) of the butter, adding more as necessary.

Cook the scallops gently for about 5 minutes on each side—the flesh turns pale and opaque when it is ready.

For the garnish:

Cut the lemon and the tomato each into 6 sections. Divide the lettuce between the shells. Dish the scallops onto this, decorate with the lemon and tomato and serve before it gets uniformly lukewarm.

These are fine as they are, but if you want a sauce, use a sharp piquant one—no eggs or cream—totally cholesterol-free. This is what I usually serve:

Spicy Tomato Sauce

A lump of tamarind pulp (about
   1-inch (2.5 cm) cube)
½ teacup boiling water
2 star anise *or* 1 teaspoon aniseed
   or fennel seed
1 teaspoon black peppercorns
1 tablespoon coriander seed
1 lb (450 g) tomatoes
1 medium onion
salt

Put the tamarind in the cup of hot water and leave to soak. (If you don't have tamarind, mix the juice of 1 lemon and 2 teaspoons dark brown sugar.)

Grind the spices and put them in a saucepan over medium heat till they darken and smell aromatic. Add the onion and tomatoes roughly cut up, and stir well. Paddle the tamarind in the water with your fingers, discard the seeds and husks, and add the softened pulp or the lemon juice to the tomato mixture. Simmer till the onion is soft—20–30 minutes. Strain by pushing through a sieve with the back of a ladle: this is very easy if you liquidise the mixture first. Add salt to taste and a little brown sugar if it is too sour for you, but remember the scallops are sweetish in flavour.

Scallops in yoghurt

I can never decide whether this recipe is a flower of my genius or a disgusting aberration, but many diners have raved about it. Others have said nothing. . . .

  18–24 scallops
  juice of 1 lemon
  salt, nutmeg and freshly ground
    black pepper
  2 oz (50 g) unsalted butter
  1 teaspoon arrowroot slaked in
    1 tablespoon water (optional)
  ¼ pt (150 ml) yoghurt

Prepare the scallops and slice into rings. Lay on a baking sheet and sprinkle with the lemon juice and seasonings. Use very little salt—¼ teaspoon at most. Leave for half an hour.

Melt the butter in a wide pan, and put in the scallops and any juice they have exuded. Mix gently, cover, and cook just till opaque, turning once or twice. Don't let the collecting juices boil, or the scallop will toughen.

Remove the scallops with a slotted spoon and keep warm. Turn up the heat and boil the juice fiercely, uncovered, till it is well reduced. If you are a purist, boil grimly till you have only about a teacupful of syrupy liquid left. If you find this too tedious, reduce to twice that and thicken with the arrowroot.

Take the pan off the heat. Dish up the scallops, either in the deep shells or in a bowl. Add the yoghurt to the juice in the pan, mixing well, but do *not* reheat, or it will curdle. Pour this sauce over the scallops.

Seafood Pie or Gougère

I make these when I end up with quantities of this and that too small to feed a whole dining room. For the pastry or gougère crust, follow the instructions under Turnover of Sole (p. 280) or Gougère of Mushrooms and Peppers (p. 270). For hearty eaters you will need to double the gougère paste quantities to serve 6 as a main course, but the filling ingredients given below are enough for 6. For a cheaper dish you can substitute firm white fish for the lobster.

For the filling:
6 scallops
12 langoustines *or* 24 prawns
1 small lobster
20 mussels
½ pt (275 ml) dry white wine *or*
   wine and water
1 bay leaf
1 small onion
2-inch (5 cm) strip lemon peel

2 oz (50 g) butter
2 oz (50 g) flour
1 tablespoon chopped parsley
½ teaspoon dried tarragon, thyme
   or basil
salt and cayenne pepper
1 teaspoon French mustard *or*
   2 tablespoons sherry
3 tablespoons cream

Cut the scallops into rounds. Shell the langoustines or prawns and the lobster, and put the shells in a large pan with the wine, bay leaf, sliced onion and lemon peel. Bring to the boil. Lay the mussels in their shells on top, cover the pan and boil for 2 minutes.

Remove the mussels from their shells, cut the lobster meat into chunks, and mix all the shellfish together in a bowl. You don't want people sulking because someone got all lobster while another had all mussels.

Strain the shellfish stock into a jug and make up to ¾ pt (425 ml) with milk or water if necessary.

Make a roux with the butter and flour. Add the stock and beat till smooth. Add all the remaining ingredients and taste. It should be highly seasoned.

For the pie:

Roll out the pastry to fit a large pie dish or 2 small ones. Lay the shellfish in the bottom, pour on the cooled sauce, and place the pastry over, gluing it to the dish with beaten egg at the edge. Brush the top with egg, and make a small hole in the middle. A ribbon of pastry over or under the lid at the edge helps to prevent shrinking and oozing. Bake for about 20 minutes in a moderately hot oven till golden brown.

For the gougère:

Bake the crust as directed. 10 minutes before it is ready, bring the sauce to boiling point. Drop in the shellfish, and cook very gently —below a simmer—till the crust comes out. Dollop the mixture into the centre of the gougère and serve at once.

The shellfish mixture can also be served over rice or another grain.

Game and other Meat

I have called this section "Game and other meat", because if I have to cook meat I prefer to use game. This is not from any liking for huntin' and shootin': in fact, I am bemused by the excitement sportsmen find in the chase. I can remotely imagine rejoicing in an unarmed victory over a grizzly bear or a rabid wolf, but where is the thrill in vanquishing a clawless, fangless, oblivious herbivore with a high velocity bullet? Be that as it may, at least the victims have led relatively unconfined lives and are hit before they know it's coming.

A rueful sportsman told us the following tale. He had arrived in Harris for fishing, having just been presented with some grouse on the mainland. These he thrust into the hands of his bed-and-breakfast lady, instructing her to cook them for his supper. After many hungry hours flogging the loch and anticipating dinner, he arrived back. There was an odd smell in the house—not entirely appetising—but he seated himself at the supper table. The landlady appeared, smiling to herself, bearing in the grouse—thoroughly cooked, but cooked guts, feathers and all.

Well done, you bad old lady! For what reason on earth should she pluck the Sassenach's grouse? A fresh hen is unpleasant enough, but a high grouse is abominable.

Pheasant

Pheasants have only recently been successfully introduced in Lewis, and for the first couple of years they tasted suspiciously like chicken. As there are no cornfields and no woods, the poor things hung around waiting for handouts of grain. Plantations have by now improved their lifestyle.

Pheasants are surprisingly meaty and one bird will serve three. Don't try to gnaw your way through the drumsticks: they are very sinewy. Boil them up with onion, carrot and celery and make a soup.

Pheasant with Apples and Rosemary

This is similar to the classic Faisan à la Normande, but the sauce is more robust, with a slightly bitter pungency from the rosemary.

2 pheasants	4 tart eating apples, *or* 2 sweet ones
2 oz (50 g) butter	and 2 cooking apples
2 medium onions	3 tablespoons brandy
4 4-inch-long (10 cm) sprigs	½ teaspoon salt
rosemary	2 tablespoons cream

Trim excess fat round the vents of the pheasants. Put ½ oz (15 g) of butter and a sprig of rosemary in the cavity of each.

Chop the onions and sauté in the rest of the butter till golden. Core the apples and peel them, or not, as you like. Cut them in quarters and turn them in the butter with the onion. Scrape all this into the bottom of a large lidded casserole or roaster. Add the remaining sprigs of rosemary. Place the pheasants on top and sprinkle with salt.

Warm the brandy in a small pan, ignite it, and pour it quickly over the pheasants. While it is still blazing, put on the lid. Cook in a moderate oven for 60 minutes, basting two or three times. You may need to add a little water.

Dish up and carve the pheasants, and keep warm. Taste the apple mixture, adding salt, and sugar or lemon juice if it seems to need it. Remove the scraggy stalks of the rosemary but leave the leaves in. Add cream if you like it, and pour this sauce over the sliced pheasant.

It is a horrible colour. If you have plenty of rosemary, lay a criss-cross of fresh sprigs over the top. Otherwise avert your eyes. The taste is fine, anyway.

Pot-roasted Pheasant

If the pheasants are tough, this is a good method.

2 pheasants
2 medium onions
2 medium carrots
3 stalks celery
1 oz (50 g) butter
salt
a bay leaf, a sprig of thyme and a
    strip of lemon peel
¼ pt (150 ml) tasty white wine or
    feeble port
1 teaspoon flour
¼ pt (150 ml) double cream
redcurrant or quince jelly or lemon
    juice—optional
chopped parsley to garnish

Trim excess fat from the vents of the pheasants. Chop the vegetables coarsely and brown them lightly in the butter. Remove them with a draining spoon to the bottom of a large lidded casserole and brown the pheasants in the same pan.

Lay the bay leaf, etc., on the vegetables and sprinkle with the salt. Put the pheasants on top, breast down, and pour the wine over them. Cook slowly, covered, on the stove top or in a slowish oven for 1½–2 hours. Turn the birds over and stir the vegetables occasionally.

Remove and carve the pheasants and keep warm. Drain most of the fat from the vegetables and stir in the flour over heat. Add a little stock or water if necessary to make a thickish sauce. Adjust the seasoning—if you used wine you may want to add a little redcurrant or quince jelly; if port, a squeeze of lemon juice. Stir in the cream, reheat without boiling, and pour the vegetable mixture into the centre of the serving platter. Sprinkle with parsley, as this one isn't a nice colour either.

Pheasant with Oatmeal Stuffing

To roast a pheasant, rub the breast well with butter, put an onion and a knob of butter inside, and roast for 40–50 minutes in a moderately hot oven, basting several times. The following recipe is for a traditional Scottish poultry stuffing. If you fill the birds with this, clean out the cavity very well first with kitchen paper, and increase the cooking time by 10 minutes. This quantity will do two pheasants.

Oatmeal stuffing
3 oz (75 g) dripping or white
    cooking fat—not lard from a
    block
1 medium onion
6 oz (175 g) fine or medium
    oatmeal
salt and pepper
¼ pt (150 ml) water

Chop the onion and fry till it begins to brown in the dripping. Put in the oatmeal and cook, stirring, till it turns pale and then begins to darken slightly. Remove from the heat, add salt, pepper and water.

Venison

We don't hang our venison long. We get stags in August, when the weather is damp and mild and putrefaction is in the air. On the seventh day the worm fastened on Ea-bani, and so on a Harris stag. We cut it up hastily and stuff it in the freezer. Hinds, shot in January and February, would last a little longer hanging, but we have no taste for decay and usually don't keep them either. Good red deer venison tastes of the heather it fed on, and hanging is more useful for tenderising than flavouring it. Venison freezes better than other meat, which is just as well when you have two hundredweights at once, and freezing makes it more tender; but it is never as good as fresh.

Try to get a well-nourished beast, but when you are preparing the meat, trim away all the fat, particularly if you are dealing with a stag's hindquarters. The stuff has a pungent odour which may turn on a hind, but it will hardly delight your dinner-guests. You will, of course, have to add other fats to make up. I find butter best.

Roast Venison with Rosemary Jelly

The best cuts for roasting are the saddle, the rump, and the top of the haunch. Weigh the meat after trimming, and calculate the cooking time at 10 minutes to the pound and 10 minutes over for medium rare, in a moderately hot oven.

To flavour and baste a 4–5 lb (1.8–2.2 kg) roast, you will need:

10 juniper berries
1 teaspoon dried rosemary
½ teaspoon salt
2–3 oz (50–75 g) butter
4 sprigs bog myrtle or thyme

Crush the juniper berries and dried rosemary with the salt, and rub this all over the meat. Butter the roasting tin thickly and squash the rest of the butter over the top of the meat and into any crevices. Baste very frequently.

You will probably have no excess fat in the gravy. Deglaze the roasting tin with a little venison stock or water, and 2 tablespoons of port. Failing port, use wine and a teaspoon of a tart jelly. Strain the gravy as it will have bits of herb-stalk in it.

Rosemary Jelly

My mother-in-law drew my attention to this lovely preserve, and now makes mine for me. Mine is murky and musty—hers is clear and fragrant. It is the ideal accompaniment with game, and also good with mature mutton.

You can use your usual apple jelly recipe, and to the apples and water add a good-sized branch of rosemary, which stews along with them. Don't try using dried rosemary; it is lacking in the essential oil which imparts the fresh flavour.

If you don't have a favourite jelly recipe, here is the method in full.

The amount of sugar required and the final yield varies depending on the condition of the fruit.

6 lb (2.8 kg) cooking apples or
    windfalls
water to cover
a few branches of rosemary
granulated sugar

Remove bad pieces from the apples but do not peel or core. Cut into thick slices, put in a jelly pan with the rosemary, and just cover with water. Bring to the boil and simmer for about 1 hour, till the liquid is reduced by one third.

Strain the pulp through a jelly bag for at least an hour, till the pulp is dry. Measure the resulting juice and return to the rinsed-out pan with 1 lb (450 g) sugar for every half pint (275 ml) of juice.

Bring to the boil, stirring to dissolve the sugar. Boil rapidly till setting point is reached (probably about 10 minutes). Test a little by dropping it on a cold plate. Let it cool and if it wrinkles when the plate is tilted, it is ready.

Pour into dry, warm jars and cover.

Venison Chops with Vermouth

This method would also work with elderly grouse, following the slower cooking after initial browning.

6 thick venison chops	½ teaspoon dried thyme
2 oz (50 g) butter	½ teaspoon salt
1 smallish onion	¼ pt (150 ml) dry Vermouth
6 juniper berries	½ oz (15 g) flour
1 × 4-inch (10 cm) sprig of rosemary	¼ pt (150 ml) game stock or water
	1 tablespoon sultanas

Trim the chops thoroughly. Chop the onion finely and brown with the meat in the butter over a high heat. Remove the onions and chops to an ovenproof dish. Lay them in a single layer.

Crush the herbs with the salt to release the aromatic oils, and sprinkle over the chops. Swill the Vermouth over the meat. To the butter in the browning pan, add the flour, scraping well to incorporate it. Stir in the stock or water, add the sultanas, and simmer for 2 minutes. Pour this over the chops.

Either (1) Leave the dish uncovered and bake in a hot oven for 10 minutes, turning once. The meat will be rare and the sauce syrupy.

Or (2) Cover with greaseproof paper or a lid and bake in a slow oven for 40 minutes, basting once or twice. The meat will be brown right through and drier, but it will have absorbed the sweetish flavour of the sauce.

A julienne of celery and potato goes well with this (see recipe p. 316).

Civet of Venison

This is a glorified stew, really, richly flavoured and aromatic. It also makes an excellent pie filling. Shoulder is the best cut to use. The really stringy ends of the beast—neck and lower legs—should be used for the next recipe.

2–2½ lb (.9–1.1 kg) venison (weight excludes bone)	1 wineglass brandy or whisky
3 oz (75 g) bacon	1 bay leaf
1 tablespoon olive oil	2-inch (5 cm) strip lemon peel
1 oz (25 g) butter	½ teaspoon dried thyme
2 large onions	3 cloves garlic
1 medium carrot	6 juniper berries
6 oz (175 g) mushrooms	venison stock or water
1 oz (25 g) flour	*To garnish:*
½ bottle full-bodied (even blowsy) red wine	triangles of fried bread or puff pastry or a few mushrooms

Trim all the sinewy and scraggy bits off the meat. It is convenient to have a dog sitting beside you who will obligingly remove the waste before you notice your own extravagance. Cut what is left into 1-inch (2.5 cm) cubes.

Cut the bacon into small pieces and sizzle it in the oil and butter till the fat runs out. Get the pan very hot and brown the meat.

Chop the onions and carrots coarsely and the mushroom stalks finely. (Reserve the mushroom caps.) Add to the pan of meat and cook, stirring, for a couple of minutes.

Stir in the flour, and follow that with the brandy, wine and herbs. Crush the garlic and juniper berries with a pinch of salt and add that too. Mix well, and simmer gently till the meat is tender—about 2 hours. Check several times to make sure the liquid has not evaporated. If your dog was taking a nap earlier, you could make stock with the trimmings and use that to top up with. Otherwise use water.

10 minutes before serving, test for salt. If the bacon was mild you may need more. Put in the mushroom caps at this stage and another splash of wine if it was unassertive.

You can garnish with triangles of fried bread or puff pastry; a few more small fried mushrooms; or just plenty of parsley, and hope no one notices you didn't do the other things.

Venison Pudding

This is a very substantial and warming winter dish. If possible, take the meat off the bones yourself: and use them to make stock which is really needed for this recipe.

For the filling:
1½–2 lb (700–900 g) so-called "stewing venison" or 3–4 lb (1.4–1.8 kg) on the bone
2 oz (50 g) dripping or butter
2 large onions
1 medium carrot
2 stalks celery
¼ lb (100 g) turnip or swede
½ oz (15 g) flour
1 pt (570 ml) venison stock, or ½ pt (275 ml) stock and ½ pt (275 ml) beer

1–2 teaspoons French mustard
1 tablespoon Worcester sauce or mushroom ketchup
1 teaspoon brown sugar
½ teaspoon dried savory or mixed herbs
salt and pepper
For the suet crust:
8 oz (225 g) self-raising flour
½ teaspoon salt
4 oz (100 g) shredded suet
water

For the filling:

Remove the bones and the toughest-looking bits of sinew. Smuggle these trimmings into a pan while the dog is out chasing cats and boil up with 1½ pt (825 ml) water. Simmer for 1 hour or till you are ready for it.

Cut the bits of venison—I'm assuming it's scraggy—into roughly 1-inch (2.5 cm) cubes. Brown them in the fat.

Dice the vegetables, not too small, and brown them with the meat. Sprinkle in the flour. Add ⅓ pt (200 ml) of the liquid and all the seasonings and simmer till the meat is tender. This will take about 3–4 hours and can be done a day or so ahead. Check every half hour for sticking and top up the liquid as necessary. Check the seasoning—it should be well-flavoured. Cool the stew somewhat.

For the suet crust:

Mix the flour, salt and shredded suet. Add enough cold water to make a soft scone-like dough. Roll out about ⅔ of it very lightly on a floured surface and piece this together to line a 2 pt (1.2 litre) pudding basin, thinly but thoroughly—about ¼ inch (6 mm) thick. Pat the remaining third out into a round to fit the top of the basin.

Fill the lined basin with the stew, using a draining spoon. Leave a good deal of the gravy in the pan: the filling should be moist but not swimming. Place the top crust over, pinching it on to the inner crust.

Cover the pudding with a double layer of greaseproof paper, greased, and with a 2-inch (5 cm) pleat down the centre to allow for swelling. Tie it up firmly—it's a good plan to anchor the paper under the basin rim with an elastic band before tying the string. The band perishes with the steam, but does no harm. Trim the ends of the paper and string so that they won't soak up the water. Set the basin on a steamer or in 1½ inches (3.75 cm) of boiling water, cover, and cook for 1–1½ hours. Don't let the water touch the paper, boil dry, or go off the boil.

Heat up the rest of the gravy and serve it separately, with mashed potatoes, and a green vegetable.

If you can't be bothered fiddling with a pudding basin, make the stew and pastry as directed. Pull the pastry into 12 lumps to make dumplings, and cook them in the simmering stew for 15 minutes.

Lamb

Out of force of habit, and to allay prejudice, we feature "lamb" on our menus, but in fact we can hardly ever get lamb in Harris. The youngest carcases we ever lay hands on are fourteen months, and they only weigh between 20 and 30 pounds. They are difficult to get hold of, because no one sees the sense of killing a beast at that weight that might grow twice as heavy, with time. It's like persuading the grower of prize vegetable marrows to harvest courgettes. The preferred local style is a nice fat wedder—a wedder being a castrated ram of 2 or more years old. They are good mutton, but doubtful lamb. The three recipes following make use of robust flavours for this reason. Try them, and your lamb will be dressed as mutton.

Lamb with Apricots

This is an adaptation of a middle eastern tradition. If the apricots are sweet, add the juice and rind of half a lemon, but it won't be as good.

    4 lb (1.8 kg) leg of lamb
    2 oz (50 g) butter
    1 medium onion
    4 oz (100 g) sour dried apricots
    1-inch (2.5 cm) piece of cinnamon
        stick
    ½ pint (275 ml) water
    salt and pepper

304

Chop the onion finely and brown it and the leg of lamb lightly in the butter. Transfer these to a lidded casserole, preferably metal, and add all the other ingredients. Bring to a simmer, and then cook, covered, in a very moderate oven for 2–2½ hours. Turn the meat twice and add more water as necessary. You should end up with the meat pulling away easily from the bone at the shank end, and a mush of darkened but still juicy apricots, without much liquid.

Rice cooked in the following manner makes an attractive border to the platter of lamb.

Rice with Pine Kernels

You could use any long-grain rice, but Basmati is very good-tempered. I never bother with washing it or any other fancy procedure, and it still cooks dry and separate.

12 oz (350 g) Basmati rice
½ teaspoon saffron strands
½ teaspoon salt
water
2 oz (50 g) butter
2 oz (50 g) pine kernels
2 oz (50 g) raisins

Put the rice in a jug or bowl to judge its volume. Empty it into a saucepan and add just over twice its volume of water. Add the saffron and salt, stir and bring to the boil. Turn the heat right down and cook tightly covered for 10 minutes. Remove from the heat, still covered, and leave for a further 5–10 minutes.

Heat the butter in a small saucepan till just browning. Add the pine kernels and raisins and stir till the raisins puff up. Serve the rice with this mixture dribbled over the top.

Lamb with Haricots

This is not meant to be "gigot aux haricots" so don't judge it accordingly.

    8 oz (225 g) dried haricot beans
    2 pt (1.2 l) water
    1 bay leaf
    4 cloves garlic
    4 lb (1.8 kg) leg of lamb
    4 oz (100 g) smoked fat bacon
    1 tablespoon olive oil
    2 medium onions
    1 lb (450 g) tomatoes
    1 teaspoon dried oregano or a few
        sprigs fresh marjoram
    salt

Boil the haricots with the water, bay leaf and 1 clove of garlic till half cooked—about 1–1½ hours depending on whether you soaked them first.

Chop the bacon and sizzle it in the oil till the fat comes out. Add the chopped onions and the remaining garlic, crushed.

Skin and chop the tomatoes. If seeds bother you take them out and strain the juice from them. Add the tomatoes to the bacon and onion.

Put all this in a covered casserole or roaster and add the haricots and their liquid. Add the herbs and salt and stir well. Put in the meat, bring to the boil, cover and cook gently for 2½ hours. Turn the meat and make sure the beans don't dry out.

If any beans are left, purée them and serve as a soup with croûtons next day.

Stuffed Shoulder of Lamb

This is a light fresh-tasting stuffing, very summery. It is also good with breast of lamb.

4–5 lb (1.8–2.3 kg) shoulder of
    lamb
For the stuffing:
2 oz (50 g) butter
4 oz (100 g) breadcrumbs
1 tablespoon chopped parsley
1 teaspoon dried thyme (or
    2 teaspoons if fresh)
1 teaspoon dried marjoram (or
    2 teaspoons if fresh)
grated rind and juice of 1 lemon
salt
For roasting:
1 oz (25 g) butter
2 sprigs rosemary

Bone out the lamb and trim the fat.

Melt the butter for the stuffing and add all the other ingredients to it. Stuff this into all the cavities in the lamb. Tie it up as well as you can: don't worry if it's untidy, but try to arrange it so that the muscle fibres all run more or less parallel.

Use ½ oz (15 g) butter to grease a roasting tin. Lay the meat on it with the rosemary and the clove of garlic split in half underneath. Smear the rest of the butter over the top of the meat. Roast in a moderately hot oven for about 1¼ hours, or longer if you like the meat well done. Baste several times.

Make gravy in the usual way and serve fresh mint sauce alongside.

Mint Sauce

¼ pt (150 ml) (loose measure) mint
    leaves
1 teaspoon sugar
1 tablespoon wine vinegar
½ tablespoon water

Put everything in a blender for 10 seconds. It will probably look frothy but it is much less work than chopping and produces a very intense flavour and colour. Use the day it is made.

Offal

The next two recipes are for offal. We never use it as part of our set dinner menu, as it is very common for people to have an aversion to it, but if you aren't one of these squeamish ones, it is all good stuff, cheap and nourishing.

These recipes date from the time when we were renovating the house before opening as a hotel. We were very hard up, and constantly hungry. We virtually lived on sheep's innards donated by a kindly butcher friend, and I evolved many ways of cooking them to vary our diet. Nowadays, our dog is the only meat-eater left in the family, and he is still catered for by the same kind friend. On holiday, I buy him offal on the grounds that no animal is killed specially for its insides. After about three days in one place, I get miserably embarrassed about revisiting the village butcher for a daily parcel of one pound of heart. I feel I am suspected of sinister practices. But Jet gulps it down with the ecstatic relish of an Aztec priest.

Casserole of Heart with Prunes

Hearts have a much more meaty texture than other offal and require long, slow cooking. If you slice them first, you can remove the unappetising stringy bits inside and the signs of fatty degeneration around the top. I think they are best in an aromatic sweetish gravy like the one below. I leave the spices whole—you could grind them, but don't use ready ground. Serve with plenty of rice or fried potatoes to soak up the tasty sauce.

5 or 6 sheep's hearts—about 2 lb (900 g) weight
1 large onion
2 oz (50 g) dripping or oil
1 oz (25 g) flour
1 dessertspoon paprika
3 cloves garlic
a 3-inch (7.5 cm) piece of lemon or orange rind
a 1-inch (2.5 cm) stick of cinnamon
a blade of mace
12 black peppercorns
2 bay leaves
1 teaspoon celery salt
1 glass red wine *or* juice of half a lemon
¾ pint (425 ml) water
12 large prunes *or* 18 small
1 green pepper

Slice onion and hearts and brown them in the fat. Stir in the flour and paprika and let it sizzle for a minute. Add everything else except the prunes and green pepper and simmer for 2½ hours, topping up the water if it boils in.

Chop the pepper and add it with the prunes.

Cook for a further 45 minutes. The prunes will absorb a lot of water, so check this.

Liver with Sage and Orange

It was always sheep's liver I had to hand, and I made some nasty mistakes with it. For instance, we had sheep's liver pâté, the most disgusting way of wasting butter next to the EEC butter mountain; and sheep's liver soup, reminiscent of sawdust suspended in sheep's pee. But one or two recipes were an unqualified success, for instance this one. Serve with spaghetti.

For the sauce:
1 tablespoon olive oil
1 small onion
2 cloves garlic
½ teaspoon salt
½ teaspoon sugar
a sprig of fresh thyme or a pinch of dried
2 teaspoons flour
1 tablespoon tomato purée
juice and grated rind of 1 large orange
¼ pt (150 ml) water
(2 teaspoons capers—optional)

For the liver:
1½ lb (675 g) liver
1 tablespoon chopped fresh sage or 1 teaspoon dried
½ oz (15 g) butter

For the sauce:
Chop the onion, crush the garlic with the salt and sugar, and sauté in the oil till tender. Add all the other ingredients and simmer for one minute. Take off the heat.

For the liver:
Slice the liver fairly thinly and fry lightly in the butter with the sage. Don't overcook—it should still show a bead of pink juice when pricked.

Pour over the sauce and reheat to simmering point. Serve at once.

Cereals and Vegetable Side-dishes

The quantities given are for small helpings on the side for 6 people, but in fact many of these dishes can form a simple vegetarian main course for 2. They are what we usually eat ourselves for supper after the guests have finished, so there is always a strong element of self-interest in my choice and preparation of these items.

Cereals

There is not much to be said about cereals except that they are not cornflakes. I suspect the British prefer roast potatoes, but I occasionally use some other juice-catcher, especially with fish.

Buckwheat with Cucumber

Buckwheat is not wheat at all—it is a relative of rhubarb. It is stuffed with minerals and bursting with protein. It is highly esteemed by the Japanese, and in Eastern Europe, buckwheat kasha was as porridge to the Scots. I'm not sure how much I like it, personally, but there's something about it—I keep trying it again.

4 oz (100 g) buckwheat
1 egg (optional)
½ pt (275 ml) water
1 cucumber
1 tablespoon snipped chives

salt
1 oz (25 g) butter
¼ pt (150 ml) yoghurt or sour cream

Beat the egg and mix it into the buckwheat. (This keeps the grains separate, but you can omit the egg if you don't mind stickiness.) Put this in a heated pan and stir till it looks dry. Pour on the water, cover and simmer till tender—about 20 minutes.

Cut the cucumber in half-inch (1.25 cm) chunks or thereabouts. Stew it gently in the butter with the salt and chives, covered, till just cooked—about 4 minutes.

Mix the cucumber into the buckwheat and pour the yoghurt or sour cream over the top.

Bulgar (or Bulghur, or Cracked Wheat)

The Bulgarians gave their name to this method of preparing wheat grain, and also to buggery, but as far as I know there is no connection between the two practices.

The wheat is sold ready husked, boiled, dried and cracked. It may be fine or coarse—use fine for Tabbouleh, the Middle Eastern salad, and coarse for a plain steamed grain or a pilaff. In any form it is delicious and easy to deal with. It has a bland yet warm flavour which goes well with all vegetables, shellfish and lamb.

Burghul Pilaff

    2 oz (50 g) butter
    1 large onion
    1 red pepper or ½ lb (225 g)
      tomatoes
    ½ lb (225 g) coarse cracked wheat
    ¾ pt (425 ml) water
    salt and pepper

Chop the onion and fry in the butter till it is translucent. Add the chopped pepper or tomatoes and the grain. Stir well to incorporate the butter. Add water, salt and pepper, cover and simmer for 20 minutes. It may need more water and further simmering. It should be tender yet dry, but is still good rather wet—better that way than gritty, so don't worry about overcooking as much as you would with rice.

For a filling main course, serve on its own with grated cheese or a lentil dish.

Rice

Recipe books are full of detailed and earnest accounts of how to cook perfect rice. Even reading them makes me tired. Below is my sloppy method of cooking rice. It works more than half the time.

I usually use organically grown long-grain brown rice, which is good-natured and tasty. If you want a white rice, basmati is not too temperamental either, and has a distinctive dry smell and taste.

Steamed Rice

12 oz (350 g) rice
2¼ times its volume of water
1 teaspoon salt if you like it

Bring everything to a fast boil, turn down the heat as low as possible, and cook covered till the water is absorbed and the grains just tender. This takes about 10 minutes for white rice and 25–45 for brown (with brown rice, a lot depends on how old the rice is, but old age will not make it inedible unless your kitchen storage area is humid or weevilly).

Once the rice is cooked, it is best if you put a folded tea-towel under the lid and leave it to sit in a warm place for 5 minutes or till you want to serve it, but you can use it at once.

Variations on plain rice

If you are following a risotto or pilaff recipe but using brown rice, *don't* cook it in the fat before adding water, even if you are directed to. This treatment hardens whole rice grain, so that it can take some bits well over an hour to soften, by which time other bits will be mushy. Cook the rice first by the method above, but take it off the heat just short of tender enough. Fry other listed ingredients, mix into the rice, and replace on a very low heat for 10 minutes to let the flavours mingle.

Two very simple variations on plain rice are rice with green herbs and rice with whole spices.

For herbs, add a teacupful of chopped fresh herbs and 2 oz (50 g) butter or 2 tablespoons of olive oil to the basic recipe.

For spices, add 4 cloves, 1-inch (2.5 cm) stick of cinnamon, 4 crushed cardamoms and a broken bay leaf, fried in 2 oz (50 g) butter.

In either case, mix the garnish into the just-cooked rice, replace the lid, and leave to stand for 5 minutes.

Vegetables

The counsel of perfection is to steam vegetables briefly and serve them plain. Wonderful—if your vegetables are tender, pristine fresh, unbloated by excess watering, and unflavoured by the swimming-pool of chlorine some nations dunk them in to rid them of bacteria. The Israelis are particularly keen on this type of purification, though I can find no reference to it in Deuteronomy. The Californians prefer a squirt of perfumed air-freshener, or is it deodorant? The South Africans seem to have confidence in their own cleanliness and don't take precautions of this sort—such a pity they're ideologically unsound: still, one better than the Chileans, whose carrots are slimy as well as fascist by the time they reach the Outer Hebrides. And now the English turnips are going to be irradiated so that the poor Scots won't know they've been out of the ground for 2 years.

You will guess from the above that my vegetable store is multinational and I am seldom in a position to serve the plain steamed perfection, at least before July when our own start growing.

Tolerable vegetables can be successfully treated, after steaming or boiling, with white sauce. Use part milk, part cooking water in the sauce, and flavour with nutmeg, cheese or parsley. Another possibility is a purée, which is especially good for a combination of root vegetables—carrot and parsnip, swede and potato. Don't believe any book which tells you to make purées ahead and heat them up later. Once the vegetable is crushed it immediately starts to oxidise, and your delicately flavoured and tinted masterpiece will taste like hospital 2 veg. if you don't serve it pretty immediately. Purées need lots of butter or cream to make them nice, but if you keep quiet you will find that calorie-conscious ladies who would regard chips as indecent proposals will lap them up: they look so very pretty and dainty.

The following recipes will restore a semblance of health to vegetables past their prime, or to overwatered imports.

Sesame Aubergines

Use only a little oil at a time to fry aubergines—otherwise you will find the whole bottle has gone, with consequent harm to your digestion.

These also make a nice first course, sprinkled with lemon juice.

2 large aubergines
salt
2–3 oz (50–75 g) sesame seeds
¼ pt (150 ml) sunflower or corn oil

Remove the tops from the aubergines and cut them into thin lengthwise slices. Salt them and leave in a colander for 45 minutes. Rinse them and drain them but don't dry.

Put the sesame seeds on a plate. Press the aubergine slices into them and fry in hot oil. Be careful—the seeds burn easily. Serve at once —they wilt.

Casserole of Aubergine and Potato

1 large aubergine
its weight in potatoes
1 medium onion
1 red pepper
½ lb (225 g) tomatoes
2 cloves garlic
3 tablespoons olive oil
juice of 1 lemon

Cut the aubergine into 1-inch (2.5 cm) chunks, salt, and leave to drain in a colander for 45 minutes. Scrub or peel the potatoes and slice. Slice the onion and pepper thinly. Crush the garlic with salt. Skin and seed the tomatoes if you prefer to, but strain and keep the juice from the seeds. Squeeze the lemon.

Get the oil hot in a deep pan. Put in the onion and pepper and cook for 1 minute, stirring once or twice. Add the potatoes, garlic, tomatoes and lemon juice. Wash and dry the aubergine chunks, and mix them in. Simmer for 15 minutes and test for salt. The aubergines may have retained enough. Simmer till the potatoes are just cooked. If there is a lot of juice, cook uncovered on a high heat for a minute or so to reduce it. The finished dish should have sheen and coherence.

Lemon Cabbage

This is about the best you can do with these sinister luminescent footballs which infest Scottish greengrocers for 9 months of the year.

1½ lb (675 g) white cabbage
1 teaspoon caraway seeds
juice of 1 lemon
¼ pt (150 ml) water
salt
a knob of butter

Shred the cabbage finely and put it in a pan with the other ingredients. Cover and cook very fast for 3 minutes. If the cabbage is still tough for your liking, cook a bit longer, but watch for drying out.

Carrot and Potato Cake

This is light and colourful, particularly good with fish.

1 medium onion
2 oz (50 g) butter
½ lb (225 g) carrots
1 lb (450 g) potatoes
½ teaspoon salt

Butter an 8-inch (20 cm) sandwich tin thickly. Chop the onion finely and sauté in the rest of the butter till golden.

Scrub or peel the carrots and potatoes. Grate the carrots and mix into the onion with the salt. Slice the potatoes thinly.

Spread half the carrot mixture in the bottom of the tin. Cover with the sliced potatoes and top with the rest of the carrot. Put a round of greaseproof or Bakewell paper on top and press down.

Cook in a moderate oven for about 25 minutes, till a knife goes easily through the centre. When you take the tin out, press the contents down again and leave for a minute or so before turning out.

Julienne of Celery and Potato

This one is good with game.

 1 small onion
 1 oz (25 g) butter
 1 lb (450 g) potatoes
 1 head celery
 salt

Chop the onion finely and sauté it gently in the butter. Peel the potatoes and cut them into strips like thin chips. (If this is too fiddly, cut them into thin slices.) Add to the onion.

Clean the celery and cut across or transversely in narrow slices. Add it to the other vegetables with a little salt and fry uncovered, stirring occasionally, for 5 minutes. Now cover the pan and cook on a very low heat till the potato is just tender, but not mushy.

This is rather pallid, though delicious, so use plenty of parsley to garnish.

Courgettes with Tomato Sauce

 1½ lb (675 g) courgettes
 For the sauce:
 1 small onion
 1 tablespoon olive oil
 1 lb (450 g) tomatoes
 2 teaspoons tomato purée
 marjoram or oregano to taste
 salt and a pinch of sugar
 a blade of mace or a scrape of
   nutmeg

For the sauce:

Chop the onion and sauté it in the oil till soft. Slice the tomatoes and add with all the other ingredients. Simmer for 5 minutes. If it is watery, add another teaspoon of tomato purée and boil fast for 2 minutes. Liquidise and strain the sauce and reheat.

Meanwhile, cut the courgettes in rings or diagonal slices ¼-inch (6 mm) thick. Steam them, or fry in a little oil, till just tender—they shouldn't be transparent. Dish up and pour the tomato sauce over.

The same sauce is very good with fried aubergine slices. It cuts their greasiness and their sombre colour.

Cucumber with Herbs

I shall never see a cucumber again without thinking of the "repulsant snozzcumbers", "the filthiest-tasting vegetable on earth" consumed in Roald Dahl's *The BFG*. "They is disgusterous! They is sickable! They is rotsome!" laments the eponymous hero of that work. So too are the bent-ended and soft-spotted cucumbers that are often all that is left to me, come Fridays in Spring or Autumn. But with a bit of judicious trimming, they can be rendered edible by the following treatment.

> 2 cucumbers
> a pinch of salt
> ½ oz (15 g) butter
> a teacup of mixed herbs—parsley,
>   chives, and mint or dill

Cut the cucumbers, unpeeled, into small chunks. To do this quickly, slit them lengthwise. Lay each half face down, side by side, slit again twice each, then cut across all the strips at ½-inch (1.25 cm) intervals.

Put the cucumber in a pan with the butter and salt in the bottom and scatter on ¾ of the herbs. Cover and cook fairly fast for 4–5 minutes. Drain and serve garnished with the remaining herbs.

This is disgusterous tepid and rotsome kept hot, but eaten at once it is scrumdiddlyumptious.

Fennel with Tomatoes

> 1 medium onion
> 1 tablespoon olive oil
> 1 lb (450 g) fennel
> 1 red pepper
> 1 lb (450 g) tomatoes
> a little basil or tarragon
> salt and pepper

Chop the onion and sauté in the oil till transparent. Slice the fennel and pepper and add to the onion. Skin the tomatoes, seed them, and retain the juice from the seeds. Crush the garlic with the salt, and add it and the other seasonings. Simmer for 10–15 minutes. If it is too liquid, boil hard for another minute or so.

This is a very pleasant sauce with plain pasta.

Gratin of Fennel

This is good enough to be served as a starter, in which case use a thicker topping of crumbs and cheese.

> For the fennel:
> 2 lb (900 g) fennel
> juice of 1 lemon
> ½ oz (15 g) butter
> 3 tablespoons water
> a little salt
> For the sauce:
> 1½ oz (40 g) butter
> 1½ oz (40 g) flour
> ½–¾ pt (275–425 ml) milk
> chopped fennel tops
> 1 tablespoon cream (optional)
> For the topping:
> 1 oz (25 g) grated cheese
> ½ oz (15 g) brown breadcrumbs

For the fennel:

Trim the bulbs, reserving the better bits of green. Slice them from top to bottom, and then across in thin strips. Put in a shallow pan with the other ingredients, and simmer till tender—about 7 minutes. Drain, keeping the juice.

For the sauce:

Melt the butter and add the flour, and when it turns pale, pour on the fennel juices and gradually add the milk. It should be thickish but still pouring. Simmer for 1 minute, add the fennel tops, and test for salt. You can add a tablespoon of cream if you want.

Put the fennel in an ovenproof dish. Pour over the sauce, and scatter the cheese and breadcrumbs on top. Bake near the top of a hot oven for 10 minutes or till the top browns and crisps.

Sweet and Sour Leeks

Leeks done like this are very good with fish and shellfish, and also on their own with a rice dish. The colour is strange, so have a bright garnish ready—lemon slices or parsley.

approximately 1-inch (2.5 cm)
   cube of tamarind pulp
¼ pt (150 ml) boiling water
6 medium leeks
1 dessertspoon sunflower oil
1–2 teaspoons brown sugar
salt

Soak the tamarind in the hot water for at least 15 minutes. Trim the leeks but keep as much green as possible. Cut them in narrow rings and dabble them in cold water to get out the grit. Drain them well.

Heat the oil and turn the leeks in it till well coated. Add the sugar and salt. Squash the tamarind in your fingers to liberate its sour juice. Press this liquor through a sieve and pour onto the leeks. Mix well, cover, and simmer for 5 minutes. Take off the lid, raise the heat, and boil till the liquid reduces to almost nothing.

Casserole of Sweet Peppers

This looks best made with mixed coloured peppers—red, green and yellow. If all green, the result is slightly bitter as well as dingy in colour. If all red peppers are used, it goes particularly well with fish or pasta.

1 tablespoon olive oil
1 medium onion
6 peppers
1 lb (450 g) tomatoes
salt, sugar and black pepper to
   taste

Chop the onion and sauté in the olive oil. Cut the peppers into ½-inch (1.25 cm) strips and add them too.

Skin and seed the tomatoes, draining the juice from the seeds. Add tomatoes and juice and the seasonings. Mix well, cover and cook slowly for 20 minutes.

If a lot of juice has formed, ladle it into a frying pan and boil it hard to reduce to a couple of tablespoons. Pour it back over the peppers. Don't boil the peppers themselves hard to reduce the liquid, as they will mush up and the skin will separate and toughen.

Potatoes

The next three recipes are for potatoes. I could have made it thirty rather than three: I love potatoes in any form, though I would stop short of the rotten ones mixed with grass, as recommended to the starving Irish by an English peer, during the blight of 1845.

Not everyone is enamoured of even the wholesome tuber: when the Macneill of Barra ordered his people to plant potatoes rather than grain so as to have a harvest even in poor weather, they planted them, harvested them, dumped them sullenly at his gate—and starved. Now their descendants plant virtually nothing else.

One of my best potato memories is of earthing up the crop one sunny June, looking straight down the orange throat of a bright-eyed corn-crake, as it craked day-long in a tussock not 10 feet away. Poor corncrakes, they are almost all gone now, prey to feral cats here and God knows what perils in Africa.

My worst potato memory is of sugaring instead of salting them, and not discovering the mistake—no, the worst was miscounting the Château Potatoes so that there were only a total of 3 pea-sized articles left to feed the last table in the dining room. Difficult to choose.

Potatoes in White Wine

I think I borrowed this recipe, more or less, from Anna Thomas's *The Vegetarian Epicure*. I was looking desperately for ways of using up not quite white wine. We had bought several cases of indifferent Soave at the end of a season, and by next April it was turning ominously amber and beery. Potatoes soak up Soave like sponges. This was a wonderful discovery. It tastes very good too.

1 oz (25 g) butter	salt and pepper
1 large onion	¾ pt (425 ml) white wine
2 lb (900 g) potatoes	chopped parsley
2 bay leaves	

Melt the butter and sauté the sliced onion in it till golden. Meanwhile, scrub or peel the potatoes and cut into large chunks. Add them with all the other ingredients, except the parsley, stirring well. Simmer, covered, till the potatoes are beginning to break up. Stir carefully now and again—don't mush it—and add more wine if it sticks. Garnish with parsley, as the colour is drab.

Skirlie Potatoes

"Skirlie" is a Scottish mixture of fried onions and oatmeal. It is used as a stuffing (see under Roast Pheasant p. 299), as a side dish with mince and boiled potatoes, or as a meal on its own.

Vegetarians can substitute sunflower oil for dripping. As long as you use plenty of onions this tastes fine; but don't use margarine: all the colourants and anti-oxidants will rise up and smite you in this combination.

As an accompaniment, this potato dish is very good with a plain rare roast.

2 lb (900 g) even-sized potatoes
For the skirlie:
1½–2 oz (40–50 g) dripping
1 medium onion
4 oz (100 g) fine or medium
   oatmeal
salt and pepper

Boil potatoes in their skins.
For the skirlie:
Chop the onion fairly finely and fry till just browning. Add the oatmeal, salt and pepper, and continue cooking till it turns pale and then begins to darken. Remove at once from the heat as oatmeal catches easily.

When the potatoes are ready, dish them, cut them into thick slices in the dish, and scatter on the skirlie.

Potatoes with Rosemary

This is very good with lamb and game.

2 tablespoons olive oil
6 × 4-inch (10 cm) sprigs fresh
   rosemary
2 lb (900 g) potatoes (preferably new)
½ clove garlic crushed with a little
   salt

A cast iron casserole is best for this. Heat the oil in it, put in the rosemary, and leave on a very low heat while you scrub the potatoes. Use even-sized small ones or cut large ones into cubes. Dry them and turn them in the oil with the garlic and salt. Cover and cook in a slow oven or on the stove top till tender—about 1 hour. Stir them gently now and again.

Colourful Mixed Salad

The North of Scotland is not good salad country. I use a mixture of anything I can get or grow that tastes or looks fresh.

We get our olive oil (through Yapp's of Mere) from Beaume-de-Venise. It is a lot more drinkable than the sticky wine of the same name, in my opinion.

For the dressing:
½ a small clove of garlic
a pinch of salt
½ teaspoon French mustard
4 tablespoons fruity olive oil
2 tablespoons wine vinegar
For the salad:
1 lettuce
a few spinach leaves
3 sprigs lovage
a small bunch of chives
a sprig of mint
2 tomatoes
½ small red or yellow pepper
2-inch (5 cm) chunk of cucumber
2 stalks of celery
marigold petals, nasturtium heads,
    bergamot, borage or comfrey
    flowers

For the dressing:
Crush the garlic with the salt, add the other ingredients, and whisk or shake. This is enough for 2 or 3 salads.
For the salad:
Wash and dry the lettuce and spinach carefully. Tear it up and put it in a big bowl. Chop the herbs, slice everything else except the flowers and add to the bowl. Sprinkle on the dressing and turn lightly with your hands. Garnish with the chosen flowers—the brighter the better.

Sweets and Puddings

I don't like sweet things much. This was not always so. Leftover pudding used to appeal to me as the main perk of the job; but two or three seasons of dining mainly on meringues and mousses led to a change of heart. For many people, though, the sweet remains the highlight of the meal, so I make conscientious efforts.

As no one is actually hungry by pudding time, the sweet course should always appeal to the eye. I usually have hasty recourse to leaves or flowers, but tastes were not always so simple. Carême, much quoted, referred to "architecture—of which the main branch is confectionery". It was hardly an exaggeration: sweet dishes had for long been a showplace for brilliant technique, fantastic display, and downright vulgarity. In earlier times it had been the custom to move to a specially decorated table or a more elegant room—in extreme cases even to a separate building such as a summerhouse—for the dessert. As if the candied fruit, syllabubs and comfits of this "last remove" were not enough in the way of sticky delights, the tables of the great were decorated throughout the feast with "subtleties", often in sculpted sugar: castles, swans, palaces, knights in armour—in one extreme instance even the Holy Ghost. A picture of Queen Christina of Sweden dining with the Pope, as late as 1668, shows the unfortunate lady seated solitarily, some 20 yards to the right of and 2 yards down from His worldly Holiness, both diners being half concealed behind the turrets and fortifications of a sugar city. Presumably they were not expected to eat them: but who did? Perhaps they were recycled? One hopes they were not fed to the poor or the dogs, to the ruin of their teeth.

Cakes

The first few recipes are not cakes in the tea-time sense, but simply puddings that will sit upright looking pretty on a flat plate.

Almond Cake with Peaches or Pears

To skin peaches or nectarines, try dropping them into boiling water for 20 seconds. It may not work: some varieties have stubborn skins, and even after this treatment the knife will leave them full of nicks, looking as if a mouse has been at them. Cover them with a swirl of cream and no one will ever know.

For the base:
3 oz (75 g) butter
3 oz (75 g) caster or light
    muscovado sugar
3 oz (75 g) ground almonds
1 oz (25 g) plain flour
2 eggs
For the top:
3–4 peaches or pears
1 tablespoon jam or jelly
¼ pt (150 ml) cream
10 almonds

For the base:
Make sure the butter is really soft. Put all the ingredients in a bowl and beat till thoroughly mixed.

Line a 7-inch (17.5 cm) sandwich tin with Bakewell paper and spread the almond mixture in it. Bake in a slow oven till just firm to the touch—about 1 hour. Cool slightly before turning out. It will be moist and fragile, not really spongey.

For the top:
Peel and halve the fruit. Blanch, toast and chop the almonds. Whip the cream till stiff.

Spread the cake with the jam or jelly—plum, apricot or quince are the best choices. Arrange the fruit round the base. Pipe the cream in swirls over the fruit and scatter on the toasted almonds.

Blackcurrant and Cinnamon Tart

This is my slapdash version of the French Tarte Canelle.
If you have any pastry left make it into biscuits.

For the pastry:
6 oz (175 g) plain flour
1 level tablespoon ground
  cinnamon
3 oz (75 g) caster sugar
3 oz (75 g) butter
2 egg yolks or 1 whole egg
For the filling:
1 lb (450 g) blackcurrants
4 oz (100 g) light muscovado sugar
2 teaspoons arrowroot

Rub the butter into the flour, cinnamon and sugar till it begins to stick like shortbread. Bind with the egg. If you use whole egg the pastry will be slightly harder. Let the pastry rest while you pick over the blackcurrants. Remove gross débris but don't worry about the odd unripe berry or the tufty bits at the end. Put the currants in a pan with the sugar over a moderate heat, till the juice runs and boils up. Simmer for 2 or 3 minutes and test to see if they need more sugar, but don't oversweeten.

Cool 2 tablespoons of the juice slightly in a cup and add the arrowroot to it. Mix till smooth, pour into the currants, and bring back to the boil, stirring. As soon as the juice thickens, take off the heat and cool.

You can use a tin of blackcurrants, failing fresh—just thicken the strained juice with the arrowroot and return the currants to it.

Roll out the pastry fairly thick and line a 7–8 inch (17.5–20 cm) flan ring. Bake blind—about 30 minutes in a moderate oven. Watch it—it burns easily.

Cool the pastry shell before removing the ring. If it looks like breaking, leave the ring on.

Pour the filling in. Don't chill: this is best at room temperature.

Serve cream separately, if at all, as it doesn't improve the appearance and not everyone likes the way it blunts the intense flavour of black fruit.

Chilled Cheesecake

This is the first recipe I ever wrote down, 20 years ago when cheese-cakes were still considered rather daring in Scotland. It is a great favourite, though far from original: I got it from a school friend's mother who I think found it in *Good Housekeeping*, so I don't know who to thank for it.

I never get it ready in time to chill thoroughly, so it usually collapses, but if you can give it a couple of hours in the fridge, it will turn out beautifully, firm yet creamy.

For the top:
3 eggs
4 oz (100 g) caster sugar
¼ pt (150 ml) double cream
12–14 oz (350–400 g) curd cheese
    (I use yoghurt cheese)
grated rind and juice of 2 large
    lemons
½ oz (15 g) gelatine
For the base:
8 digestive biscuits
1 oz (25 g) Demerara sugar
1 oz butter

For the top:
Line the base of an 8-inch (20 cm) cake tin.
Separate the eggs. Whisk the yolks with the sugar and lemon rind till thick and light. Do this over a pan of steaming (not boiling) water if you are not using an electric mixer, to speed things up.

Melt the gelatine in the lemon juice and blend with the yolk mixture. Don't have the mixture cooler than room temperature or the gelatine will form strings.

Half whip the cream and mix it into the curd cheese. Add this to the first bowl.

Whisk the egg whites till very stiff and fold them in lightly. Turn the mixture gently into the prepared tin.
For the base:
Crush the digestive biscuits and mix in the sugar. Add the melted butter and sprinkle the buttery crumbs evenly on the cake. Press down lightly and chill, overnight if possible, then turn out and decorate—you can use cream, fresh soft fruit, grated chocolate or green leaves.

Chestnut Cake with Apricot Sauce

When turned out, this pudding bears a superficial resemblance to a block of choc ice at a kids' party, but beware! It is extremely solid and should be served in thin slices. The greedy may well wish to come back for more.

For the cake:
4 oz (100 g) butter
3 oz (75 g) dark muscovado sugar
1 tin unsweetened chestnut purée
2 oz (5 oz) cocoa
1 oz (25 g) white sugar
3 tablespoons water
½ teaspoon vanilla essence
For the sauce:
4 oz (100 g) sour dried apricots
½ pt (275 ml) water or a little less
honey
apricot brandy
For decoration:
¼ pt (150 ml) cream (optional)

For the cake:

Beat the butter and muscovado sugar together in a cursory way. Turn the chestnut purée out of the tin and mash it well. Mix it with the butter and sugar.

Mix the cocoa, white sugar and water to a paste and simmer for 2 minutes. Cool slightly, but while still warm add to the chestnut mixture. Add the vanilla essence and beat everything hard together —the warmth of the sauce will help to make everything blend.

Line a loaf tin with foil or Bakewell paper and pour in the chestnut mixture. Chill well.

For the sauce:

Stew the apricots in the water till soft. Liquidise, with the juice. Sweeten to taste with honey and apricot brandy.

To serve:

Turn out the cake on a plate. Either pour over a little of the sauce just before serving and pass round the rest, or decorate with cream and hand the sauce separately.

Chocolate Chestnut Cake

Chestnuts are not everyone's cup of nut. My father was a doctor, and every Christmas he got about a hundredweight of assorted chocolates and candies from grateful patients, which kept us all munching till spring. In the early sixties, to everyone's disgust, a new confectionery fashion entered middle class life—marrons glacés. Box after box poured in, and piled up, despised, in a corner of the hall cupboard. About the end of February, having run out of chocolates, I discovered I liked them. Then I discovered I liked them better with cream. The pile of marrons grew smaller and I grew larger. At school I read of a similar grossness which afflicted the Mossynoeci, "flabby and very white, fattened up by feeding on boiled chestnuts", according to Xenophon.

Theirs were not even boiled with sugar, let alone served with cream. This cake has both of those and chocolate too. I invented it to use up sweetened chestnut purée bought in error—what else can you do with the stuff?

    8 oz (225 g) dark chocolate
    ¼ pt (150 ml) water
    1 tin sweetened chestnut purée
    3 eggs.
    2 oz (50 g) sugar
    ½–¾ pt (275–425 ml) double
      cream

Melt the chocolate in the water over gentle heat. Separate the eggs. Whisk the yolks with the sugar till thick and pale.

Blend half the chocolate into the chestnut purée till smooth. If you haven't a food processor, it may help to put the purée through a mouli or sieve first.

Fold the chestnut mixture gently into the whisked yolks and sugar. Whip the egg whites stiffly and fold them in too.

Put discs of Bakewell paper in the bottoms of 3 7-inch (17.5 cm) sandwich tins and divide the mixture between them. Bake in a very moderate oven until just firm—about 40 minutes. Leave in the tins to cool. The cake will sink, but remain light and moist.

For the filling:

Cool the rest of the chocolate mixture, whip the cream stiffly, and combine, leaving slightly marbled. Use this to sandwich and coat the cake.

Hazelnut Meringue Cake

"Tell me, how do you get the skins off your hazelnuts?" a knowledge-able guest once asked me.

I was very embarrassed. It had never occurred to me to skin hazelnuts. When she explained how she toasted hers in the oven and rubbed them in a rough cloth, I realised why hazelnut meringue in smart places is rather dry and brown. I prefer it like this—moist, slightly gooey, with untidy nibs of nut in it. But if you want to do things properly, toast and rub them, then grind very finely.

For the meringue:	For the filling:
4 oz (100 g) hazelnuts	½–¾ pt (275–425 ml) double cream
4 egg whites	3 peaches or ¾ lb (350 g)
9 oz (250 g) caster sugar	raspberries or 4 oz (100 g) strong
1 teaspoon vinegar	chocolate melted in
½ teaspoon vanilla essence	3 tablespoons water

Grind the hazelnuts. Whisk the egg whites very stiff. Add the sugar, vinegar and vanilla essence, and whisk again till glossy—not too long or it will liquefy. Fold in the nuts.

Divide the mixture between 3 sandwich tins with lined bases—I use a 6-inch (15 cm), a 7-inch (17.5 cm) and an 8-inch (20 cm) tin and make a volcano-shaped cake, but 3 7-inch (17.5 cm) tins are fine.

Bake in a very moderate oven till pale brown and crisp—about 45 minutes. To loosen, run a knife round the edge of the pans. Turn out and peel off the papers before they are completely cold, or they may stick.

For the filling:

Whip the cream stiffly. If you are using chocolate, have it melted and cool and add it to ⅔ of the cream. Use this to layer the cakes and spread the top, and decorate with the plain cream. You can add nuts and grated chocolate.

If you are using fruit, peel and slice the peaches, saving an unsliced half till it is time to decorate as peaches go brown quickly; or pick over the raspberries, keeping back the best berries for the top. Use half the cream for the layers, and the rest of the fruit. Decorate the top with the remaining cream, adding the reserved fruit at the last minute.

You can use tinned raspberries, but drain them very well. Use some of the juice to tint the cream for the top.

A combination of chocolate *and* fruit is very good.

Any meringue is best filled 2 or 3 hours ahead, but I don't like it left longer, as it loses all its texture.

Meringues

Meringue desserts are well liked, and they are about the only useful way of using up egg whites—unless someone has mistakenly drunk weedkiller on your premises: take the egg whites raw for that.

A lot of cooks find problems with meringue making. Take my husband for example. One day I left him with 4 egg whites, a bag of sugar, a whisk and an oven set at 100°C/200°F. "Can you make meringues?" I asked, and rushed out. Some hours later, I got back and looked in the oven, where a dozen or so pallid biscuit-shaped objects were deliquescing ominously.

"I thought they would rise," he said, feebly.

Here are a few hints for meringue making:

(1) Have everything as dry as possible. Even a damp day or a steamy kitchen can cause ooziness or sticking.

(2) Use *fresh* eggs, don't get more than a spot of yolk in the white, and whisk only when you are ready to bake; all these things will affect the amount of air you can incorporate.

(3) Use Bakewell paper for lining if you can get it.

(4) Don't have too high a heat—the meringue will swell, crack and ooze. It will taste lovely, but stick like superglue.

(5) If you do end up with paper firmly stuck to your meringue, turn it over on the tray. Wring out a cloth in warm water and leave it pressed to the paper for 10 minutes. The paper should then lift with the help of a knife. If it doesn't, repeat the process till it does.

(6) If nothing works and you end up with smashed and sticky remnants, don't despair. Mix them lightly with whipped cream, flavoured if you like with chocolate, vanilla or a liqueur, and layer with fruit or toasted almonds. See the recipe for Summer Trifle (p. 336) for an example.

The basic meringue mixture is as follows:

4 egg whites
8 oz (225 g) caster sugar

Whisk the egg whites till very stiff, but still slightly shiny. Add 1 oz (25 g) of the sugar and whisk again. Fold in the rest of the sugar with a metal spoon or a spatula and bake at once.

Have tins lined before you start with Bakewell paper or 2 layers of greased greaseproof paper or foil. Bake in a low oven until crisp and dry—2 hours minimum.

For ordinary meringues, make 16 even-sized blobs. When cold, sandwich with cream and decorate with a glacé cherry and a bit of angelica if you like vulgar bright colours, as I do.

For a meringue cake, make 4 small or 3 larger flat rounds. When cool, sandwich and spread them with cream or buttercream flavoured with chocolate and coffee—6 oz (175 g) chocolate and 2 teaspoons instant coffee melted in 5 tablespoons water, added when cool to ½ pt (275 ml) whipped cream. You can call this Gâteau Diane, though it isn't quite.

Alternatively, sandwich with cream and fresh fruit, and decorate imaginatively with swirls of cream, some strawberries, flowers or leaves. This is also not quite, but call it a Vacherin. It's as good as.

Things in Bowls

If you have a nice cut glass or glazed bowl, you needn't fear failures with sweets. Fallen cakes, broken meringues, collapsed moulds and liquid creams can all be made to look tolerable in a pretty container, with the addition of whipped cream, fruit or nuts. The recipes below, though, I have actually evolved with cut glass in mind, rather than as rescue operations.

Several of these recipes call for gelatine. To get an even, light texture without strings, timing and temperature are both important. The egg yolk mixture must not be too cold, or the gelatine will form hard lumps as soon as it touches it. Once the gelatine is incorporated, keep an eye on it, as it may set very quickly: fresh lemon juice in particular can have that effect. You can put the bowl into cold water to start it setting, but don't forget it. The cream (if any) should go in just as the yolk mixture starts to thicken. Don't try to cut work by whisking egg whites in advance: they will begin to lose their airiness at once. And above all, don't use the sort of egg that says Week 42 on the packet when you are living in Week 48. Warmish gelatine is an ideal growing medium for all sorts of bugs, and all sorts of bugs thrive in ancient battery eggs.

Strict vegetarians may baulk at gelatine, as it is made from boiled sinews. Agar-agar is a substitute, but you only need ¼ as much, and it has to be boiled in some of the liquid from the recipe till it gels. The caramel mousse in this section will stiffen reasonably without any gelling agent at all.

Caramel Mousse

Caramel is very easy once you are used to it, but be prepared for blackness and the fumes of Hell if you haven't tried it before.

Be careful when handling a pan of hot caramel. Always wrap a teatowel round the hand holding the pan, and if you have to add water tilt the pan away from you and hold it under a drizzling tap, unless you are incapable of judging quantities. If you have to use a measuring jug, cover the hand holding that as well.

In this recipe, more yolks than whites will give a creamier, closer texture, but I prefer the lighter effect of equal proportion. Like all caramel sweets, this is very good with fresh fruit, especially oranges.

3 eggs, *or* 4 yolks and 2 whites
1 tablespoon water
8 oz (225 g) granulated sugar
¼ pt (150 ml) water
1½ teaspoons gelatine melted in
  2 tablespoons water
½ pt (275 ml) double cream

Beat the egg yolks till thick and pale.

Dissolve the sugar slowly in the tablespoonful of water over gentle heat, and when it is clear, raise the heat as high as possible. Have ready a drizzling tap or ¼ pt (150 ml) water in a jug, and a covering for your hand. Put a little cold water in the sink.

When the syrup has gone from gold to amber to a rich russet brown, take the pan quickly and dip the bottom of it in the water in the sink. Trickle in the ¼ pt (150 ml) water, and when the explosions subside, put the pan back on the heat briefly and stir till the caramel is dissolved.

Cool the caramel for 5 minutes. Meanwhile dissolve the gelatine and whip the cream, but not the egg whites yet.

Pour the caramel onto the egg yolks. If you are using an electric beater do this while the whisk is turning at high speed: otherwise whisk like mad immediately afterwards, in case the caramel sets stickily in the bottom of the bowl. Whisk till pale and thick again. Stir in the gelatine, and cool the mixture. It will set before it is really cold, so when it is tepid, whisk the egg whites stiff. Fold in half the cream, followed by the egg whites, and turn into a serving bowl. Decorate with the rest of the cream.

Once you are confident with caramel, you can set some of it hard for decoration. To do this, oil a small baking tin. When the caramel is brown, dip the pan in the sink as directed to stop it darkening any further, and pour a thin layer of it into the tin before adding the water. When this sets, break or crush it and scatter it on top of the mousse. Caramel absorbs moisture quickly, so don't put it on till you are almost ready to serve, or it will sweat.

For the same reason, some good news. If you stick up your pans with unsuccessful caramel, they will usually wash clean after a soaking, unless utterly carbonised.

Cold Orange Soufflé

3 eggs
2 oz (50 g) caster sugar
grated rind of 2 oranges
juice of 3 oranges
juice of 1 lemon
2 teaspoons gelatine
¼ pt (150 ml) double cream
For decoration:
10 walnut halves
1 tablespoon caster sugar

Separate the eggs. Whisk the yolks till thick with the sugar and orange rind. Dissolve and melt the gelatine in 4 tablespoons of the orange juice.

Add the rest of the juices to the cream and whip till it holds a peak. Stir the gelatine into the egg yolks. Don't have the yolks too cold or it will string.

As soon as the mixture starts setting, fold in the cream. Whisk the egg whites stiffly and fold them in too. Turn into a bowl.

For decoration:

Put the walnuts and sugar in a small heavy pan on a medium heat till the sugar melts, then turn up the heat till the mixture browns and bubbles. Have ready an oiled baking tin, pour the caramelised walnuts onto this and push apart quickly with a metal fork. Just before serving, place them on the mousse.

If you don't fancy caramelising, decorate with grated chocolate or fresh orange segments.

Frangipane Cream with Plum Compôte

The texture of this cream bears an unfortunate resemblance to cold semolina pud, but the taste is very delicate and distinctive. It goes well with a compôte of red plums.

On the subject of red plums, I once had a tray of them in the shed where I keep the fruit and vegetables. One night they disappeared. The box was there, but the plums were not. Everything else was as before. The following day I reached into the paper sack of carrots—and reached—and reached—no carrots either! We were mystified. Neighbours' boys playing practical jokes? Light-fingered campers? We rigged up a makeshift burglar alarm against further raids, but nothing else happened. We looked askance at the suspected campers, and grumbled.

A couple of weeks later, we smelt a rat—a dead one. We moved everything in our search, including the pallets on which the fruit boxes stood. We didn't find the rat but we found his treasures, now much decayed—40 red plums and 30 carrots: not even nibbled, but stored up in red and orange glory for him to gloat over. Vanity, vanity! It was so pathetic I cried. We bought a humane rat trap and baited it with Stilton to catch any other marauders. The Stilton was appreciated. In the course of a fortnight our visitor ate about a pound of prime Stilton, rejecting dried-up cheddar crusts. But he always left before we got up in the morning. Late one night we crept in and caught him at dinner. We took him to the local rubbish dump to try his fortunes there. I hope the local gang didn't scrag him.

For the Cream:
3 egg yolks
3 oz (75 g) sugar
¾ pt (425 ml) milk
2 teaspoons gelatine melted in
   2 tablespoons water
finely grated rind of 1 orange
3 drops almond essence
1 tablespoon orange flower water
   (if it's the concentrate, use only
   3 drops)
2 oz (50 g) ground almonds
¼ pt (150 ml) double cream
10 split toasted almonds

For the Compôte:
1½ lb (675 g) red or black plums
¼ lb (100 g) light muscovado sugar
2-inch (5 cm) strip orange peel
2 cloves
1 glass port or red wine

334

For the Cream:

Blend the egg yolks with the sugar. Boil the milk, pour it on to the egg yolks, stirring all the time, and return the mixture to the pan. Cook very slowly till it thickens slightly but do not boil, or it will curdle. Pour this custard into a wide bowl. Add the dissolved gelatine, and everything else except the cream. Cool, stirring occasionally, until it begins to set. Whip the cream and fold it in, and turn it into a serving bowl. Decorate with toasted almonds.

For the Compôte:

Stone the plums if you prefer to. Put all the compôte ingredients in a pan and let the contents boil up once. Reduce heat to very low and barely simmer till the plums are just soft. Add more sugar if necessary, but don't lose the slightly bitter plum taste by oversweetening. Chill before serving.

Rose Cream

This recipe is plagiarised from Damask Cream in Theodora Fitzgibbon's *A Taste of the West Country*. I make it less creamy. It is very simple and unusual.

For the junket:
1½ pt (825 ml) milk
2 oz (50 g) caster sugar
1 tablespoon rosewater
a drop of red colouring
1 teaspoon essence of rennet
nutmeg
For the top:
¼ pt (150 ml) double cream
1 tablespoon rosewater
red rose petals

For the junket:

Warm the milk and sugar to blood heat. Add the rosewater, colouring and rennet. Stir well, and pour into a glass bowl or 6 individual ones. Set in a warm place without moving until firm. Grate nutmeg over fairly liberally. Cool.

For the top:

Half-whip the cream and rosewater and pour it over the junket. Chill. Scatter rose petals on just before serving.

Summer Trifle

This is best if you make your own sponge cake and use it very fresh, but you can substitute bought sponge fingers. The lack of custard and the addition of egg white to the whipped cream make it lighter and fresher than a Christmassy trifle

Actually the kind of trifle I like best is the solid institutional sort, with bloated sponge cake suspended in red jelly of the consistency of gristle, topped by 2 yellow inches of unyielding custard, if possible made with dried milk powder. But the honest old school-party trifle is hard to find these days; its sophisticated descendant is beautified with sweet and slimy preparations of sodium alginate, Saccharin and citric acid—no-cook custard, instant jelly and sort of shaving foam on top. Only the hundreds and thousands are what they always were, and they were the only bit I didn't like.

For the sponge cake:
2 eggs
2 oz (50 g) caster sugar
2 oz (50 g) plain flour
For the filling:
4 tablespoons apricot brandy or
    strawberry or raspberry liqueur
2–3 peaches or nectarines
½ lb (225 g) strawberries
For the top:
½ pt (275 ml) double cream
1 egg white
1 pt (570 ml) volume broken
    meringues or ½ pt (275 ml)
    macaroons

For the sponge:
Preheat the oven to 200°C/400°F. Grease an 8-inch (20 cm) sandwich tin and line the base. Whisk the eggs and sugar till very light and thick. Fold in the flour gently and turn into the tin. Bake till just firm—about 8 minutes.
For the filling:
Peel the peaches and slice all the fruit, but save the best few strawberries for the top. Pour the liqueur over the sliced fruit.
Line a bowl with the cut up sponge cake and put the fruit on top.

For the top:

Whisk the cream and egg white separately till fairly stiff and combine gently. Fold in the meringues or macaroons, not crushed but in rough pieces. Pile this onto the fruit and decorate with the reserved strawberries. Chill for an hour, when the meringue will have begun to melt pleasantly.

Syllabub

This recipe also makes a refreshing ice cream to serve with peaches or melon. If you freeze it, take it out and mash it a couple of times or it will separate.

> juice of 2 lemons
> ¼ pt (150 ml) white wine, dry or
>   sweet
> caster sugar to taste—1–3 oz
>   (25–75 g)
> ½ pt (275 ml) double cream
> nutmeg or cinnamon

Whisk the cream with the sugar till fairly thick. Add the juice and wine in 2 or 3 instalments, whisking between additions to a soft peak. Taste for sweetening. If the cream looks as if it will take it without curdling, add a little extra wine. Turn into a glass bowl or 6 long-stemmed glasses, and sprinkle the chosen spice over.

You can serve brandy snaps, macaroons or fresh fruit with this.

Ices

I am not going to describe the correct procedures for making various sorts of ices. They are fiddly and tiresome like many correct procedures, and you can make ices of character without knowing anything about them. The following are all personal experiments. Do try your own—you can use anything from avocadoes to evaporated milk with cocoa.

To freeze, preferably use a flat-bottomed metal container on the bottom of the freezing compartment—not on top of other packages.

Butterscotch Ice Cream

This is quite a lot of bother but extremely good.

8 oz (225 g) dark muscovado sugar	a further 2 tablespoons water
4 oz (100 g) butter	3 eggs
⅛ pt (75 ml) water	¼ pt (150 ml) double cream
a pinch of salt	For decoration:
½ teaspoon vanilla essence	20 toasted almonds

Put the sugar, butter, ⅛ pt (75 ml) water and salt in a heavy pan and boil for 2 minutes on a high heat. It will froth up and then subside, glooping vigorously. (It should be at 110°C/220°F, jam temperature, certainly no hotter.)

Remove it from the heat and add the vanilla and the second dose of water.

Whisk the eggs till pale and thick, and pour in ¾ of the warm butterscotch, beating the while if possible. Continue whisking till it is light and fairly thick again, by which time it should be nearly cool. Whip the cream to a soft peak and fold it into the mixture. Turn into a shallow metal dish and freeze for 2 hours. It is a rich mixture, so it won't go crunchy, but if you don't beat it now and again during freezing, it will separate into a lighter and darker layer. I rather like it that way.

Keep an eye on the rest of the butterscotch, which is for a sauce. If it gets too sticky, heat it up with a little more water and cool again. If it is too runny, heat it to boiling point and stir in 1 level teaspoon arrowroot slaked in 1 tablespoon water.

To serve, pile the ice cream in a serving dish layered with the sauce and toasted almonds.

Milk Ice

This simple recipe comes from my mother-in-law. It's a very light and refreshing ice, but it goes rock hard if kept, so eat it at once—it will be no strain to do so.

I have tried the same method using 1 tablespoon rosewater instead of vanilla, and that is also very good.

1 pt (570 ml) milk	1½ teaspoons gelatine
vanilla essence to taste	3 oz (75 g) sugar

Mix the gelatine and sugar in a pan and add the milk. Heat, stirring, till dissolved. Add vanilla essence to taste (I like it quite strong). Cool, and then freeze. Inspect it every half-hour and mash it a few times after it begins to crystallise.

Cardamom Ice

This and the next two ices are made in the same way. The three together make a sophisticated party sweet. If you plan to do this, make a double or triple quantity of custard, and divide into 3 bowls for flavouring, before adding the egg whites.

> 3 eggs
> 1 pt (570 ml) milk
> ½ teaspoon agar agar (or
>   2 teaspoons gelatine dissolved in
>   2 tablespoons water)
> 2 oz (50 g) light muscovado sugar
> 20 crushed cardamoms

Separate the eggs. Boil the milk with the agar agar (but if you are using gelatine, just melt it and keep it aside). Make a custard with the milk and egg yolks and cook over a very gentle heat till it thickens lightly. Pour it into a wide bowl and add the sugar, and the gelatine if you are using it.

Crush the cardamoms, remove large bits of husk, and add to the custard. Cool the bowl in a sink of cold water, stirring occasionally.

When the custard is cool and beginning to set, fold in the stiffly whisked egg whites. Freeze for 1½ hours, mashing after each half hour.

Cinnamon Ice

Substitute 2–3 teaspoons ground cinnamon for the cardamoms.

Heather Honey Ice

Instead of the sugar, add 2 tablespoons heather honey, and omit the spices.

Hot Puddings

I only use hot puddings on Sundays, as a simple hot English pudding with cream seems a good complement to the Sabbath Lobster Mayonnaise. I often make fruit pies, or if not, one of the following. These are popular with everyone including our dog Jet. Six days a week he sleeps soundly till the main course is served, then stations himself immovably in the breach between kitchen and serving hatch, to intercept tasty morsels on their way to and fro: but he doesn't care for lobster, so on Sundays his pre-prandial slumber is extended till the pudding is broached. His favourite is apple pie (with the cloves removed before he is served) but that is so well known it hardly needs a recipe. Here is his second choice:

Queen of Puddings

½ oz (15 g) butter
1 pt (570 ml) milk
grated rind of 1 lemon
2 oz (50 g) fine breadcrumbs
1 oz (25 g) granulated sugar
2 eggs
½ lb (225 g) home-made jam
4 oz (100 g) caster sugar

Heat the milk with the butter, lemon rind and granulated sugar and pour over the breadcrumbs. Butter a 2-pint (1.2 litre) baking dish. Separate the eggs. Beat the yolks into the bread and milk and pour this custard into the dish. Bake in a very moderate oven till just firm —about 40 minutes. Cool slightly.

Whisk the egg whites very stiffly and fold in the caster sugar. If you happen to have an extra egg white handy, use it, with 2 oz (50 g) more sugar.

Spread the jam on the cooked base. Raspberry jam is traditional, but plum and blackcurrant are very good too: don't use anything too sweet. Pile the meringue on top, sealing the edges, and return to the oven till the top is crisp and brown—about 30 minutes.

Hot Chocolate Pudding

This and the next pudding look rather like failed soufflés—not surprisingly, as they consist of similar ingredients combined in a different manner.

For the sauce:
½ oz (15 g) butter
1 tablespoon golden syrup
1 tablespoon dark muscovado
   sugar
1 tablespoon cocoa

For the top:
½ pt (275 ml) milk
3 oz (75 g) sugar
2 oz (50 g) butter
2 oz (50 g) flour
1 oz (25 g) cocoa
3 eggs

For the sauce:

Melt all the ingredients together and bring to the boil. Pour into a greased 2-pint (1.2 litre) baking dish.

For the top:

Whisk the cocoa, sugar and egg yolks together till well mixed. Add the butter cut in small pieces, the flour and milk, and whisk again. Beat the egg whites very stiff and fold gently into the mixture. Pour it over the sauce and bake for 45–50 minutes in a very moderate oven. It should be sticky and dark at the bottom and spongey on top.

Hot Lemon Pudding

4 oz (100 g) sugar
2 oz (50 g) plain flour
1½ oz (40 g) butter
juice and grated rind of 2 lemons
3 eggs
½ pt (275 ml) milk

Separate the eggs and cut the butter into small pieces. Put all the ingredients except the egg whites in a bowl and whisk with a rotary whisk for 1 minute. Whisk the egg whites stiffly and fold in. If you only possess one whisk, make sure it is washed and dried before attacking the egg whites, as any moisture will prevent them fluffing up.

Fold the egg whites into the mixture and pour into a greased 2-pint (1.2 litre) baking dish. Bake for 45–50 minutes in a very moderate oven.

Bananas Flambées

Andrew claims to have invented this method on a yacht somewhere, but as the recipe he says he used is entirely different except that it contains bananas, either he can't read or he tippled too much of the rum. It is best with a home-made vanilla ice cream, therefore not on a yacht, unless a very advanced one.

> 6 bananas (underripe work best)
> 2 oz (50 g) butter
> 2 oz (50 g) dark muscovado sugar
> 1 tablespoon raisins ·
> 4 tablespoons rum, or more

Slice the bananas in 4 lengthwise and then across once. Melt the butter in a frying pan and put in the bananas. When they turn yellow, add the sugar and the raisins. Turn carefully till everything is hot.

Warm the rum. If you want the bananas in a fancy serving dish get the dish very hot and turn them into it: if it is cool the rum won't blaze. Light the warmed rum and immediately pour over the bananas.

Breakfast

Breakfast has meant different things in different times and places. There is an eighteenth century painting in the Musée Condé entitled "Das Austern Frühstuck"—Austrian breakfast—depicting a company of elegantly dressed young gentlemen starting the day with oysters and champagne. Most of us would not relish oysters for breakfast. The clue to the evident self-satisfaction of this party is perhaps to be found in their activities of the previous night: oysters were much esteemed for aphrodisiac properties, both to stimulate and to restore. The young gallant might down a dozen or so oysters between engagements, as the harassed executive gulps black coffee.

Samuel Johnson was downright in his praise of the Scottish breakfast above all others. "If an epicure could remove by a wish in quest of sensual gratification, wherever he had supped, he would breakfast in Scotland," declared the sage.

I have kind feelings for Dr Johnson because he loved his cat Hodge, and so I am pleased to think that he would have enjoyed our breakfast at Scarista. We start with a cold table of fresh fruit juices, fresh fruit, stewed dried fruit, yoghurt, muesli and other cereals. This is followed by porridge with cream; kippers, bacon, sausages, black, white and raisin-speckled sliced puddings, fried tomatoes, mushrooms, fried bread, eggs; scones, oatcakes, wholemeal toast; and a choice of various coffees and teas.

The vigilant reader (if not bored into quiescence by this catalogue) will have noticed the presence of bacon and sausages. Free range? Yes, of course, though sadly not local. It was a very narrow squeak. When we decided to abandon all factory-farmed produce, bacon was the

343

greatest difficulty. We could ban poultry and pork without anyone really noticing the lack, and augment the deficiencies of our laying hens by applying to a fellow hen-keeper; but bacon seemed impossible. With a week to go before the start of the new season, we gritted our teeth and prepared for ill tempers at baconless breakfasts. Then we heard of Ann Petch in Devon (her address is at the end of this book) who rears rare old breeds of pig and from them produces superb sausages, bacon and hams. A few days after my nervous 'phone call, the first Datapost parcel arrived. Since then all our pigmeat has come in this manner—a special van with a jolly postman on overtime makes the round trip of 110 miles from Stornoway to deliver our sausages. The quality of Mrs Petch's products is unbeatable. The quality of life enjoyed by her pigs looks unbeatable too. We went to see them on our next trip South and shot our whole reel of holiday film on studies of jowly Middle Whites, alert Tamworths, dapper Berkshires and blowsy Gloucester Old Spots. We saw the well-sprung van they go the slaughter house in too, and it looked as stress-free as such a conveyance could be, certainly more comfortable than a Harris bus. Watching Mrs Petch's pigs, I almost felt they had got a decent bargain, and I am not prone to feel that about meat animals.

Fresh Fruit Juices

If you have an electric juice extractor, you can make juice from almost anything, but the only sorts we use are grapefruit and orange. The best method for these is an aluminium hand-juicer. The important thing about fresh fruit juice is that it should be *fresh*. Kept in the fridge overnight, it is hardly distinguishable from the bottled type in taste, and in appearance it is decidedly worse, as the flecks of fruit and the oil from the zest rise to the top.

Dried Fruits

It's a mistake to go straight for the big, brightly coloured moist-looking stuff in sealed packets. Buy your dried fruit from a health food store. Sniff around the sacks and boxes (but surreptitiously, or they may eject you). The best dried fruit has an intense perfume, reminiscent of its fresh sun-warmed self dipped in wine. Don't be put off by small wizened fruits with a powdery white coating: this is just the natural sugar crystallising on the skin. Fruit that is very plump and shiny has been treated with foreign substances (hair oil?) and fruit that is very large was grown in conditions conducive to size and tastelessness: think of Golden Delicious Apples, size 1.

Here are a few types of dried fruit that may be unfamiliar, whose looks alone would not persuade you to buy:

Apricots—Hunza

These are very small whole wild apricots from the Hunza Valley on the borders of Afghanistan. Beautiful must be the mountains whence they come, but you would never guess it to look at these little mud-coloured marbles. Taste them, though, and you will be astonished. They are lusciously sweet, almost buttery. Anyone who has read *The Magician's Nephew* will be reminded of Digory's toffee tree. The kernels are good to eat, too, if you are not inhibited about crunching the stones.

Apricots—Turkish unsulphured

Dried apricots are usually treated with sulphur to retain their colour. These are dark brown, with a rich, warm scent, like heather honey.

Apricots—unprepossessing wizened halves

You sometimes come across small, dry-looking apricots, unevenly coloured from rusty red through orange to greenish yellow. They are usually cheap. Buy them—they are very sour, but have an intense flavour. Use them in savoury dishes, or with other sweeter fruit such as figs, if they are too sharp on their own, or sweeten them cautiously with honey and cinnamon.

Figs—Turkish

The best ones are not over large, but squashy, dark and blooming with crystallising natural sugar. They need very little cooking and are very good without any, instead of sweets.

Prunes—70/80 runts

Prunes are graded by number per kilo. 30/40 are huge and bland, 50/60 are sweet and juicy with a good flavour, and 70/80 are invariably very wrinkled and sour. These smallest cheap ones often have the most pronounced prussic flavour, more than a hint of almonds. As with apricots, use the sourest in savoury dishes, or with a sweeter dried fruit, or add some light muscovado sugar.

I never bother to soak dried fruit. Cover liberally with water, bring to the boil, and simmer very gently till almost tender. The fruit will continue to plump up as it sits in the warm juice. It will keep, covered, for several days.

Fresh Fruit Salad

If you are serving fruit salad for breakfast, it should be sharper and lighter than after a meal, so forget about sugar syrup and liqueurs. I peel apples and peaches for guests, but I prefer them unpeeled personally. If you don't peel, slice finely.

    1 small melon or pineapple
    2 apples
    2 oranges, or 1 orange and
        1 grapefruit
    2 peaches
    1 banana
    ¼ lb (100 g) grapes
    juice of ½ lemon

Peel the fruit as necessary and cut into even-sized slices. To get pithless segments out of citrus fruit, peel round and round like an apple and cut out the flesh with a fine saw-bladed knife, leaving the membrane behind. Catch any juice and add with the fruit. Put in the lemon juice, but you may not need it if you used grapefruit.

Muesli

Wholefood muesli mixtures are generally very good these days, but try this for a special occasion. You should use the combination of grains labelled "muesli base" for this. If you can't get hold of it use porridge oats—*not* a sweetened packet muesli. I like the mixture fairly sharp, with yoghurt and no cream, but this depends on individual taste. It is quite tolerable to substitute a mixture of evaporated milk and fruit juice if you have neither cream nor yoghurt, or use all fruit juice. Milk is too bland.

This mixture is quite passable next day, but it is much better eaten at once, when the textures are distinct, with a bit of bite to the grains and dried fruit, and no suggestion of mushiness. It doesn't suit everyone even then—Andrew always refers to it as cold porridge.

1 dessertspoon each of:
    raisins or currants
    dried apricots
    shelled but not skinned nuts
juice of 1 orange and 1 lemon
1 dessertspoon of well-flavoured
    honey
about a teacupful of sliced fresh
    fruit
1 large tart apple
3–4 tablespoons muesli grains
¼ pt (150 ml) yoghurt or cream, or
    rather more

The night before you intend to make the muesli, chop the first three ingredients coarsely together. Stir the honey into the fruit juices and add the chopped mixture and the sliced fresh fruit. Do not peel anything that has edible skin. Chill this mix overnight.

Next morning, grate the whole apple into the bowl, without peeling or coring. Add the muesli grains. Put in enough cream, yoghurt or a mixture of both to make the consistency slightly sloppy—it should *not* resemble porridge.

Taste for sweetness/sharpness. Add more honey, brown sugar or lemon juice, as required.

Garnish with streaks of cream, attractive-looking fruit such as grapes or strawberries, or mint leaves.

Yoghurt

Yoghurt is delicious with stewed dried fruit for breakfast, and has, of course, a multitude of other applications. You can use any sort of milk, pasteurised or not, skimmed or whole, dairy or soya.

Home-made yoghurt is much superior to bought. I used to think patent yoghurt makers were cissy, but after 10 years of struggling to keep batches going in muffled bowls and vacuum flasks, I gave in, and sheepishly bought the cheapest model available at Boots'. Since then I have had consistently perfect yoghurt.

I use a new commercial starter every 6 weeks or so, but skilled hands can keep it going much longer. The first starter I ever battled with was fearsomely rugged. It didn't come in a hygienic bottle or packet—it was fished out of a bubbling bowl of yoghurt by the friend who presented me with it, and looked like a sprig of tough cauliflower. Every evening I offered it a bowl of warm milk, and every morning it had gobbled most of the offering and trebled in size. I drained off whatever it had left (which had turned into a very tangy, effervescing yoghurt) placed the Thing gingerly in a sieve, and washed it ritually three times in running water. Then another libation of milk. By the end of a week it was consuming 2 pints a day and had attained the size of a football. Eventually I plucked up enough courage to put it in the dustbin, but for some time I expected retribution to follow.

Use live yoghurt but not as live as that. Failing instructions with your patent machine, proceed like this:

Have the milk just above blood heat—hot to the touch, but not so hot you can't stick a finger in it. Clean the finger first: warm milk quickly picks up bacteria. If you are using fresh dairy milk, boil it and cool it to the correct temperature; if you have processed milk, heat it. Whisk in 1 teaspoon of live yoghurt, or your starter. Pour into a yoghurt maker, or vacuum flask, or put in a covered bowl in a warm place, insulated with a towel. Investigate at intervals after 3 hours. When the milk thickens, remove it to a cool place. It is best made every day, but will keep up to a week in the fridge.

Porridge

If you use no-cook oats you will end up with wallpaper paste. In fact any sort of rolled oat is just about as bad. Use oatmeal: it comes in pinhead, medium and fine, according to preference. The best porridge I ever ate was my grandmother's, made with fine oatmeal and a lot of salt. She served it in shallow plates. It went satisfyingly solid, so that one could excavate milk rivers and lakes in it. Somehow it was never gelatinous, as mine is if I make it that thick.

In my home area, those over the age of porridge landscaping dunk it spoonful by spoonful in a cup of milk or cream. The top of the porridge is always sprinkled with dry meal, and no one *ever* puts syrup, honey or sugar on it. Indeed, the very thought of this abomination is so disgusting that to this day I can hardly bear to handle the plates where it has been perpetrated.

This quantity is for only 2 servings, as you are unlikely to find many porridge lovers together in time and place.

3 oz (75 g) oatmeal
¾ pt (425 ml) water
1 flat teaspoon salt

If you are in a hurry in the mornings, soak the meal overnight. Then you need only bring it to the boil, stirring, and it will thicken almost at once. Pinhead meal will need 2 minutes cooking even if it has been soaked, 10 minutes if it hasn't. I use fine with a third of pinhead for texture's sake.

Don't overcook porridge and above all don't let it form a skin. It will develop a steamy flavour like the smell of an old-fashioned wash-day.

Serve liberally sprinkled with dry meal, with milk or cream. Please don't put sugar on it.

Kippers

Bought kippers are scorned by addicts of home smoking, who claim, with justice, that they are insufficiently long in smoke and dyed a silly colour. Nevertheless, if the herring were fresh, even a commercial kipper can be very good. You should never need extra fat to cook a kipper. Heat a dry frying pan, put in the kippers flesh side down, cover with a lid and cook for 2–3 minutes. Turn them over and cook a further minute. You should get about a tablespoonful of evil-looking oil draining from 2 kippers. If you haven't, suspect them of old age. If they make you belch kippery fumes all day, they were certainly past it, or else you are pregnant.

Kedgeree

Kedgeree is a good way of using a small quantity of fish—a couple of smoked whiting or the catch of an unsuccessful fly fisherman. If kept hot it goes very stodgy, so have everything ready, even the previous evening, and just mix at serving time. It will only take 2–3 minutes.

    4 oz (100 g) long grain rice
    4 eggs
    ½–¾ lb (225–350 g) fish
    3 oz (75 g) butter
    salt and freshly ground black
        pepper
    chopped parsley

Cook the rice. Hardboil and chop 3 of the eggs. Cook and flake the fish.
    When ready to serve, get the butter very hot in a frying pan. Add first the rice, then the fish, then the eggs, allowing each ingredient to heat through before adding the next. Season to taste. Beat the fourth egg, mix it into the rice, and serve at once, garnished with chopped parsley.
    You can make a similar vegetarian dish in exactly the same way, using lightly cooked vegetables instead of fish. Leeks and mushrooms are best. Add some grated nutmeg.

Eggs

Egg production is so fiendishly cruel that I must reiterate its horrors. In a battery cage, a hen has little more room than the page you are reading. To live life-long in such conditions is for her as it would be for you to spend your whole life in your wardrobe, with four other people. Imagine if one of them was a bully, and pulled your hair out, or even bit holes in you. Imagine if the floor of the wardrobe was of wire mesh, and you were barefoot. If that reads like one of Amnesty International's torture files, that is just how it is.

Poached Eggs

To get perfect results, use a rather wide, shallow pan with at least 1½ inches (4 cm) of water in it, over a high heat. Break the first egg into a cup. As soon as the water boils up, slide the egg into it, bringing the cup down to the level of the water. Do the same with the other eggs in quick succession. After the last egg is in, let the water boil up fiercely. Remove from the heat, cover and let stand for 2 minutes. Try to take the eggs out in the order they went in—this is not difficult with up to 4 eggs.

Scrambled Eggs

Scrambling eggs in large quantities is not a success. Allow 1–2 eggs per person depending on what else you are serving. Don't use too much milk (a common practice) or you will get a flavourless curdled custard.

    4 eggs
    1 tablespoon milk
    ¼ flat teaspoon salt
    ½ oz (15 g) butter

Whisk the eggs, milk and salt in a bowl. Melt the butter in a heavy-bottomed pan, pour in the eggs, and stir over a medium heat till you have flakes of egg forming and the rest of creamy consistency. Take off the heat at once, and continue stirring till the flakes predominate. There should still be liquid egg coating them, and it should have a nice satiny sheen. Dish hastily, and eat at once.

As for fried eggs, I can't offer much advice. Frying eggs isn't an area in which I excel. I dislike using a lot of fat, and never believe how much is required to cook an egg. I can't baste them without burning myself, and as I usually cook everything on the highest possible heat, I toughen and brown the undersides. All the same a Scarista fried egg is still a lot better than the recurrent hotel horror of stale battery eggs fried slowly in rancid commercial cooking oil.

Scots turn their eggs—thrifty with fat. When they are almost cooked, flip them over for half a minute before serving. I achieved notoriety at an early age by shouting after an elderly head waiter in a very proper establishment, "I like my egg turned!" A lot of heads turned too, I recollect my parents' faces vividly. My daughter recently avenged them by bellowing in an echoingly empty café in Yorkshire, "*This* isn't real cream!"

Puddings—Maragan

A marag is a pudding—black, white or spotted. They are dearly loved in the Islands. Those we buy and slice for breakfast frying are obtained in plastic skins from Charles Macleod, butchers in Stornoway, who are rightly proud of their puddings. The true traditional marag, though, is made at sheep-killing time, to use up the blood, suet and stomach from the carcase. Some housewives are superb pudding makers, but it is rather a dying art.

Don't be squeamish about these. Better eat the outsides of a sheep one week and the insides the next, than eat the outsides of two and waste the rest.

White Pudding

1 sheep's stomach	6 oz (175 g) suet
¾ lb (350 g) medium oatmeal	salt and pepper
½ lb (225 g) onions	water

Wash the stomach, inside and out, under a cold running tap. It should be used warty side out.

Chop the onions and suet finely. Mix all the ingredients together with enough water to make a slightly sloppy consistency. Fill into the skin, a bit more than half full. Tie or sew the skin up firmly, leaving enough slack for the meal to swell. Prick all over with a darning needle. Place in a pan of simmering water and boil for 2 hours. Remove from the water and cool. Slice and fry for breakfast or high tea.

Fruit Pudding

a sheep's stomach	3 oz (75 g) sugar
¾ lb (350 g) plain flour	a pinch of salt
6 oz (175 g) suet	mixed spice (optional—only in
a handful of raisins	moderation)

Wash the stomach as directed for the previous recipe. Chop the suet finely. Mix all the ingredients together with enough water to make a crumbly dough. Finish as for white pudding.

Black Pudding is the third of the local pudding trinity and the most popular of all. There is no point in giving directions, as it requires fresh sheep's blood. The local slaughter house will reserve the necessary when they kill anyone's sheep, so it is still commonly made at home in the Islands. It tastes quite different from English black pudding, which is made from pig's blood.

Marmalade

I hate making marmalade. When I'm shredding, I absent-mindedly put the pips in the peel bowl and vice versa. I forget how many pounds and how many pints before it comes to the cooking stage. I watch it for hours and it doesn't boil, then go away and leave it and it boils over. This year it boiled over to such effect that trickles of marmalade are still oozing out of crevices in the cooker 3 weeks later. And I don't even like the taste of it. Still, as marmalade goes, this is a good recipe, more fruity than some. It makes about 18 lb (8 kg).

    7 lb (2.2 kg) Seville oranges
    2 sweet oranges
    3 lemons
    14 pt (8.4 l) water
    12 lb (5.4 kg) sugar

Have ready a large bowl for the peel and a smaller one for the pips. Separate them as follows:

Cut each fruit in quarters. With a saw-edged knife, cut out the pips in a chunk. Most of the flesh will come too, but this doesn't matter. Put these chunks in the smaller bowl.

Shred the peel across in ¼-inch (6 mm) strips and put it in the other bowl.

Now cover both pips and peel with water, measuring the quantity you use, up to the full 14 pt (8.4 l). Leave for 24–48 hours.

Spread a square of muslin or a tea-towel in a sieve over a third bowl. Pour in the pips and their water. Tie up the cloth firmly, reserving the liquid that has gone through.

Now put that liquid, the bag of pips, the contents of the peel bowl and water to make up the 14 pt (8.4 l) into a jelly pan. Bring to the boil and simmer slowly till the peel is soft enough to break instantly at a pinch. This takes 1½–2 hours.

Remove the bag of pips, draining it well and returning the juice to the pan. Add the sugar and dissolve. Bring back to the boil and cook fairly rapidly till a little sets on a cold plate—the boiling temperature should be about 110°C/225°F. This will take a further ¾–2 hours, depending on how hard you boil it. Longer, slower cooking will produce a darker marmalade with a more barley-sugar flavour.

Remove the pan from the heat and take off any scum with a cold metal spoon. Allow the pan to stand for 15 minutes, then stir to distribute the peel evenly. Ladle into hot dry jars and cover.

You can use part muscovado sugar—about ⅓—if you like a slightly treacly flavour and a very dark colour. Be prepared for a much heavier scum and a poorer set though.

Thank goodness it only happens once a year.

Baking and Suchlike

"She wadna bake and she wadna brew
  Nickety, nackety, noo, noo, noo,
For fear o' spoilin' her gentle hue . . ."

That was the wife of the wee cooper o' Fife. Perhaps her stove was like mine. My oven is deep and my arms are short, and much branded with incautious groping into the dark recesses. When the wind blows, as it usually does, the hot-plate glows orange, and my face cooks as much as my pancakes.

Everything baked that we use in the hotel is home-baked, with the exception of one item, of which more later. Fortunately, Harris women are wonderful bakers, and I have ducked out of many baking jobs which I would otherwise make a mess of, as I tend to forget about things in ovens till they start smoking. Many of the recipes in this section are with grateful acknowledgements to friends who bake for me.

Yeast Doughs

There is a misplaced mystique about breadmaking. It is really very easy, and needn't be time-consuming. You don't have to knead the stuff till your back is breaking and you don't need to let it rise twice—these are left-overs from the days of huge troughs of dough and home-cultured yeasts, when producing an even texture took both skill and muscle. You needn't hover over the dough while it rises: give it

½ an hour by a steaming saucepan, 2 hours in a not very warm kitchen, or overnight in the fridge, depending on what suits you.

Here are a few hints for the baker who has tried and failed:

(1) Have your yeast mixture nicely warm, but *never* uncomfortably hot.

(2) Don't make your dough too dry. It should be soft like scones or suet-crust, not firm like short pastry.

(3) Cover the rising dough with a damp tea-towel. If the top dries and hardens it will prevent the rest from rising.

(4) Don't rest the dough-filled tins on a very hot surface, or the bottom will harden before it can rise.

Flour

For most doughs, I use stoneground organic wholewheat bread-flour finely milled. Some organic wholewheat flours are "soft", i.e. low gluten, and make very dense bread. They are not always labelled, so it may take a bad experience or so before you learn what is what. A finely ground flour rises more easily than a coarse one, anyway. It is also a better bet for all-purpose cooking: you can use it for sauces, sponges and pastry, even though it is ostensibly for bread. If you are using wholewheat flour all the time, you may find it worth while buying a sack from a wholefood shop or wholesaler. Buy 100% wholewheat or wholemeal. "Wheatmeal" has had the bran removed.

For white bread, use only strong white flour. Unbleached has a slightly better flavour. Strong white flour tends to toughen sponges and pastry, but it is good for batters and not noticeable in sauces.

Other flours, such as oat and rye, are low gluten, so if you want a well-risen bread, you should use at least ¼ weight of hard wheat flour. But a dense un-British bread can be very good.

Yeast

Three kinds of yeast are generally available:

(1) Fresh yeast. This usually comes in a compressed block. You need 2 oz (50 g) for 3 lb (or a 1½ kilo bag) of flour. Mash it with 1 teaspoon of sugar till it goes runny. Add a cupful of the warm water required for the recipe and leave it till it foams. Add the rest of the liquid and proceed.

(2) Dried yeast. This is granulated. Use 1 oz (25 g) for 3 lb (1.5 kg)

flour. Sprinkle it into the warm liquid with 1 teaspoon of sugar, stir, and leave till it goes frothy.

(3) Instant yeast. This is almost a powder. Use 1 oz (25 g) for 3 lb (1.5 kg) flour, or a sachet as directed. Mix it into the flour, *not* into the liquid.

Don't be fooled by the apparently wholesome lack of sugar in type 3: instant yeast is encouraged to perform by various chemicals, which you can read about in the small print under the pretty picture. For the other types, sugar is just a convenient quick "food" to get them started. It is not absolutely necessary, and you certainly don't need the tablespoon or more recommended in many recipes, unless you like the taste. It's worth noting that large quantities of sugar, salt, melted fat or oil all inhibit the action of yeast. Certain fancy doughs containing these can be alarmingly slow to work, but will get there in the end.

All breads freeze reasonably well in the short term. Freshen them up by crisping the crust for 5 minutes in a moderate oven. After a week in the freezer, though, yeast doughs become progressively more crumbly.

Wholemeal Bread or Rolls

This quantity makes 3 loaves or 36 rolls.

2 oz (50 g) fresh yeast *or* 1 oz (25 g)
   dried yeast
1 teaspoon sugar
1½ pt (825 ml) warm water
3–3¼ lb (1.4–1.5 kg) wholemeal
   flour
1 level tablespoon salt

Treat the yeast as directed in the general remarks. Mix everything together and knead till coherent and elastic. Divide between greased loaf tins or make small balls, placed ½ inch (1.25 cm) apart on greased baking trays. Cover with a damp tea-towel and leave, out of draughts, till doubled in bulk. Bake in a hot oven—30–40 minutes for loaves 10–15 for rolls.

Test for readiness by poking the bottom. If it retains your fingerprint, give it another 5 minutes.

Jack MacWilliam's Wholemeal Bread

Jack's superb bread cuts and keeps much better than the basic recipe above. He bakes me 6 loaves every week and we use them for packed lunches and breakfast toast. It is so good that it takes an inhuman amount of will-power not to gobble any leftover toast that comes back to the kitchen immediately.

    1 tablespoon cooking oil
    1 flat tablespoon malt extract
    ¼ pt (150 ml) boiling water
    50 mg vitamin C (this is a yeast
       accelerator)
    1 flat tablespoon salt
    1¼ pt (700 ml) lukewarm water
    2 sachets instant yeast
    3¼ lb (1.5 kg) wholemeal flour

Stir the malt and oil into the boiling water, till well mixed. Crush the vitamin C tablets and salt and dissolve in the lukewarm water. Mix the yeast into the flour.

Pour the liquids into the flour and knead well. You may need up to ¼ pt (150 ml) extra of warm water.

Form into 3 loaves and leave to double in bulk. Bake in a hot oven—about 40 minutes.

Butteries

Butteries are a wondrous speciality of Aberdeen and the surrounding district, a relation of the French croissant. When I was a girl, every little bakery, of which there were many, had its own jealously-guarded recipe, and its own passionately loyal customers. Some bakers added a little sugar, some a splash of vinegar. Some used fat or milk in the basic dough. Some rolled thin, others squat. Some baked brown and crisp, others light gold and melting. We called these articles simply "rolls", judging no other bread worthy of the name, and they arrived in a paper bag on the doorstep, warm and fragrant, before 8 o'clock. They were considered stale by lunchtime. Not any more, I'm sorry to say; except in a very few country bakeries the modern version is flabby, coarse and cellophane-packed. Perhaps it is just as well: I fear my consistently ample girth is a consequence of an early addiction to these delectable pastries.

The simplest way to make these is to separate off a third of a batch of ordinary white bread dough and proceed from the first rolling. If the dough is too warm, it will be difficult to roll, so do this on a cold surface. If your butter is soft, spread it onto the dough as you would spread a slice of bread. If it is very cold, or better still frozen, grate it on a coarse grater. These methods are both much quicker than pinching off tiny pieces to cover the surface.

1 lb (450 g) strong white flour
1 teaspoon salt
½ oz (15 g) dried yeast *or* 1 oz
(25 g) fresh
1 teaspoon sugar
½ pt (275 ml) lukewarm water
6–8 oz (175–225 g) butter or
mixed butter and other fat
extra ½ oz (15 g) butter for the
tops.

Treat the yeast according to the general directions. Mix the flour and salt. You can rub in 2 oz (50 g) of the fat if you want a very tender crumb.

Pour the yeast liquid into the flour and knead till smooth and silky. Cover with a tea-towel and leave in a warm place till double in bulk. Knead again. (This first rising is not essential, but it is an improvement. It makes the dough easier to roll.)

Roll the dough out on a floured cold surface, about ¼ inch (6 mm) thick. Starting from the left, dot ⅔ of the surface of the dough with ⅓ of the fat. Fold the right hand side over the middle section and the left hand side over that. Crimp down the edges and give the dough a half turn, so that the right hand fold now faces you.

Repeat this rolling, spreading and folding twice more, and if there are streaks of butter coming to the surface, do it again.

Now roll out about ¼ inch (6 mm) thick. Cut into about 12 rectangles. Fold the corners underneath and flatten slightly. Place on a baking tray, leaving ½ inch (1.25 cm) between to allow for spreading. Pinch the extra ½ oz (15 g) butter into flakes and put 1 on the top of each buttery. Put the tray in a warm place till they are well-risen and puffy looking, but don't give them so much heat that the butter melts and escapes.

Bake in a moderately hot oven for 10–15 minutes. When you take them out, spoon any fat which has run out back over the butteries, and leave to cool on the baking tray.

Oatmeal Bread or Rolls

This is a pleasant change from wheat bread. The rolls are very good warm for breakfast. This quantity makes about 30.

2 lb (900 g) fine oatmeal
2 teaspoons salt
1¼ pt (700 ml) warm water
2 oz (50 g) fresh yeast *or* 1 oz (25 g)
    dried yeast
1 teaspoon sugar
½ lb (225 g) wholemeal flour

Mix the oatmeal and salt with 1 pt (570 ml) warm water (1¼ pt (700 ml) if you are going to use instant yeast). Leave to stand in a warm place for 1 hour.

Treat the yeast as directed in the general instructions, using the other ¼ pt (150 ml) water unless it is the instant type. Add it to the oatmeal with the wheat flour.

Mix thoroughly. It will be very sticky, so use only one hand at first. Add some extra flour if it is too intractable, but this dough remains rather soft. Form into loaves or rolls and leave covered with a damp cloth. It takes a little longer to double in bulk than an all-wheat bread. Bake as for wholemeal bread.

Afternoon Tea

Many innocuous people have a dream of driving on a lovely sunny afternoon to a country retreat, there to drink tea out of pretty cups and to consume fresh scones and home-made jam, with other delights. Some of them still come hopefully to our door. Sometimes there is no answer, if we have seen them coming and bolted up the hill. Sometimes they find me in my gumboots, with a bucket of potatoes, and ill-tempered. Sometimes they are greeted by our small grimy daughter and her equally unclean friends. Sometimes they are molested by our hens, who peck their toes if they are wearing sandals. Whatever happens, *they don't get any tea*. This is extremely mean of us, but between 2 and 4 in the afternoon, the sight of a prospective guest is as a crucifix to a vampire.

Come 4.30, we bow to the inevitable and concede (grudgingly) that residents at least have to be allowed tea. Some of them are in a pitiable state by then. They have motored all round the island looking for a pub to have lunch at, or walked 5 miles to the nearest shop only to discover it's Sunday.

Tea is unelaborate but elegant, with a silver tea-service, pink cups, warm scones and home-made jam, and cream if there is cream to spare. It is really better if there is no cream, as people always eat it and then feel bilious at dinner time.

Pancakes

Known as dropped scones or Scotch pancakes outside Scotland. Syrup makes them a more even brown than sugar, and sour milk gives a lighter result than fresh. The lightest and most velvety brown I have ever encountered were Mrs Peggy Macaskill's. She advised using water rather than milk.

    4 oz (100 g) self-raising flour
    pinch of salt
    2 teaspoons syrup or caster sugar
    1 egg
    about ¼ pt (150 ml) milk, thick
       sour milk if possible

Sift the flour and salt. Drop in the egg, the syrup or sugar, and half the milk. Beat hard till the mixture is smooth. Add more milk to make a thick batter and beat again till bubbles form. If there is time, let the batter stand for half an hour.

Heat a heavy frying pan till very hot—it should sizzle when you grease it. Don't over-grease: wipe the fat off again till the pan just shines.

Drop tablespoons of the batter on to the hot surface. As soon as bubbles rise and break, flip the pancakes over. They will only take seconds for the other side.

Keep them folded in a clean cloth till they have cooled, and use the same day.

Scones

Every housewife in the Hebrides has her own ways of making scones. Some leave them plain, others sweeten with syrup or sugar. Most people pat lightly rather than roll, and cut the dough into wedges or rectangles rather than rounds. Tops are left attractively floury, not glazed. I have collected these recipes from three of our helpers, but I never get as good results as they do.

Morag Macleod's Scones

Use sour milk for the best taste and lightest texture.

    1 lb (450 g) self-raising flour
    ½ level teaspoon cream of tartar
    ½ level teaspoon bicarbonate of
        soda
    2 oz (50 g) sugar
    3 oz (75 g) margarine
    2 eggs
    milk to mix—sour if possible

Add cream of tartar and bicarbonate of soda to the flour and rub in the margarine. Mix in the sugar. Stir in the beaten eggs and enough milk to make a soft dough.

Do not knead the dough. The less handling it gets the better the scones. Roll out gently ½ inch (1.25 cm) thick. Cut into pieces and bake about 15 minutes in a hot oven.

Mary Ann Macsween's Scones

    2 lb (900 g) self-raising flour
    ½ teacup sugar
    2 oz (50 g) margarine
    1 tablespoon syrup or treacle
    2 eggs
    about ¾ pt (425 ml) milk

Mix the flour and sugar and rub in the margarine. Add the syrup, eggs and enough milk to make a soft dough. Pat out very lightly about ½ inch (1.25 cm) thick. Cut into oblongs and bake in a very hot oven till well risen and golden brown—about 10 minutes.

Kathleen Morrison's Wholemeal Scones

8 oz (225 g) plain flour · a pinch of salt
8 oz (225 g) wholemeal flour · 4 oz (100 g) margarine
1 level teaspoon bicarbonate of · 2 oz (50 g) sugar
  soda · 1 egg
2 level teaspoons cream of tartar · milk to mix

Sieve the plain flour with the bicarbonate of soda, the cream of tartar, and the salt. Add the wholemeal flour and mix well. Rub in the margarine and add the sugar.

Beat the egg with a little milk and mix into the dry ingredients with a knife. (Don't use too much milk—this is a slightly drier dough than the other recipes given here.)

Turn onto a board floured with wholemeal. Knead lightly into a round. Cut into 8 or 10 wedges and bake in a hot oven till golden brown—10—15 minutes.

Victoria Plum Jam

My mother makes all the jam we use. This one is my favourite, excellent for tarts and sponges as well as on scones.

Makes about 12—14 lb (5.5—6.5 kg).

7 lb (3.2 kg) Victoria plums
7 lb (3.2 kg) sugar
½ pt (275 ml) water

Remove the stems from the plums. Rinse and drain them. Slit them down one side—this helps to free the stones on cooking. Put them in a pan with the water and cook gently till they are soft and the skins are tender.

Take out some of the stones and crack them with a hammer. Reserve the kernels.

Add the sugar to the plums and continue cooking, stirring till the sugar dissolves. Boil fairly hard for 20—25 minutes, till a little sets on a cold plate. Add the kernels to the boiling jam a few minutes before the end of the cooking time.

Take off any scum—a cold metal spoon is best for this. Remove the stones (they will mostly have risen to the top). Pour the jam into hot dry jars and cover.

Oatcakes

There are as many oatcake and bannock recipes in the Western Isles as there are grannies and aunties. The best are often made by octogenarians or even nonagenarians. I hasten to add that neither of the ladies who contributed these recipes is in that group yet.

Some people melt the fat, put in more raising agent or omit it altogether. Others add flour, to make handling easier, or sugar and extra fat to produce a more biscuity texture. Any type of oatcake can be cooked entirely in the oven, without using a girdle, or the first side can be done on the girdle and the drying out in the oven. The one feature common to all Hebridean oatcakes is their hefty thickness: elsewhere they are usually made thin and crisp. I remember years ago taking a present of oatcakes I had made to an elderly Harris lady. I had made them Aberdeen style—with melted dripping and not more than 1/8-inch (3 mm) thick. She eyed them with disapproval, and half an hour's conversation could not persuade her I had really intended to produce wretched things like that.

We always keep oatcakes for breakfast and to serve with cheese after dinner. Usually Morag makes them; if I do them myself, I forget my early training and use Joni's recipe.

Morag Macleod's Oatcakes

 1 lb (450 g) oatmeal
 6 oz (175 g) self-raising flour
 ½ teaspoon bicarbonate of soda
 5½ oz (165 g) margarine
 ½ pt (275 ml) warm water

Mix all the dry ingredients together. Rub in the margarine till it resembles breadcrumbs. Add warm water and mix with your hand till it forms a stiffish dough. You may need a little extra water—if it is too dry it will crack on rolling out.

Put the dough onto an oatmeal-floured surface, form it into a ball, and roll it out about ½ inch (1.25 cm) thick. Do all this without a pause, as once the dough cools it will become dry and difficult to work.

Cut into oblongs and bake in a moderately hot oven for 20–30 minutes. The oatcakes should look pale and dry when they are done.

Joni Wilson's Oatcakes

    1 lb (450 g) fine oatmeal
    ½ teaspoon bicarbonate of soda
    pinch of salt
    4–5 oz (100–150 g) margarine
    1½–2 tablespoons hot water

Rub the fat into the dry ingredients till it sticks together. Add the hot water, enough to make it hold together in one lump, but don't make it soggy. Pat out ¼ inch (6 mm) thick, either in several 7-inch (17.5 cm) rounds or in one sheet. Cut into triangles if you made rounds or oblongs if you didn't. Bake on a greased girdle till they go firm, then transfer carefully to a baking tray. Dry them off in a moderate oven for about 15 minutes. Don't let them burn.

Other Savoury Biscuits

Morag's oatcakes made me ashamed of the bought crackers offered alongside them with cheese, so I evolved the next two recipes last season. Unfortunately, they were so popular that I spent half the day baking more and more of them, and by the middle of the summer I had run out of enthusiasm for it.

If you don't care for sweet biscuits, try these instead; they don't need cheese or butter.

Caraway Biscuits

    10 oz (275 g) plain flour
    ½ teaspoon salt
    1 teaspoon caster sugar
    1–2 teaspoons caraway seeds
    1 teaspoon ground coriander or
        grated lemon rind
    6 oz (175 g) butter

Rub the fat into the dry ingredients till you have a cohesive dough like shortbread. Roll out ⅛ inch (3 mm) thick. Cut into rounds and bake in a moderate oven till pale golden—10–15 minutes.

Stripey Biscuits

> 8 oz (225 g) wholemeal flour
> 1 level teaspoon baking powder
> a large pinch sugar
> a large pinch salt
> 4 oz (100 g) butter or margarine
> 3 egg yolks
> 2 tablespoons sesame seeds
> 2 tablespoons poppy seeds

Mix the dry ingredients except the seeds, and rub in the fat. When the mixture begins to stick together, bind it with the beaten egg yolks.

Keep back a little egg yolk and mix it with a teaspoon of water. This is for glazing.

Roll out the dough about ⅛ inch (3 mm) thick, as near an oblong as possible. Push and trim it to square it off. Brush the whole surface with the egg glaze.

Sprinkle the 2 kinds of seed in alternate stripes across the dough. Cut into fingers at right angles to the stripes. Be careful lifting them onto the baking tray as they lose the seeds easily. Bake in a moderate oven for 10–15 minutes.

Lena Maclennan's Shortbread Biscuits

These are to be found in the tins on the bedroom tea-trays. They are one of the greatest delicacies of the house. I have discerned meek and law-abiding guests smuggling them into their cars; the tin of many a dieting lady has been found mysteriously empty by evening; penniless honeymooners who couldn't afford dinner have lived on these and love. On Lena's baking day, a procession of assorted children and dogs (only three of each, but it seems like more) trots between her kitchen and mine, bearing empty and full tins in expectation of fragrant rewards fresh from her oven.

> 2 teacups plain flour
> 1 teacup cornflour
> 1 teacup icing sugar
> ½ lb (225 g) butter

Rub all the ingredients together into a firm dough. Roll out thinly (⅛ inch (3 mm)). Cut into small rounds and bake in a moderate oven till crisp and golden—10–15 minutes.

Pat MacWilliam's Rich Fruit Cake

Pat is the other half of the one who makes the bread. This rich, moist cake embellishes packed lunches. It is good eaten at once and even better after a few weeks' maturation. I think the specially fruity taste comes from Pat's home-candied peel, so I include the recipe below.

10 oz (275 g) butter	1½ lb (675 g) currants
10 oz (275 g) caster sugar	6 oz (175 g) candied peel
7–8 eggs	4 oz (100 g) almonds
14 oz (400 g) plain flour	4 oz (100 g) glacé cherries
1 dessertspoon mixed spice	grated rind of 1 lemon
a pinch of salt	juice of ½ lemon

Preheat oven to 160°C/325°F. Line a deep 8–9 inch (20–22.5 cm) round tin.

Sieve the flour with the spice and salt. Pick over the currants. Chop the peel, cherries and almonds.

Cream the butter and sugar till light. Beat in the eggs one by one. Add the flour mixture alternately with the fruit. Mix in the lemon rind and juice.

Turn the mixture into the prepared tin. Bake in a slow oven for 1½ hours, then reduce heat to very slow and bake a further 2 hours. Turn off the oven and leave the cake in for a further 15 minutes.

Candied Peel

8 oz (225 g) orange and lemon peel
8 oz (225 g) granulated sugar
½ pt (275 ml) water

Remove loose pith from the peel, as you use the fruit. Save the peel in the freezer till you have enough. Chop it, pour boiling water over it and leave it overnight.

Drain off the water. Cover with fresh cold water, bring to the boil and simmer till tender—at least 20 minutes. Drain.

Put the sugar in a pan with ½ pt (275 ml) water. Dissolve and bring to the boil. Add the peel and simmer till the syrup is almost absorbed. Cool and pack in plastic bags or cartons.

Sweets

One Christmas when we were very hard up I solved the present problem by giving everyone home-made sweets. For days on end I hung over boiling syrups, beat fudge, worked fondant, pulled Edinburgh Rock and dipped chocolates. The Turkish Delight bounced, the brittle deliquesced, and the chocolates dulled. I burnt the bottoms out of 2 saucepans and most of the skin off my fingers. Since then I have refused to have anything to do with confectionery.

Marzipan

Even Andrew can make this without instruction. It keeps very well in a box in the fridge.

> ½ lb (225 g) ground almonds
> ½ lb (225 g) caster sugar
> 1 large egg
> 1 tablespoon of any fruit liqueur
>   (you can also use rum, sherry or
>   rosewater)

Mix all the ingredients to a putty-like consistency. If it is too sticky, add more almonds and sugar. Pinch off small balls and decorate with nuts.

You can also use this to stuff dates and cover Christmas cakes.

Pat MacWilliam's Fudge

Don't be incredulous about the quantity of vanilla essence. The butter offsets it—very good indeed.

> 1 lb (450 g) pale soft brown sugar
> 1 large tin condensed milk
> ½ lb (225 g) butter
> 1 tablespoon milk
> 1 dessertspoon vanilla essence

Put everything but the vanilla essence in a heavy pan. Heat slowly till the sugar dissolves, stirring all the time. Bring to the boil, still stirring. Boil for 15 minutes—keep stirring. Beat slightly, stir in the vanilla essence, beat again. Pour into a greased Swiss Roll tin. Mark into squares before it is cold.

Soft Cheeses

We usually serve one or two fresh soft cheeses after dinner, for those who are daunted by the venerable aspect of the Stilton and its colleagues.

Yoghurt Cheese in Oatmeal

Yoghurt cheese is excellent for cheesecakes or any recipe that calls for curd or quark. The whey is nutritious too—very good for hens.

> 1 pt (570 ml) yoghurt
> 2 tablespoons pinhead oatmeal

Line a sieve with muslin and set it over a bowl. Put in the yoghurt and drain for at least 6 hours. Salt the curd if you want to, and roll it gently into a sausage inside its muslin. Put the oatmeal on a flat plate (pinhead, the coarsest, is best). Roll the curd out onto the oatmeal and scoop more meal over it. Keep it in the fridge till you are ready to serve it. Use within 24 hours.

Crowdie and Cream

Well! Here it is at last—the food that Finlay J. Macdonald has made Scarista famous for. Quite likely you only bought my book because of his *Crowdie and Cream*. No one can better describe this traditional delight than Finlay: "Once the cream had been removed, gallons of thick sour milk were left over every week, and the sour milk, when it was stood on a warm fire, converted into crowdie, which floated to the surface of tangy, refreshing whey—the ideal drink for hot days of peat-cutting or haymaking. . . . But the greatest delicacy of them all was the crumbly crowdie mixed with fresh cream, which piled high on a fresh oatcake, spread with fresh butter, combined into a flavour with an inbuilt memory. Crowdie and cream! The bitter and the sweet blending. . . ."*

As you can gather from this, crowdie is usually made from the skimmed milk left after the cream has been taken off to make butter, but you can use whole milk. Pasteurised milk is unlikely to work, though: it turns thin and putrid, not thick and sour. Mary MacDonald,

* *Crowdie and Cream* by Finlay J. MacDonald (Warner Books, 1992).

the Scarista postmistress, often gives me a present of some crowdie, and it is her method I give below. The basic crowdie freezes very well, she tells me, but don't add the salt and cream till you are ready to use it.

8 pt (4.6 l) skimmed milk
salt
double cream

Leave the milk in a warm place to sour and thicken. Now stand it on a very, very low heat. If you have a solid fuel stove, the hottest part of the top other than the cooking area is ideal. Leave it overnight. If you can't manage such a low heat, use the lowest you can for several hours. The milk will separate into curds and whey—Mary says it is best when the curd sinks, which it doesn't always do. Drain off the whey.

To serve, mash some crowdie with a little salt and add cream to taste—I find about 3 tablespoonfuls to 4 oz (100 g) cheese is right.

You can add chopped chives or other fresh herbs to crowdie. It isn't authentic, but it makes a pleasant change.

Some Dinner Menus

Mostly you will have your own ideas about dinner parties. Personally, I have never been able to use the menu sections at the back of cookery books. During my cooking life, I have always been without at least one of the essentials they tend to assume: cash—an oven—shops—and where on earth do you find lengkuas root?

The present menus are no more resourceful, but perhaps some well-organised hosts and hostesses will manage to use them. They are in the Scarista House style, but rather simpler, as when I am cooking for hotel guests I don't have to sit at table with them and make light conversation while the kitchen burns down.

A few hints:

(1) Plan your party according to the season. No use having the cash, the oven, the shops—even the lengkuas root—and then discovering there's no asparagus till next May.

(2) Pay attention to colour and texture, as well as taste. Don't have red soup followed by red gravy, or a savoury and a sweet mousse at the same meal. If you get caught out, seize a few green leaves for colour or some chopped nuts for texture to vary the effect.

(3) Food is meant to nourish. Don't overcook everything or keep it warm for ages: better to stick to a simpler meal with some cold items that can be ready before your guests arrive. And don't stuff them silly: cream and egg yolks with everything and pie followed by pie may seem mouthwatering when you're feeling ravenous as you plan your dinner, but by half way through the meal it will become a pain in some part or other of everyone's anatomy.

These menus are arranged in twos—a fish and a meat main course

371

for each part of the year.* Underneath is a vegetarian main dish which can be fitted in to either menu.

Without injury to the balance of the meal, you can scrap the pudding and serve whatever fruit and/or cheese is good at the time. Don't forget celery, radishes, figs, dates and nuts, all of which make a leisurely and convivial ending to a meal, if you don't want to bother with a sweet. Pass the port, please.

Spring

1. Nettle Soup

   Liver with Sage and Orange
   Spaghetti
   Steamed Carrots

   Caramel Mousse

   Wine: Gamay de l'Ardèche
   or red Sancerre

2. Grapefruit Water Ice

   Mussels with Fennel
   Oatmeal Rolls
   Salad

   Hot Chocolate Pudding

   Wine: Muscadet

Vegetarian alternative: Courgettes with cheese

Early Summer

1. Borshcht

   Stuffed Shoulder of Lamb
   Fresh Mint Sauce
   Potatoes with Rosemary
   Spring Cabbage

   Hazelnut Meringue Cake

   Wine: full-bodied claret,
   e.g. Cissac

2. Cauliflower Soufflés

   Baked Salmon with Raita
   New Potatoes
   Courgettes with Tomato
   Sauce

   Butterscotch Ice Cream

   Wine: Vouvray or Montlouis

Vegetarian alternative: Spicy Stuffed Tomatoes

* I have given wine suggestions. If you notice a preponderance of Loire and Rhône wines and wonder why, write to Robin Yapp for elucidation. One of his recent lists was mainly in classical Greek so it may not elucidate everything. Address at the back of the book.

Late Summer

1. Avocado and Walnut Salad

   Venison Pie
   Julienne of Celery and Potato

   Summer Trifle

   Wine: red Rhône, e.g.
         Châteauneuf du Pape

2. Melon with Blackcurrant Water
   Ice

   Scallops in Oatmeal
   Spicy Tomato Sauce
   Carrot and Potato Cake

   Almond Cake with Peaches

   Wine: Sancerre

Vegetarian alternative: Spinach Soufflé Flan

Autumn

1. Pepper Fritters and Tomato
   Granita

   Lamb with Apricots
   Rice with Pine Kernels
   Steamed Calabrese

   Syllabub

   Wine: Rioja, e.g. Vina Ardanza

2. Apple-stuffed Mushrooms

   Turbot with Dill Sauce
   Burghul Pilaff
   Colourful Mixed Salad

   Queen of Puddings

   Wine: white burgundy,
         e.g Meursault

Vegetarian alternative: Aubergine Pizza

Winter

1. Carrot and Orange Soup

   Pot-roasted Pheasant
   Skirlie Potatoes
   Lemon Cabbage

   Bananas Flambées

   Wine: light burgundy,
         e.g. Fleurie, Rully

2. Curd Cheese Ramekins

   Halibut with Mushrooms
   Buckwheat with Cucumber
   Casserole of Sweet Peppers

   Chocolate Chestnut Cake

   Wine: dry rosé, e.g. Tavel or
         Sancerre

Vegetarian alternative: Gougère of Mushrooms and Peppers

How Carnivores Can Cope with Vegetarians

It is becoming increasingly common for people who are not vegetarians themselves to be faced with the problem of catering for vegetarians. So if you are a parent of alternative offspring or a police officer with the cells full of ALF detainees, read on.

The chances are your charges will be vegans. This means you have to forget about the "We can always give them cheese or eggs" theory. Vegans do not eat anything of animal origin, so dairy produce, eggs and honey are debarred. You will have two headaches: how to provide enough daily protein, and how to produce variety.

Take the protein question first. It is worth remembering that in Britain and America we eat far more protein than we need, on average. Particularly for adults, it is not necessary or even healthy to consume large quantities of concentrated animal protein—meat, fish, eggs, cheese and milk. Still less do we need animal fats—certainly not two or three times a day.

"Breakfast, Dinner, Lunch and Tea
    Are all the human frame requires",

concluded Henry King, who chewed Bits of String, and was Early cut off in Dreadful Agonies. But he could have been wrong. If he had stuck to string and missed out the bacon and egg, roast beef, fried mutton chops, iced cakes and buttered scones, he might have been alive and well, albeit, like most vegans, lanky. For the secrets of vegan eating are the proteins, vitamins and trace minerals in unrefined carbohydrate foods. All whole grains, pulses and nuts and the flours and pastes made from them provide satisfactory nourishment. Furthermore, if you eat a grain and a pulse at the same meal (not necessarily cooked together), the proteins are better utilised by the body. Ethnic food all over the world shows instinctive understanding of this fact—peanuts with millet, lentils with rice, beans with pasta, sesame paste with pitta bread. Reckon on a combined dry weight of 4–6 oz (100–175 g) per serving for a satisfying meal. Sprouting seeds such as mung and alfalfa are also nutritious. Raw and cooked fruit and vegetables are as good for vegans as for everyone else, but it is even more important not to peel or overcook everything, as these practices are a great waste of nourishment and a sure way of cementing up your innards.

So much for the serious business of nourishment. But what about enjoyment? Endless bowls of brown rice and lentils imply a dismal monotony. But have a browse through the ethnic recipe books which are on sale everywhere nowadays, particularly from Middle Eastern and Indian cuisine, and you will get plenty of ideas for gingering up the basic grain/pulse combination (lengkuas root?). One visit to a Pakistani grocer or a delicatessen should arm you with sufficient spices, condiments and oils to keep you experimenting for months. By that time your pestilent teenager will have taken up some other fad anyway, but who knows, you may have got a taste for the stuff yourself.

Remember that a vegan diet is perfectly acceptable to any vegetarian, but not vice versa, so if in doubt cook vegan. Particularly, vegetarians who are so for humane reasons will be revolted by non-free-range eggs. Anyway, vegetarians are bedevilled by cheese omelettes, which everyone from best friend to expense-account restaurant thinks are very good for them, and you will win esteem and affection by giving them a nice plate of beans instead.

Whether you are dealing with vegans or other vegetarians, if you have to provide more than just the occasional meal, avoid two pitfalls. Keep clear of processed foods, particularly if your vegetarian is rigorous. On the whole (the exceptions are usually confined to healthfood shops) such foods contain meat by-products, animal fats, battery eggs—quite likely hoof-and-horn meal, under some long chemical name. By the time you have read the labels carefully, you might as well have bought raw ingredients and made it yourself. The other mistake to avoid is always sticking to traditional English-style cooking, substituting lentils (say) for meat and vegetable margarine for lard or butter. This can produce very heavy and greasy results, and very fattening too. When I was at university in Aberdeen, the local bakers' answer to vegetarians (there weren't many, and I wasn't one of them) was a macaroni pie—a pie shell made with white flour, filled with white pasta in cheese sauce, with a lid of mashed potato on top. There was a baked bean version too: indeed they are both still around, and can fill a gap in a hungry student, but the general principle is not healthy. Refined carbohydrates, such as white flour, soak up any amount of fat, and lack proper nutrients. The end result is stodgy and unwholesome. I am reminded of some guests we once had, who had, they assured us, taken to a high-fibre diet—then newly the rage. But they had to abandon it because they gained so much weight: "It was all the baked beans we had to eat," they explained. Well! the beans may have been fibrous before they got in the tin, but by the time they are eaten, the fibres have swelled to saturation point, permeating them with an unholy solution of white sugar, white flour, water and vinegar. So go easy on the macaroni and chips and the baked bean crumble. Use *whole* foods —warts and all.

Some Useful Addresses

For information on factory farming and how to combat it:
Compassion in World Farming
5a Charles Street
Petersfield
Hants GU32 3EH
Tel. (01730) 264208

For a helpful list of stockists if you have trouble getting hold of
free range eggs:
British Free Range Egg Producers' Association
Valley View Farm
Stoodleigh
Tiverton
Devon EX16 9QA
Tel. (01398) 351422

For free range meats and country foods (mail order and callers):
Ann Petch
Heal Farm
King's Nympton
Umberleigh
Devon EX37 9TB
Tel. (01769) 574341

For non-intensively reared meat:
Wholefood Butchers
31 Paddington Street
London W1
Tel. (0171) 486 1390

For Rhône and Loire wines (particularly good with the recipes in this book):
Yapp Bros.
The Old Brewery
Mere
Wilts BA12 6DY
Tel. (01747) 860423

Index

Warner Books now offers an exciting range of quality titles by both established and new authors. All of the books in this series are available from:

Little, Brown and Company (UK),
P.O. Box 11,
Falmouth,
Cornwall TR10 9EN.

Fax No: 01326 317444.
Telephone No: 01326 372400
E-mail: books@barni.avel.co.uk

Payments can be made as follows: cheque, postal order (payable to Little, Brown and Company) or by credit cards, Visa/Access. Do not send cash or currency. UK customers and B.F.P.O. please allow £1.00 for postage and packing for the first book, plus 50p for the second book, plus 30p for each additional book up to a maximum charge of £3.00 (7 books plus).

Overseas customers including Ireland, please allow £2.00 for the first book plus £1.00 for the second book, plus 50p for each additional book.

NAME (Block Letters) ....

....

ADDRESS ....

....

....

☐ I enclose my remittance for ....

☐ I wish to pay by Access/Visa Card

Number ☐☐☐☐☐☐☐☐☐☐☐☐☐☐☐☐

Card Expiry Date ☐☐☐☐